This cavalcade of grace now stands, it speaks in

silence, its story is this land.

Where in this wide world can man find nobility without

pride, friendship without envy, or beauty without

vanity? Here, where grace is laced with muscle, and

strength by gentleness confined.

He serves without servility; he has fought without

enmity. There is nothing so powerful, nothing less

violent; there is nothing so quick, nothing more patient.

Canada's past has been borne on his back.

All our history is his industry; we are his heirs,

he our inheritance.

Ladies and gentlemen… The Horse.

THE SPRUCE MEADOWS STORY

ISBN 0-9681141-0-5

Published by: Spruce Meadows

Cover design: A. Hordos Designs Ltd., Calgary, Alberta

Cover photos: Katey Barrett, Al Savage

Printed by: Ronalds Printing,
a division of Quebecor Speciality Group

The Southern Family

"The Spruce Meadows Story is a vivid testimony to Marg and Ron Southern, their family, friends and employees on how a shared passion for the horse can - with thoughtfulness, leadership and the pursuit of excellence – develop into an internationally recognized role model.

The lively description of the process will help organizers of show jumping competitions at all levels around the world to further the popularity of the sport."

(Charles E. Barrelet, Swiss Chef d'Equipe.)

"The Spruce Meadows Story is a testimony to an institution and is historically presented in a fascinating way. It is interesting and yet amusing. It offers so many anecdotes from so many great horsemen and horsewomen that it is just plain fun.

In my opinion the book will be a MUST for any horse library."

(George H. Morris, former United States Olympic Team member and now one of the sport's most highly regarded coaches.)

"Colourful and funny, it is a book packed with anecdotes and a lot of good lessons for the future of equestrian sport. The book is at the same level as the great adventure of Spruce Meadows itself.

Honesty and integrity are real words at Spruce Meadows, and it is also one of the merits of Ken Hull's book to insist always on reflecting this point."

(Swiss journalist, Alban Poudret, author of several top-selling equestrian books.)

"Ken Hull has chronicled the creation of the Spruce Meadows legend in an informative and intriguing fashion that leaves the reader with a stronger understanding and appreciation of the sport of show jumping."

(Ian Millar, dean of Canadian show jumpers.)

"It will be a sorry day for me when I am no longer Chef of the British team and cannot go back to Spruce Meadows. I back everything the stars have said in the book about Spruce Meadows. We all love it, despite the weather, and only hope we can keep coming forever."

(Ronnie Massarella, British Chef d'Equipe.)

FROM THE AUTHOR

Researching and writing this book was a four year project of pure delight. Editing it for publication, however, was a task beyond the patience of a journalist who has been programmed by a lifetime of daily deadlines.

I therefore remain forever in debt to those who took time from their busy lives to greatly improve this publication. To my wife, Margie, for all the encouragement and a million little tasks; to the Southern family for the endless hours of interviews and editing; to Sue Archibald for the painstaking final read; and to those at A. Hordos Designs Ltd. for their creative touch.

But none of it could have happened without my daughter, Sheryl Dalik. As a young rider she exposed me to the magnificence of this sport and continues to educate me about it on an almost daily basis. For the book she set up more than one hundred interviews, transcribed every tape, proofed every word, helped select every picture, and in the end, designed and laid out every page.

It is, by all measurements, her book and I dedicate it to her with my eternal gratitude.

Ken Hull

Day One
The Beginning

The silence is so appropriate, yet it is a masquerade soon to be exposed. Couched by the beauty of nature's bounty, it appears almost irreverent to taint this tranquility with human intrusion.

But it will happen tomorrow. It always does on the first day of competition. The flow begins as a trickle, but by the weekend a torrent of humanity will flood the grounds of Spruce Meadows.

In all shapes and sizes, and for as many reasons as one can conceive, fans always embrace the Spruce Meadows MASTERS. For most it has become a tradition - a special gift they present to themselves to cap the close of another wonderful summer.

For Marg and Ron Southern, architects of the vision that has become Spruce Meadows, their reward is the happiness which settles so comfortably on both the young and the old. They speak so gracefully of the help they have received, the friendships they have forged, and the gratitude they feel they can never, despite their oratory eloquence, properly and completely express.

This is Spruce Meadows, a contradiction of sorts when one examines the previous blueprints of the world's other great show jumping centres. This all shouldn't have happened . . . or at least not this quickly.

Does anyone truly understand all of the reasons why, in two fleeting decades, Spruce Meadows has become arguably the best show jumping venue in the world? Probably not. But there are some haunting explanations and theories that collectively spin a fascinating story of a success that all of us should be fortunate enough to experience once in a lifetime.

As this tournament unwinds, the five-day attendance tally will eventually settle at a record of more than 145,000 spectators . . . an achievement that traditionally is short-lived. It took just twenty years for Spruce Meadows to become the most popular show jumping venue in the world.

Who would have ever believed it? Where are the sceptics now?

> No one has ever been able to explain conclusively just why this sport has captivated the hearts and imagination of a city whose sophisticated population is approaching one million.

They were in abundance in the mid-seventies - lining up to dance on the grave of this daring new sport venture. Today, however, they're part of the universal chorus that sends its crescendo of praise crashing into every corner of the global show jumping community. No one has ever been able to explain conclusively just why this sport has captivated the heart and imagination of a city whose sophisticated population is approaching one million.

Calgary, the metropolis that renders the heartbeat to a vibrant Canadian prairie, has always been home to a small but hardy group of show jumping fans.

Perhaps it is an inherited trait passed on through the generations by those turn-of-the-century Calgarians who for several years had made show jumping the hottest ticket in town.

On April 9, 1912, the long-ago-departed Calgary News Telegraph went into vivid detail reporting that: "Almost a thousand people were crushed in a surging mass before the entrance of the Horse Show building at the commencement of the opening performance last night."

It was, the writer intimated ". . . a miracle that the Easter finery in which Calgary society had adorned itself was not torn to shreds in the scramble."

Under the headline "All Other Horse Shows Will Date From This," the coverage consumed no less than seventy-two column inches of gushing prose that focused primarily on what was worn by the city's social set.

The competition, quite clearly, was not a test of courage among horses, but was a highly contested tournament of adornment among Calgary's elite.

And that, with some notable exceptions, is pretty well the hat with which this sport was crowned for decades to come - not only in Calgary, but throughout North America. Reports of its triumphs seldom managed to break loose from the social pages, and when it did happen, very little interest was expressed.

Show jumping, it seemed, was destined to remain an event where the best seats were measured not by how well you could see from them, but how well you could be seen in them.

No one, however, counted on the magic of Spruce Meadows. On June 3, 1976, a boring, slumbering sport was transformed into an entertainment spectacle that changed the face of show jumping in Canada, in North America and around the world.

On that first day of competition a dozen people - accounting for the body of the audience - looked somewhat strange as they lined the sideline of the show jumping ring. They clapped their hands, hesitantly, to the classical beat of "Radetzky's March." It was the only march ever composed by Johann Strauss, and it is doubtful he could have ever imagined a more unlikely setting for its presentation.

Spruce Meadows' fans are among the most knowledgeable and supportive in the world

Equally bewildered by the display of so much enthusiasm by so few, was a shy, young French Canadian who had just recorded the first ever clear round in the Spruce Meadows International Ring. Enjoying the music's peppy flow, he directed the snaking line of ribbon winners in a "Victory Ride" before the handful of applauding officials. He wasn't sure what he had done to deserve such attention. After all, it was only a $2,500 opening day stake class and the jumps hadn't been that big.

That rider was Jean-Guy Mathers who had left his St. Adele, Quebec home only days before for an adventure into the unknown . . . a show jumping competition in the hinterlands of the Canadian West at a sparkling new facility called Spruce Meadows.

No one at the time would have been brazen enough to suggest that over the next two decades, Jean-Guy's "Victory Ride" would be cloned many times by the greatest riders in the sport.

Every competing Olympic, World, European and North American champion would eventually trace Jean-Guy's route around what has become perhaps the greatest ring in global show jumping.

Jean-Guy had launched a tradition. But did anyone realize it at the time?

With the exception of Marg and Ron Southern, probably not. Each would later confess that in the beginning not even they were all that certain of the significance of their creation.

Spruce Meadows did not rise from typical beginnings. Ron Southern admits the spark that ignited it all showed no early signs of exploding into the raging success it became. It was a truly spectacular growth, but one not always totally under control.

A few, including elder daughter Nancy, believe the absolute picture was always vivid in her father's mind.

"He had to know to lay it out the way it is," said Nancy. "I can remember driving around looking at properties with my father in the early seventies and not really understanding what it was he was talking about."

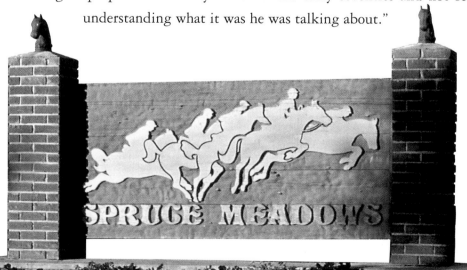

The Southern Family - Linda, Marg, Ron and Nancy.

They found one site not far from where Spruce Meadows is now. It was an old farm of only eighty acres nestled into the contours of the Rocky Mountain foothills. A natural rise in the middle of this property dominated its topography.

Ron quickly surveyed the land and told his daughter they could build a jumping ring at the bottom of the hill, the banks of which would then provide natural seating for the fans.

"He knew all along."

Nancy conceded that while her father may not have known precisely how Spruce Meadows would evolve, he did know "it was going to be great." "He had been to Hickstead in England and knew that he wanted to have thousands of people enjoying the sport here as well."

If such a belief needed affirmation, Nancy suggested that those in doubt need only look at the one hundred and sixty acres her mother and father finally purchased for Spruce Meadows.

"It was flat enough yet had sufficient contour that it was going to be an interesting piece of land. And there was enough to ensure that expansion, and even further land purchases, would not be difficult.

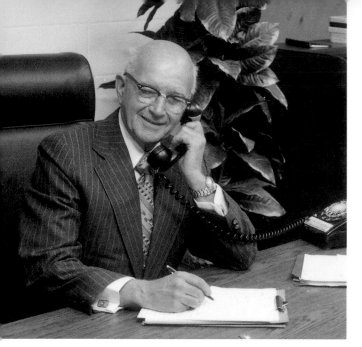

The late S.D. Southern.

"Nor can you ignore the fact that Pamela (world-renowned course designer Pamela Carruthers of Little Fosse, England) was invited to start laying our courses before the buildings even went up. I don't think he thought it would be everything that it's come to mean for so many different people, but I do believe he wanted it to be a world-class facility," concluded Nancy.

Ron Southern is one of the easiest men in the world to understand. He speaks clearly, never in generalities. And while he does not suffer fools easily, he has a forgiving quality that allows them at least one chance. He is also one of the most focused visionaries this sport and the business world has ever known, or likely ever will.

Together with wife Marg, a woman as uniquely gifted as her husband, they have earned the deepest respect among leaders of commerce, politics and sport around the world.

Personality insights that have been so carefully thought out by those close to both Marg and Ron provide a deeper appreciation for their diversity, as well as their uncommon honesty in sharing triumphs with others. The accolades have been earned in an epic of enterprise.

They have earned their wealth, but only part of their affluence can be measured in dollars. The monetary balance in their lives runs a distant runner-up to the immense pride shared in family, in business and in Spruce Meadows.

They are a partnership. Marg Southern operates not in his shadow, but boldly and squarely beside him.

Together they struggled through the lean years of ATCO Ltd. - now a multi-dimensional model of conglomerate efficiency, that in 1948 was started on a bankroll of $2,000 each from Ron and his moonlighting, fireman father, the late S.D. Southern.

S.D. Southern was earning the princely sum of $218 a month in 1948, not enough to realize his dream of sending his only child to university. He needed more income and the idea of a business venture was born. To finance the concept he took his mustering-out pay from the Royal Canadian Air Force, while Ron's contribution came from the toil of several summer jobs.

> If it is accepted that no man truly knows or understands the intricate complexities of another man's mind, then it should also be decreed that those who would come closest to unravelling these inner mysteries would probably be their children.

What began as a backyard family venture, renting little yellow utility trailers, matured into ATCO Ltd. It is one of Canada's premier corporations with just under $4 billion in assets, and almost $2 billion in sales from four operating groups employing more than 6,600 people.

The make-up of this world-wide organization, which went public on Jan. 9, 1968, changes almost yearly as its Chairman and Chief Executive Officer, Ron Southern, leads a team of extraordinary directors and officers in the search for new and profitable endeavours around the world.

In 1995 the ATCO lineup included an equity position in twenty-eight companies in Canada, the United States, Hungary, Australia, the United Kingdom and Europe.

In the vast majority of instances the ownership position is one hundred per cent, and rarely less than fifty. Interests range from drilling companies to a strong local, national and global equity in utility and power corporations, including a fifty per cent share in the mammoth Thames Power Limited in Great Britain.

Appropriately the family holding company is called Sentgraf Enterprises Limited, named after Nancy Southern's first horse.

Although Ron is more often linked to the strategic planning of Spruce Meadows, he and others are quick to lay the credit for transforming it into reality at the scurrying feet of Marg.

"There are terrific people running Spruce Meadows," he said. "The compliments and tributes for that should go to Marg. She is something

(photo by Cansport)

Linda Southern-Heathcott aboard Advantage Chrysler.

and not just because she is my wife. I've never seen anybody work like this lady. It's not unusual for her to spend fourteen and fifteen hours a day here (Spruce Meadows) - year round. She is intelligent, articulate and caring. She leads by example."

Security guard reports confirm the details of her unusual hours. The reports demand that guards enter the names of those discovered on the grounds after midnight. One name and one name only dominates that list ". . . Mrs. Southern was here until 2 a.m. . . . 3 a.m. . . . 4 a.m." and on occasion, "Mrs. Southern was still here when my shift ended at 7 a.m."

If it is accepted that no man truly knows or understands the intricate complexities of another man's mind, then it should also be decreed that those who would come closest to unravelling these inner mysteries would probably be his children.

Nancy Southern and Little Lion competing in the late 70's on the International Ring.

Marg and Ron Southern have two daughters: Nancy, born in 1956 and Linda, born in 1963. Because both have played, and must continue to play, a vital role in the development of both the ATCO Group of Companies and Spruce Meadows, their insights are invaluable.

It is suffice to describe each as fiercely independent, vastly different from the other, and blessed with the best - and they confessed "some of the other" - traits of their parents.

Linda Southern-Heathcott is very direct, analytical in a probing fashion, and able to grasp the significance of a situation very quickly. That helped her to become one of the best show jumpers in the sport.

She described her father as a master of motivation.

"In the kindest form, he is sort of like a mad-scientist. I believe he challenges himself because it's all a bit of a game to him. He must find out how much he and others can achieve and how much they can do," she said.

When challenged by a son-in-law as to why he continued to sit on as many as ten corporate boards at a time, Ron replied it was an educational opportunity he would never want to waste. Each company, he explained, was pushing the envelope on its respective technology. Each directorship, therefore, provided him with an opportunity to learn and take that world-class experience back to his own boardroom.

Both daughters offer unique descriptions when asked to frame the roles of their parents as they see them:

"He creates the plan and then Mom is the one that makes sure it gets done," said Linda. She described her father as a bit of a dreamer ". . . but a dreamer in the very best way. He can visualize what is going to happen five years down the road, whereas I never look at life that way. I need to get things done so they are finished by the end of the day."

In looking at her parents Linda said there is no doubt they very much complement each other.

"He's much more outgoing, and very, very loyal. Dad has very strong beliefs, and when it comes to right from wrong everything is black and white with R.D.," Linda said fondly referring to her father by the initials of his given names - Ronald and Donald.

Linda said it has become an inside joke among family and close friends because her mother has trouble saying "no" to her father when it comes to more expansion for Spruce Meadows.

"Well, I guess she does say no, but he doesn't always listen and maybe that's a problem. For him there's no such word when it comes to Spruce Meadows. Dad likes to look into the future and grow all the time, whereas Mom and I are trying to get a grip on things that are happening today.

"That's really hard on her because I think she would easily say, OK, let's not get it (Spruce Meadows) any bigger. Let's just try and hold it where it is for now."

The importance of control with quality, however, is of vital significance to her father as exemplified by the extraordinary results enjoyed at Spruce Meadows. Nancy, the catalyst that subtly led to the creation of Spruce Meadows, adopts a philosophical edge to her responses about her parents. Like her father, she analyzes the impact of each question, being careful not to misrepresent her feelings or understanding of the issue.

Although her role with Spruce Meadows will - many would say "must" - remain active, she has been groomed to succeed her father as head of the ATCO Group of Companies and is actively pursuing that challenge as its Deputy Chairman. The Southern family controls approximately seventy-five per cent of the voting shares in ATCO.

Nancy and Little Lion share some laughs with visiting school children.

Nancy, seven years older than Linda, is married to show jumper/trainer Jonathan Asselin. It is almost certain that among their three children, and Linda's two (at the time of writing), a show jumper or two will emerge.

Nancy's insights into her parent's personalities are both tender and insightful.

Albert Kley, Ron & S.D. Southern and Heinz Loewe, Spruce Meadows' first Breeding Master.

"I think my Dad is a great man. I have no problems thinking of him in the same thought as a Winston Churchill or any of the great generals of the world."

In a macro-sense, she continued, her father is "all-giving" and "more than anyone else I know, thinks for the betterment of the whole."

Nancy likened her mother to Florence Nightingale since it is the individual's well-being that is always foremost in her mind. "One is a strategist, and one is the helper - the healer that really wants to be a part of people's lives by giving something of herself to them."

Her father, continued Nancy, is at his happiest when he can sit at Spruce Meadows on a Saturday morning and watch the horses free-jumping, or share some thoughts with Linda as she works her young horses.

"For my Mom, it's when she can get away completely and play eighteen holes of golf - something that seldom happens. She drives herself much harder than my Dad and I believe has a more difficult time in relaxing.

"He seems to just be able to shut off completely when he needs to. She is always worrying about the details, which he doesn't do. She's worried that somebody isn't going to do something."

Her father, said Nancy, is constantly after her mother to slow down and delegate even more of her responsibilities to others.

"But she's so sneaky," mused Nancy. "Do you know that she will smuggle folders of work home from the office and then wait until my Dad is asleep and work from midnight to dawn?"

Both have a strong passion for the horse and the sport of show jumping.

"He has always appreciated achievement," said Nancy. "It doesn't matter what it is that you achieve, he sees it as the most precious thing in the world."

Within show jumping, she concluded, there are a lot of great coaches but few of them have the ability to motivate their athletes. Her father is an exception and utilizes the talent even though he is no longer a coach in the true interpretation of the word.

"There isn't anybody else that stops riders to tell them genuinely and with so much sincerity, how proud he is of them and their accomplishments. I think that's really important and no one else does it in this sport."

Equally, when somebody disappoints Ron Southern or goes against the rules, the hurt is intense.

"It hurts him as much if Linda or I did something terribly wrong," Nancy said with emotion. "A lot more so than my Mom. She is very forgiving. R.D. doesn't always come across as being that kind of a person, yet he will forgive anyone, anything."

Her father takes it very personally, explained Nancy, when a rider breaks a rule at Spruce Meadows, or does something to jeopardize what he's trying to build for them.

"Yet there are one or two riders that just want to throw it back at him, and that really does cut deep. For a few it has become a test of egos. They recognize what's here, but they don't want to be ingratiated. In so many ways they test him to the limit."

Both Marg and Ron were exceptional athletes in their youth, and Marg once played on a basketball team coached by Ron. Their competitive instinct, suggests Nancy, is part of the driving force that overcomes the threat of exhaustion that stalks them during tournaments.

"But you can't, as an athlete, play the same game all your life. You have to find some ways of recreating that for yourself."

For that reason, Nancy believes the Spruce Meadows tournaments are her parents' eternal games. "I don't think it's necessarily their happiest times, but it's the challenge that excites them. It is enjoyment, but it is also a competition for them."

Marg and Ron Southern shared many a common purpose in reaching a decision to build Spruce Meadows. They also had a deep-seated personal impetus to do so.

It is important to remember that before Spruce Meadows, show jumping was not part of the Southern family's make-up or heritage. Marg Southern lived out the dream of every young girl and rode bareback from dawn to dusk while growing up on a farm in rural Alberta. But she never competed.

It is unlikely that Ron ever thought twice about a horse until daughter Nancy began following "cow pies" as a toddler in the open field behind an ATCO factory near Airdrie, Alberta.

"I was thinking there's a lot of country out there and if I can find cow pies then eventually I would find horses," recalled Nancy.

Eventually her pleas for a pony reached the right ears at the right moment, and before they knew it the Southern family was "into horses".

It would still take several years before talk of a complex anything close to Spruce Meadows would take place, but the seed had been planted.

Through the late sixties and early seventies, Nancy's love for the sport continued to flourish, and Linda began burning up the pony divisions.

By the time Nancy was 14 she was competing in the open division, winning often enough to attract the intense interest of her parents.

Albert Kley, Spruce Meadows' Riding Master, had been brought to Calgary from his native Germany in 1970 to teach the children of several interested Calgarians - including the Southerns - the European traditions of riding.

He worked directly with long-time trainer and sport promoter Joe Selinger, and all of the lessons took place at Joe's St. George's Stables located just a few miles southwest of what ultimately became Spruce Meadows.

(photo by Rick Maynard)

Albert Kley with one of his first groups of students - Michelle Gendall, Linda Southern, Deirdre Campbell and Elizabeth Peters

Albert who spoke only one word of English the day he arrived - "Yes" - recalled that initially only Marg Southern would appear with the girls on lesson days.

"And then one day Mr. Southern began coming regularly," said Albert. "At first he wouldn't say anything. But he watched everything. He never took his eyes off of the horses and the riders."

Before long he seldom missed a lesson. His silence gave in to a constant flow of probing questions, all related to the horse.

"I had never met anyone like him," said Albert, a man Ron Southern still looks upon as a singular source of superb horse knowledge. "He was so determined to learn everything, and every question he asked was important."

Marg suggests her husband's interest in the sport intensified at the same time he was seriously struggling to stop drinking. It was a battle he ultimately won, and it is not a coincidence that his victory over the bottle paralleled the growth of his interest in the sport of show jumping. He quit drinking in 1972, a year before the first shovel of dirt was turned at Spruce Meadows.

At that time Nancy was doing very well in the junior division and Joe Selinger suggested a trip to the Toronto Royal Fair, a massive step for someone as young and inexperienced as Nancy.

"Ron was so busy, but I told him that Joe really thought she could do it. Ron, being as competitive as he is, asked me if I really believed this, and I told him 'Yes.'"

He had business in Toronto anyway, so he set aside some time to watch his daughter compete. Unfortunately, it was not one of her better showings. He was, however, captivated by the intensity his daughter displayed toward the sport and moved by her determination to become very good at it.

"That particular time was when Ron was drinking quite a lot," said Marg. "He was trying not to, but he was an alcoholic."

Nancy, however, didn't know until one night in 1967 that her father even had a drinking problem.

"I remember him coming home and being really drunk that night and it really bothered me. And often, when we would take our family vacation with my grandparents, I can remember Mom being very sad and that also really bothered me."

The turnabout was sudden and closed a chapter of mixed blessings for the Southern family. The next chapter, and all those succeeding it, always featured a horse among its main characters.

"I was going really well on the horses, and Dad stopped drinking. It all came as such a relief to my Mom. She just wanted to help pursue this as far as she could and really support him. She recognized he needed something other than his work and us girls. She saw his interest in the horse and the sport of show jumping as something he could really sink his teeth into."

Ron has always spoken openly about his brawl with alcoholism.

He even jokes that if Nancy had been bowling the day he entered sobriety instead of riding ". . . Spruce Meadows may have become one of the world's largest bowling alleys."

Marg presents the ATCO Cup to Barbara Simpson-Kerr at the 1979 Spruce Meadows MASTERS

Marg said that she became completely dedicated to the building of a riding facility when in the summer of 1972, prior to the 1972 Munich Olympics, she learned that Barbara Simpson-Kerr (who had accumulated the most points in the Canadian Show Jumping Team Trials) was going to be included on the team to attend the Munich Olympics but would be competing only in the individual event and not in the important team competition.

Barbara had two marvellous mounts and two of Canada's best at that time, Australis and Magnor. Possibly there were reasons unknown to Marg that determined the selection of Canada's other riders to represent Canada in the team competition but Marg had heard that the decision to exclude Barbara was that she was a woman and would not be able to handle the pressure.

Barb was one of the sport's most daring athletes, as aptly demonstrated several years earlier. When her riding peers from throughout the world refused to tackle the new Irish Jumping bank at Hickstead, she scoffed at the claims of danger. She was not only the first to attempt the foreboding bank, she handled the challenge with ease.

Hearing what happened to Barb, said Marg, was the turning point.

"Something cried out that this is not fair. Here is a kid from the west (Barb) and even though she was the best, she was only going to be an alternate."

Ironically a second Calgary rider, Norma Meyers, also should have been selected to the Canadian Olympic Show Jumping Team that year. But like Barb, Norma was also rejected. Her father actually sued the Canadian Equestrian Federation over that decision and won the judgement two years later - too late of course to correct the monumental wrong that had been commited.

"Neither Ron nor I ever wanted to become involved in the politics of this or any other sport. But it didn't seem right that there wasn't a place in the west where kids could be taught to ride and have the opportunity to compete under conditions equal to those in the east."

It seemed sad to think, added Marg, that so many good young riders would never develop because their parents couldn't afford to send them down east or into the United States for competition.

"We decided that we would build a facility where young riders could train."

Decision to Build

At first glance, the decision to proceed with Spruce Meadows prompted legitimate challenges.

It truly appeared to be an unlikely project, by unlikely people, in an unlikely location for an unlikely sport.

Although the economy was on the skids, the cost of the project - although not nearly as much as most suspected - was still significant.

The Southerns, although by now fully emersed in the sport of show jumping, were still mere neophytes when compared with the depth of experience enjoyed by Organizing

Committees at other global competitions. Many of them could rightly boast of decades, sometimes even centuries, of collective expertise.

The Irish Royal Dublin Society held its first horse show in 1864. Two years later show jumping events were held in Vienna, and a few years after that in Holland, Belgium and Italy.

Calgary, in the early nineteen seventies, didn't really offer any conclusive reasons as to why show jumping would catch fire as a huge spectator sport.

As a locale for any major sport it was enjoying only limited success. The professional football franchise was courting bankruptcy as it struggled to fill the thirty-thousand seats of McMahon Stadium, and the National Hockey League Calgary Flames had not yet arrived in town.

Several attempts at professional soccer and basketball failed miserably. Only minor league professional baseball, "A" and then "AAA", attracted steady crowds in the five thousand to ten thousand range. But even that squad threatened to pull up their bases and move into the U.S. when City Council balked at pouring tax dollars into park renovations. The Flames, in 1994, used the same ploy in a successful attempt to negotiate an upgrade of the Olympic Saddledome, an arena heralded as the finest in the world when completed for the 1988 Winter Olympics.

It was not a problem exclusive to Calgary. Fans of professional sport around the world were beginning to challenge tradition by demanding more for their entry dollar. Instead they were being asked to pay more to support outrageous salaries, yet the lack of commitment on the part of some players was painfully obvious.

In Europe, the traditional hotbed of show jumping, crowd numbers began to drop drastically as the introduction of more North American sport, presented in its traditional flamboyant manner, ate away at prime time television and prime sponsorship.

Without television and sponsorship commitment, survival at any level is virtually impossible for any sport in any country.

And while one could present a case due to the strong historical link between Western Canada and the horse, show jumping in Calgary in the seventies was not exactly a must on many entertainment calendars.

There were some very strong attempts being made to at least preserve the sport at the limited level it enjoyed, and those responsible were extremely dedicated.

The Calgary Horse Show, an indoor presentation sponsored by the Calgary Exhibition and Stampede, was reasonably healthy after more than three-quarters of a century. But its format was mired in tradition as it attracted more coverage on the society pages than the sport pages of Calgary's newspapers.

It was a bleak day for the sport, however, when the Stampede shelved the show forever in 1985. That is not the case with another show jumping-related organization which managed to celebrate its 50th anniversary in 1993. The Alberta Light Horse Association continues to foster and promote the sport among young riders. Pony Clubs also do an exceptional job of introducing the sport of show jumping to youngsters.

Horse show organizers of that era could always count on the following, but not much more: a handful of parents, grandparents and friends for an audience; three or four dominant riders of the ilk of a Barb and John Simpson, Gail Ross or Norma Meyers; and a couple of young hot prospects like Nancy Southern, Frank Selinger or Mark Laskin. Results were predictable and prize money seldom covered expenses.

Given the consistent failure of most other sports to attract significant crowds in Calgary, it seemed unlikely that show jumping's limited appeal could possibly justify the massive expenditure necessary for Spruce Meadows.

"You can accept the unlikely sport in the unlikely location as being correct at the time," said Ron, "but you must now look at all of the benefits that flow from this unlikely sport and unlikely location.

"I don't know how you describe it, but really, it was an exquisitely correct sport for that location, improbable as it may have seemed at the time."

Ron remembers the look in the eyes of both his and Marg's parents when they broke the news of their decision to build a world-class show jumping centre.

"All four were people of very modest education who had really come up the hard way," he said. "Spending this much money in this way seemed so improbable to them. Yet each of them, from the very beginning, did what they could to help us. My Mom and Dad picked rocks from the fields which are now our competitive rings, while Marg's parents hand-pulled weeds from around the farm houses."

Once the site had been purchased, initially one hundred and sixty acres now expanded to three hundred and fifteen acres, the period of design began ". . . and that was great fun."

The parcel chosen was superb. A former cattle feed lot, it began at the toes of the Alberta foothills and then flowed ever so gently into the western shadows of the Canadian Rockies that stood rigidly at guard just forty miles away. With the exception of a

> "You can accept the unlikely sport in the unlikely location as being correct at the time, but you must now look at all of the benefits that flow from this unlikely sport and unlikely location."
>
> (Ron Southern)

rugged patch of scrub willow and ragged aspen and poplar trees, the land was void of anything green. Like the heritage it served, this land was rough, ready and waiting for whatever mankind or the elements dare throw at it.

A ribbon of asphalt bordered its northern edge, merging with a super highway that jammed the throat of Calgary just three kilometres to the north.

In a quest to escape from the pounding heartbeat of the city, or some relief from the sweat its concrete frame squeezed from inhabitants, the site did offer promise as a potential oasis to soothe both mind and body.

"Our first thought was, 'how are we going to do this?'" recalled Ron. "We couldn't find any books on the subject, and the few we found on stable building didn't really seem to apply to North America."

Instead family members packed cameras and measuring tapes and headed for Europe, several times. Their visits focused primarily on Germany and England where they visited the show jumping shrines of Hickstead and Aachen, as well as the small and large family stables so prominent in both countries.

From cattle feed lot to show jumping venue, the Spruce Meadows grounds have undergone a major transformation since 1962.
(Picture is taken from southwest corner of property)

At Hickstead they took measurements of its famed bank and Devil's Dyke, and then introduced themselves to owner Douglas Bunn when he rode over from his nearby manor to see who had invaded his privacy.

The Devil's Dyke, is probably the most frightening addition ever made to show jumping. Riders must ask their horses to jump into what at first glance appears to be an open grave. Over the years, at both Hickstead and Spruce Meadows, the Devil's Dyke has consumed more show jumping aspirations then all other jumps combined.

There is a little-known tourist attraction within twenty kilometres of Hickstead that is actually called "Devil's Dyke". A very attractive restaurant awaits all visitors, otherwise people use the locale to fly small model airplanes.

(photo by Cansport)

The terror of the famed Devil's Dyke is explained by Ron to an eager audience during a Spruce Meadows "Walk On".

According to legend it is said the Dyke was dug by the devil in an attempt to flood the many small villages in the area. In fact it is a natural formation in the chalk hillside with sides rising over three hundred feet.

Upon their return to Calgary, in a room papered with pictures of what their complex might become, the Southerns began negotiations with Calgary architect Wolfgang Wenzel.

"We kept pushing ideas around with him, making things bigger and bigger. Fortunately for us now, we also decided on sites for buildings and locations for courses."

With the exception of a few close friends, Marg and Ron didn't tell many about their pending venture. One they did share the dream with was Max Ritchie, who was so taken with the concept he immediately committed to supporting junior riders. Not a

shovelful of earth had been turned, yet Spruce Meadows had its first sponsor all locked up. The Ritchie Family Junior Grand Prix became a fixture for fifteen years until the all-junior July tournament was expanded into what is now the Spruce Meadows NORTH AMERICAN.

Upon seeing the big rings at Dublin and Hickstead, Ron knew the first priority was to sever ties with North American tradition, where most rings were not much larger than indoor ice arenas. The sport needed a scope that couldn't be attained in a restricted area.

The whole development exercise of Spruce Meadows, he stressed, was not unlike the one undertaken by himself and Marg thirty years earlier with ATCO.

They would visit every mobile home show in North America, taking three or four days to explore as many as three to four hundred mobile homes and then meet with representatives.

"There wasn't one manufacturer that we didn't thoroughly exhaust in terms of how we could build our business. You might say we did the same for Spruce Meadows."

Course Designer Pamela Carruthers was already coming to the city for the Calgary Horse Show and Ron invited her to lead the way in designing and then supervising the building of the outdoor courses of Spruce Meadows.

It was a task she accepted with enthusiasm. It was certainly not an unfamiliar challenge for this talented designer. A dozen years earlier she had done the same at Hickstead and earned international accolades for her masterful creation.

The same fervour that drove the creation of ATCO took command of the creative juices stimulating the planning of Spruce Meadows.

"We kept asking '. . . what is the knowledge out there. Let's get a hold of it. Let's try and assimilate it. Let's try and apply it.' I don't mean we talked that way, it had just become second nature to us," Ron said.

Family consensus was important, but it seldom came easy. There were huge debates.

Do you, for example, put blue clay down in the stalls as recommended by everyone in Canada, or a harder surface?

"Almost everybody said we had to put clay down because it was better for the horses' feet. Yet in Europe, where they had cobblestone down, the stalls were so much cleaner and the horses seemed fine."

A trip to Winfield Farms outside of Toronto confirmed their preference. Multi-millionaire industrialist and race horse breeder E.P. Taylor had spared no expense in assuring the best for his recently-completed complex.

"And I'll be damned if he didn't have blacktop down in all his stalls," said Ron.

At one point the Southerns considered building a smaller riding hall and stable in conjunction with an already existing facility somewhere in the area.

Bas French, a close friend who became Competitions Manager at Spruce Meadows, remembered helping to talk Ron out of it. Perhaps knowing his friend better than most, Bas didn't want to put limits on what he could sense was becoming far more than a family stable.

"I've always been involved in land and believe everyone should have a piece of dirt," said Bas. "Buy the land, don't lease it," was his message and the Southerns heeded the advice.

The day finally came when the contract was ready to tender. The building contract called for construction of the Riding Hall which included: the 240' by 85' riding ring; an office area and upstairs lounge; and the two major horse barns, East and West Meadows with twenty four stalls each.

To this day, and despite the addition of some magnificent buildings over the years, nothing equals the spell-binding grandeur of that original structure.

Like an eagle in majestic flight, the Riding Hall endures as a sentinel in the heart of its kingdom. Its circular grass courtyard, undoubtedly one of the most photographed spots in Alberta, is home to a family of life-size bronze horses that create wonderful memories for every youngster or adult that eagerly climbs upon them.

In those early, pre-construction periods, not everyone was entirely convinced that what would ultimately blossom on the site of this former feed lot would be strikingly beautiful.

One man with mild doubts was Albert Kley. Although he initially had committed himself to only a one-year contract when he came to Calgary, he was quickly persuaded by the Southerns to stay on longer and join Spruce Meadows as its Riding Master.

It was a wonderful opportunity and set the mold for a life-long friendship between

Marg & Ron with "Family of the Horse" bronze statues that grace the entrance to the Riding Hall.

himself and the Southern family. But on his first visit with Ron to the Spruce Meadows site, made long before the start of construction, Albert confessed he had some doubts about his decision to stay.

He remembered the land being very messy. That, however, was nothing unusual for a cattle feed lot and Albert knew it could easily be cleaned up.

"But then Mr. Southern and I found this old red barn. It was just barely hanging together and attached to it was this little shed in even worse condition.

"Mr. Southern said he wanted to fix this barn and I said to myself: 'Wow, what kind of a start is this?'

"I was worried because he always told me he wanted a real nice stable, and now he was telling me his first priority was to fix this old barn. I wasn't sure at that moment that I really wanted to become involved in this."

The barn was refurbished and still stands proudly, subject of an annual pampering spree from maintenance staff. Again, its restoration serves as a reminder of the property's roots, and to the Southerns, that is important.

The cost of the Riding Hall project was far less than most people suspected. Rumours had the project costing as much as $10 million which simply fuelled speculation the family was crazy for spending that kind of money on a very improbable dream.

The Spruce Meadows Riding Hall still sparkles in its grandeur.

That initial contract, however, was let to Oland Construction of Calgary for far less - $1,060,000.

"At that time construction was in an absolute ditch, and we felt there would never be a more economic time to build," said Ron. "If we waited three or four more years, Spruce Meadows probably never would have been built because the cost would have been prohibitive."

Oland Construction may have built Spruce Meadows, but let there be no doubt as to who supervised that construction.

"Marg was the Project Manager on Spruce Meadows, and they don't come any tougher," said Ron.

"That was a tremendous amount of money for us and we wanted it right. It was a killer of a winter and it was tough to keep the concrete from freezing. Besides it was an absolutely different design from anything ever seen in Alberta, a project manager's nightmare, yet there was Marg directing the operation," said a very proud Ron Southern.

Marg was at the site every day and stayed from dawn to dusk. "I knew what it was costing us personally, so if it's your own dollars you're going to make sure it's being done right."

She tendered every phase of the job herself, and insisted on sitting down with each of the successful bidders before they moved onto the job site.

"I told them they had the right to withdraw right then because I would be out every day and would be making certain it was being done as if it were my home. I wasn't exactly loved by those who came out, but I think they respected me." Many came back afterward and told her that, at the very least, they always knew where she was coming from.

Marg Southern will not accept anything less than one hundred per cent effort from those working with her or for her. In return, no one will treat you with a greater respect, no matter what your station.

The Riding Hall was completed in the late winter of 1975 and was officially opened during a moving ceremony the evening of April 13, 1975.

Midway through the program a bronzed shovel was presented by S.D. Southern to his son along with a brief explanation to the crowd that such presentations were indicative of good luck when new barns were opened in Europe. Retired from ATCO, S.D. played an active role in the early years of Spruce Meadows and many of the jumps he handcrafted are still being used.

Benny, a horse Nancy credits as the "life and pulse of Spruce Meadows" was a member of that opening night cast and delighted the crowd by presenting Ron with something to scoop into his gilded shovel. S.D. smiled broadly as he watched his son get on with the job.

Spruce Meadows was now ready for competition. It had taken that first major step on its celebrated journey to global prominence.

Day One Continued:
Press Conference

Today, twenty one short years after those opening ceremonies, a press conference will again be noticeably void of the past warmth provided by both S.D. and Ina Southern, who passed away in 1990 and 1987 respectively. Even Benny, who enjoyed a majestic life that carried him into his early thirties, is now also gone.

Their spirits linger, however, and they would be deeply delighted with what is unfolding today before a vast collection of show jumping's top riders and most prominent journalists.

This MASTERS has the potential to become one of the most significant show jumping competitions of the decade, and that claim survives measurements against World Championships and Olympic Games.

Media from throughout Europe, Mexico, the United States and Canada - one hundred and twenty eight will be accredited before the tournament ends - await tomorrow's first day of competition. Today they are on the prowl for a good story and good food. Spruce Meadows' Press Conferences are known to produce the best of both.

The focal point of all questions is the German team. Everyone wants to know if they can repeat their conquests of just weeks before when they stunned the sport by sweeping three of a possible four medals at the World Equestrian Championships in The Hague, Netherlands.

It was an awesome display of riding power by the Germans who were paced by Franke Sloothaak. He was flawless at the World Championships putting together four faultless rounds to edge Michel Robert of France for the individual gold. He fits the title well and has a wonderful delicacy about what he does with horses. They demonstrate tremendous confidence for him, knowing when they enter the arena they have been well-prepared for anything. He is also among the best tacticians when it comes to a jump-off.

Germany's Franke Sloothaak and Weihaiwej - 1994 World Champions

Michel Robert, who won a team gold in the 1982 World Championships and individual and team silver medals at the 1994 World Championships, is among the fifty-two world-class riders also seeking a note of revenge at this MASTERS.

Not in recent memory, neither here nor in Europe, has such an intense concentration of the world's top show jumpers and horses been amassed for either a non-Olympic or non-World Championship event.

The Germans appear invincible. In addition to Sloothaak, the entry includes World bronze medallist Soren Von Ronne and Ludger Beerbaum, fourth at The Hague, winner of the 1992 World Cup Final and also Olympic Champion from the '92 Olympics of Barcelona.

But those who know this sport will quickly tell you that sure bets are for suckers. Results are as unpredictable as Calgary's fall weather, and wizened observers of this sport seldom speak boldly, or loudly, of pending victories in fear of having to explain such foolishness later.

The only thing totally predictable is that all results will be known in five hotly-contested days. Any attempt now at serious prognostication will almost certainly make liars of all messengers.

For as dominating as the German entry appears, one only has to look at the all-star entry gathered against it. A record eight countries were invited to send teams to this MASTERS and individuals from seven others are also here.

Among the eight teams lined up to compete in the Bank of Montreal Nations' Cup five days from now, seven finished among the top ten at the 1994 World Championships. They include: Germany - gold; France - silver; Switzerland - bronze; the United States - fifth; Great Britain - sixth; Canada - seventh; and Ireland - ninth. The eighth and final entry is a vastly improved contingent from Mexico, a respectable thirteenth at The Hague.

The queue of individual talent is even more stunning. The top eight riders from the World Championships will face off again at Spruce Meadows.

All have their sights focused on the riches of the International Division where ten competitions collectively tempt them with almost $1.1 million in prize money. (The next year, 1995, this sport's first $1 million weekend broke new sponsorship ground.)

Ludger Beerbaum - 1992 Barcelona Olympic Games gold medallist

Among events, of course, is the sport's richest competition, the $725,000 du Maurier International. As long as you finish the course, even if you are last, you will receive $3,000 as reward for just being good enough to be among the best. The winner pockets $230,000.

Eight past du Maurier winners are here this year, including two-time winners Nick Skelton and John Whitaker of Great Britain and home-grown super hero, Ian Millar. Is it possible one may become the first three-time winner?

Ron Southern opens the Press Conference, and as is tradition, he seldom wastes an opportunity to thank people for their contributions toward the growth of Spruce Meadows, or to tell an audience about what, with their help, Spruce Meadows has returned to the community,

Today, before the local, national and international press, he unveils results of an economic impact study done by the Calgary Convention and Visitors Bureau. The figures pertain to the 1993 MASTERS and were compiled using the Tourism Economic Assessment Model (TEAM) that was developed by the Canadian Tourism Research Institute of the Conference Board of Canada. The study was unsolicited, but compiled to help evaluate the economic impact of sporting events on a city.

The MASTERS, he explains, had a full-trip spending impact of $48.3 million and a total industry output for the province's Gross National Product of $67.2 million.

"Now those may not be large figures in the scheme of the billions that nations talk about, but let's think about it for a minute. From this facility and a cattle feedlot, we are now providing the equivalent of 1,101 full-time jobs in this community. That's what enterprise is all about."

The fact that not one of the sports reporters in attendance wrote about, or broadcast those figures was of little concern to Ron. He knows their priority in being there is to focus on show jumping, not economics. But he was humbled by those figures and they deserve the best audience he can give them.

He looks about the room and acknowledges the presence of some old friends, as well as some newcomers to the Media Conference. Among the familiar faces are Alan Smith of the London Daily Telegraph, acknowledged by his peers as the most knowledgeable show jumping journalist in the world. Beside him stands Bob Langrish, the sport's top freelance photographer, operating out of England.

The Calgary media also enjoys the warmth of Ron Southern's praise.

"What we have here in Calgary, in our media, makes this the best city in the world for the coverage of our sport. We could never have done this without you telling your story to the people of Canada, and now to the world."

The coverage didn't come easily.

Discovering Spruce Meadows

Because the sport had very little public following in Western Canada, it was virtually impossible to interest local and regional media in covering early tournaments.

Not to be deterred by such a minor setback, Spruce Meadows' media staff would do it for them in hopes that eventually reporters and broadcasters would come to accept the news value of show jumping.

Live voice reports, several times a day, were fed to every radio and TV station that would take them - local or otherwise. Every report was different, thus guaranteeing each station something exclusive.

Live stories were filed to the wire services, all done in accordance with specific writing styles. At the end of the competition, wrap-up stories went out to virtually every major show jumping magazine in Canada and throughout Europe. As many as fifteen different articles on the same tournament, ranging in length from one to six pages, were pounded out with a commitment to deadlines and style.

Every sponsor that had an internal newsletter was given a story detailing the specifics of their event, and every weekly newspaper that had a home town rider win at Spruce Meadows - Junior or International - received an exclusive story along with a picture of the triumphant rider.

Although an exact count wasn't taken, it is estimated that as many as sixty different stories appeared around the world about that first MASTERS Tournament in 1977, every one of them by Spruce Meadows media staff.

The Calgary Herald was the first to embrace the sport, assigning a sports writer to show jumping after the first Spruce Meadows tournament in 1976. Publisher Frank Swanson became one of the sport's most enthusiastic supporters and aided greatly in its permanent abandonment of the social pages. Finally, show jumping had found the home it deserved - in the Sports section. Within a few years all Calgary radio and television stations, together with daily and regional newspapers, were covering Spruce Meadows live. The international media was not far behind.

To gain more credibility for Spruce Meadows' competitions within Europe, Marg and Ron Southern invited key journalists to travel free to Calgary to cover the MASTERS.

It wasn't, however, a seat wrapped in luxury. In fact more than a few reporters were a bit surprised to find themselves on the same plane as that transporting the international horses. Among the first to make the journey was Dutch journalist Jacob Melissen.

"It provided me with the most beautiful experience of my whole life," Jacob said of his 1982 flight aboard a Flying Tigers cargo plane. Flying the old Polar Route, the plane had to stop in Frobisher Bay, N.W.T. for refuelling. It attracted the curiosity of several Inuit, most of them children.

"They had never seen horses in their life, and we invited them into the plane to show them the likes of Deister (Paul Schockemoehle's great jumper) and Towerlands Anglezarke (Great Britain's most successful jumper in the early eighties with Malcolm Pyrah).

"It was a wonderful feeling. I felt like a missionary in the middle of Africa. To this day I can still hear their laughter."

From the outset, Marg and Ron always made themselves available to the press, no matter how large or small the paper or TV station may have been.

Marg, often accompanied by Nancy or Linda, would get out of bed for a 6 a.m. radio talk show that promised her only seconds on a program that at best had a very limited audience.

As a result, together with a policy that insists on total honesty with the media from all staff and volunteers, Spruce Meadows continues to enjoy a uniquely positive relationship with reporters.

"Our relationship with the media, whether here or at ATCO, has always been based on total candor, genuine sincerity and absolutely no duplicity. There is no alternative to honesty," said Ron.

"From the standpoint of the cynical media, reporters have not gone out of their way to find criticism of Spruce Meadows, simply because they see it as the best," said John Quirk, publisher of Horses Magazine, the oft-quoted bible of show jumping during the eighties

> "Our relationship with the media, whether here or at ATCO, has always been based on total candor, genuine sincerity and absolutely no duplicity. There is no alternative to honesty."
>
> (Ron Southern)

and nineties in the United States.

"I don't write the positive things I do about Spruce Meadows because I like Marg and Ron Southern. I write because of me, and that is because I really believe it."

Marg Southern explained that since both she and Ron grew up in sport, dealing with the media was not something new to them.

"We found that whenever you co-operated with the media, and gave them honest information, they used it properly. But so often people expect the media to know details which should have been, but weren't, provided for them," said Marg.

To acquaint broadcasters and scribes with the lighter side of show jumping, the Southerns launched family media days. Horse rides were provided for their children, and a competition over small jumps was organized for reporters. Those who participated never again mocked the difficulty when talking about the sport.

The key to growth in any sport is television and the Southerns were quick to realize that national, and ultimately international coverage was essential to future successes.

Without national television coverage it would be difficult to keep sponsors, and without sponsors the sport simply couldn't survive at the level needed to sustain the Spruce Meadows dream. Before either would happen, however, the stands had to be filled with spectators.

Early sponsors didn't always have representatives at their events, content

The arrival of international horses on a German Air Cargo chartered 747 is an event eagerly awaited

D-ABZA

(photo by Al Savage)

to offer sponsorship packages because they believed that if the Southerns were involved, it had to be good. Most, in fact, initially put up the money more as a favour to the Southerns than as testimony of their belief in the sport.

This was fine in the early years, and actually allowed Spruce Meadows time to build gates. When sponsors did eventually show up expecting large crowds, they weren't greeted by empty bleachers.

Within a few short years, however, the head offices of many of these sponsors were asking for some tangible evidence of the sport's popularity. Some got that through newspaper clippings, but others wanted some national television exposure.

Initially only one or two of the weekend events attracted the interest of television, which meant that even though they weren't always being used, the cameras were visible around the courses.

Johnny Esaw was Vice-President of CTV Sports when he first met Ron Southern in 1976. The network, at the time, was still doing the Royal Winter Fair and Johnny told Ron that he was happy to stick just with that.

"Show jumping just didn't fit right coming from Alberta," Johnny thought at the time. "Calgary was wild west country, not equestrian territory. I kept measuring show jumping with what I was seeing at the Royal."

The CBC changed his mind. The people's network bought its way into the Royal Winter Fair leaving CTV out in the cold.

"Under the circumstances I now thought I'd better take a look at Spruce Meadows and Ron Southern," said Johnny.

The two met in Toronto and he told Ron that while his interest was now slightly tweaked, he wasn't prepared to pay anything for the broadcast rights.

"But I suggested that if he was interested in contributing to the production, then maybe we could reach a deal." Ron didn't hesitate and for $15,000 he bought himself some national television exposure for Spruce Meadows.

Johnny Esaw, the man who nurtured figure skating into a television production giant, had reason to gloat. It is unlikely anyone else in the world would ever again convince Ron Southern to pay for a service he should have been paid for.

"Well he always said he would get it back," said Johnny, "and it didn't take him long." Television contracts for the three Spruce Meadows tournaments are now comfortably into the six figure bracket.

The more he saw of Spruce Meadows, the better Johnny Esaw liked it. He was also amazed by the marketing genius of Ron Southern who told him right from the start that if he could get television exposure, he would also get serious sponsorship.

Ron told the CTV producer he would give the sponsors giant billboards, but Johnny would have to get them on television. That, said Ron, would lead to new revenues for

> Throughout television's hectic development years, no one seemed to notice that Spruce Meadows had a fascinating little television coup of its own taking shape.

both as well as a far stronger sport for riders and the public. It got Ron off the hook in terms of production support, and got Johnny Esaw into show jumping "much, much deeper than I ever anticipated."

"I thought I knew a lot about packaging and sponsorships, but it was nothing compared to what I learned from Ron. Those who put in the greatest amount of money receive the greatest support. That was his theory and I believed in it one hundred per cent.

"Programs are worth so much in value to the company and in air-time. But you can make it worth so much more if you do more, and to do more we had to have extra dollars." That theory was proven in a major sponsorship package negotiated with the Bank of Montreal in the early eighties.

After Johnny Esaw retired from CTV, rival CBC managed to wrestle the contract away in 1991. Give Johnny Esaw and CTV a lot of credit for some extremely innovative approaches to the sport, including great exposure for the riders through personality profiles.

CBC introduced Spruce Meadows to big-time production. Under the guidance of Alan Clark, Head of CBC Sports, crew numbers tripled and the packages, highly polished and professional, were also superb testimony to the many attributes of the sport.

Throughout television's hectic development years, no one seemed to notice that Spruce Meadows had a fascinating little television coup of its own taking shape.

In 1985 something called Team Spruce Meadows (TSM) was created, primarily to deal with Linda Southern's move to professional rider status. Nancy Southern, although no longer a competitive rider, was part of TSM and would appear on behalf of sponsors to promote the sport as well as their products.

Eventually TSM blossomed into a far more comprehensive entity with Nancy as President and Ian Allison as Vice President, a young man who started his career at Spruce Meadows as a seventeen-year-old maintenance worker.

Spruce Meadows Television, which now produces programming for more than half a dozen sport networks in the United States and Europe, had a most humble beginning.

Ian, who was doing some on-camera work during the tournaments for CTV, received a call from Nancy in April of 1985. Nancy had already established herself as one of the sport's most knowledgeable colour commentators, and was also working for CTV during the Spruce Meadows tournaments.

"How'd you like to do a television series?" Nancy asked Ian.

Nancy interviews Canadian Team member John Simpson (1977).

Canadian Tire associates in Calgary had put together $10,000 and wanted to sponsor a television series about Spruce Meadows. That became the foundation of a program called "Spruce Meadows Today", the same series that continues to air around the world today.

The production delves deeply, and with insight, into all facets of the horse's world, as well as those humans whose lives are so richly touched by it. A trip to The Hague or New Zealand for coverage of the World Championships or a national tournament is now as commonplace to the Spruce Meadows Television production team as a quick local hit on the Spruce Meadows breeding program.

The production crew is held in such high esteem internationally, tournament organizers at Aachen chose Spruce Meadows Television from among the world's best to produce its competitive programs.

That confidence was not quite so evident back in 1985 when, through CTV's Calgary affiliate CFCN, a production deal was struck for five half-hour "Spruce Meadows Today" programs. The only marketing commitment was a promise from CFCN that it air the shows "sometime" and do its best to convince Edmonton affiliate CFRN to do the same.

Today the "Spruce Meadows Today" series can be seen across Canada on all CTV affiliates and is syndicated nationally as well on TSN.

By 1988 Ian and Nancy had succeeded in selling the program to independents across Canada, and it was time to try and crack the lucrative U.S. market.

After being politely told to catch the next plane home by all of the major players in California, Ian dug in and set up camp outside the offices of a station in Bakersfield.

"That station's Director of Programming thought I had other business in town and saw me in thirty minute breaks over three or four days," said Ian. "I even went to his riding lesson with him, and finally we struck a deal."

Although the station was relatively small, its signal was carried on the cable systems and that meant "Spruce Meadows Today" would find its way into the monster markets of Los Angeles and San Francisco. The station was also owned by publishing and media giant McGraw Hill which just happened to own ten other stations in the western U.S.

Nancy, meanwhile, was developing contract interest with the sport network ESPN, but it would take an amazing turn of events to ice the deal.

"I met with ESPN president Bill Grimes, and although he seemed committed to take our show, Spruce Meadows wasn't really what interested him," said Nancy.

ESPN really wanted rodeo from the Calgary Stampede and asked Nancy if she knew who held the U.S. contract rights.

"I didn't, but I called home and found, believe it or not, that the Calgary Stampede was not being aired anywhere else in the world except Canada."

Nancy confidently suggested to the ESPN boss that if a deal could be struck on "Spruce Meadows Today", she would deliver him the Stampede as well.

(photo by Al Savage)

Nancy with Ian Allison, Vice President, Television & Media Services, in the television broadcast booth overlooking the International Ring.

"In the first two years they thought they had a windfall in the Stampede, but still weren't really all that interested in Spruce Meadows."

Nancy, however, changed their minds with some nifty entrepreneurial manoeuvres reminiscent of those shown by a young man selling trailers many years before. She was tired of waiting for Mohammed to show up at the mountain. She decided to taunt the biggest players of all by showing up at the doorstep of the Cannes Television Festival. Before going she struck a deal with ESPN that gave them forty percent of revenues if they helped her sell "Spruce Meadow Today" production at the Festival.

"It turned out to be a real eye-opener. "Spruce Meadows Today" made more money for them internationally than the Calgary Stampede."

Supporting the series since it began airing in the U.S. has been Chevron Corporation, headquartered in San Francisco, a proud association they maintain to this present day.

Spruce Meadows Television has since switched its affiliation to Prime Sports Network which offers a potential audience of fifty-three million viewers.

Tournament coverage and the "Spruce Meadows Today" series can be seen on TSN which reaches six million Canadian households and Sky Sports in the United Kingdom carries Spruce Meadows to a potential three million viewers there.

The Spruce Meadows team continues to expand its production schedules, now covering six of the events not contracted for by CBC.

A new state-of-the-art edit suite is now in place at Spruce Meadows and with state-of-the-art digital and three-dimensional equipment in place, has the capacity to meet the most sophisticated production needs.

(photo by Al Savage)

Pollyanna Hardwicke-Brown, Advertising Manager, and Jeff August, Production Specialist work on the "Spruce Meadows Today" television opening in the edit suite, located in the Spruce Meadows Media Center.

Day One Continued:
Riders' Meeting

Following today's Press Conference, riders gather for what has become a meeting of both controversy and delight - always taking place the day before competition begins.

It's time for the traditional Riders' Meeting, and "Yes", the veterans remind fresh, new faces, "it is compulsory no matter how many others you have attended in the past".

The golden rules of Spruce Meadows are spelled out in detail at the sessions. Misunderstand them, or even worse, ignore them, and you threaten to dislodge the primary building blocks of Spruce Meadows' foundation - honesty and integrity.

If one searched for an unyielding edge to Ron Southern's personality, it will emerge at these meetings. The Riders' Meeting has become a window into the evolution of show jumping at Spruce Meadows the past two decades, and when it comes to rule enforcement, the view hasn't changed.

Although the focal point of today's meeting inevitably will concentrate on rules and decorum, Ron also uses it as an opportunity to philosophize on subjects that might range from global economic strategy to the importance of family values.

All riders must attend the meetings and discussion is directed as much toward the first-time junior as to the Olympic champion.

He tells riders he is well aware of the time spent talking about rules and regulations, but stresses why following them is so vital to the integrity of the sport. What is said today, however, can't match the fire of his impassioned appeal for fairness delivered at the 1992 NORTH AMERICAN Riders' Meeting.

That session began quietly enough as Ron simply told riders that Spruce Meadows was in the business of creating dreams, and then working hard to turn them into reality.

"And we've done that in a genuine belief that we were helping you, the athlete. When we first entered this sport, what we noticed amongst other Organizing Committees and the athletes competing there, was the constant collisions and friction around rules that didn't make any sense to me.

"Spruce Meadows," he continued, "tried to develop guidelines that made common sense, not only to organizers, but also to riders. There is no guarantee what was done is correct," he stressed, "but everything done at Spruce Meadows is an honest attempt to better the sport for competitors, fans, sponsors and owners.

Ron addresses athletes at traditional Rider's Meeting held the day prior to each Spruce Meadows tournament.

"I hope that the best friends you have in this sport will be the people you meet at Spruce Meadows. Everything we've done here has been done to give you pride, to give pride to the sponsors who support you, and to give pride to the people that come to watch you."

Traditions are Launched

At the first Spruce Meadows tournament in 1976 Ron directed ribbon recipients on how to handle the "Victory Ride".

As they lined up for presentations, he told them they were to "go around in a little circle, and to do so at a gallop. We're going to be standing there clapping our hands and when you come by us, you're going to take your hat off for the sponsor."

The looks from those riders were somewhat incredulous.

"Everybody was saying, 'Wait a minute. It's windy and there's nobody else here but you'. The only people more embarrassed than those clapping were the eight riders who by now felt the party was really going downhill," said Ron.

"But they came by in a whirly-gig fashion, got their hats off and we created some tradition and a little bit of pride."

Graeme "Butch" Thomas, who rode for the New Zealand Olympic Team before taking up residency in California in the early seventies, was among the handful of non-Canadian riders who competed at the first Spruce Meadows tournament.

Linda Allen, a superb rider before back injuries re-directed her career toward course designing, joined Butch on that trip and recalls his reaction to some of Ron's early edicts.

"We were walking out of the Riders' Meeting and Butch was upset with Ron's edict that riders must remove their hats when being presented with a ribbon or prize from one of the sponsors. He said he would never be back at Spruce Meadows because he wasn't about to take his hat off to somebody standing on the ground."

He told Linda that as far as he was concerned they could give him his cheque later and he would go home.

"But I did notice he took his hat off without complaint, and he's been back to just about every show since. We still tease him about it."

Butch, together with wife Lu, became among the most successful riders ever at Spruce Meadows, and son Guy has since taken up where his father left off.

There are some riders who hang spell-bound on every word uttered by Ron at those meetings, and not surprisingly, Ian Millar is one of them.

"I love to listen at those Riders' Meetings," said the man who has attended far more than most others. "They're great because Ron almost always has a new theme."

(photo by Rick Maynard)

California's Butch and Lu Thomas have been great friends and supporters of Spruce Meadows.

Ron jokes that his messages may get repetitious, but that's only because the seriousness of some topics is so grave he feels obligated to repeat it often.

"But if you listen carefully, there's always a new theme or new direction," said Ian. "Sometimes it's clear he walked in with the idea in mind, other times I believe that he got up there and then the spirit has just moved him in a direction.

> "If you sit there and listen and watch carefully, you see how the man's (Ron Southern's) mind works. His knowledge is quite remarkable."
>
> (Ian Millar)

"I very much take them as lessons. I love his delivery. If you sit there and listen and watch carefully, you see how the man's mind works. His knowledge is quite remarkable. What he knows about so many things and what makes things work and why they work . . . he is a real, real leader.

"We as a sport and industry are so fortunate to have the likes of Marg and Ron Southern. It may be decades again, if ever, that the sport sees people like them."

Kind, sincere words from a man eminently respected throughout the show jumping world.

It may also explain why Ron Southern spent so much time at the 1992 NORTH AMERICAN Riders' Meeting carefully revisiting rules and regulations. This was the first Riders' Meeting since the 1992 Spruce Meadows NATIONAL, the tournament at which Spruce Meadows suspended Ian Millar for rapping a horse in a warm-up ring.

The suspension was by far the highest-profiled negative incident in Spruce Meadows' history, and marked the first time the public had discerned even a hint of gloom descend upon this upwardly positive facility.

Three stewards said they saw Ian on a horse called Winchester jump an offset fence just before he entered the International Ring. For the record, Winchester had won the speed class on opening night the evening before, but in this class he didn't even place.

Simply put, an offset fence is an oxer where the top bar on the first standard is set higher than the top bar on the second standard, the reverse from normal.

Inevitably the horse will focus on the second standard and rap his legs sharply on the top rail of the first. It is illegal, and should not be tolerated even at the schooling level. Since time eternal, however, there have always been some riders who use the procedure to wake up lazy horses.

There are also varying degrees to the seriousness of different rapping procedures. They include such barbaric practices as hitting the horse with bamboo poles, two-by-fours and even setting spiked rails. Under anyone's definition, jumping an offset fence of the nature that Ian was involved with, was minor. But it was also very much against the rules.

Ian immediately denied knowledge of the offset fence stressing that he would never, under any circumstance, jeopardize his reputation by deliberately, and blatantly jumping an illegal fence in full view of stewards, fellow competitors, and cameras surveying the practice areas.

The stewards, however, were adamant the infraction had taken place, and Ian could offer no evidence that it hadn't . . . only that if it had, he was not aware of it at the time.

The rules clearly state that the guilty party be disqualified from the tournament and all prize money forfeited. The perpetrator would also be suspended from competing at Spruce Meadows for the remainder of the year. Ron simply read from the rule book and Ian was yanked from the warm-up ring just minutes before he was to have taken Big Ben into the evening's featured class.

"I wanted to throw up when I got that infraction report," Ron told that 1992 gathering of riders. "We haven't instituted these rules to try and catch people. Believe me, that is the last thing we want."

A press conference was immediately called to discuss the suspension. Ian was invited to attend to explain his position, and he did.

Both men appeared to be physically devastated by what had transpired. The two individuals who had done more for Canadian show jumping than any others, were suddenly locked in an ugly and unwanted conflict.

"I wish more than anything else in the world that this had not happened," Ron told reporters at the press conference. He then announced his decision which would have effectively booted Millar off the grounds and not allowed him back for twelve months. It would have meant Ian could not come back for the 1992 MASTERS.

The decision, he announced, would be reviewed the next morning by the Organizing Committee. Members of that committee included he and Marg, Tournament Secretary Joanne Nimitz, and long-time friends and Spruce Meadows volunteers, Bas and Anne French - Competitions Manager and Volunteers Co-ordinator respectively.

They met for four hours the next day and announced their decision at a second Press Conference. The penalty would not be nearly as stern as initially set out, but more severe than many believed it would be.

Only Winchester was suspended for the remainder of the tournament, and only earnings from that horse would be forfeited. Ian was suspended from competing on any horse, including Big Ben for forty-eight hours from the time of the incident. Since the infraction happened on Thursday, the second day of the competition, Ian and Big Ben would miss two crucial events, but would be able to compete in the major weekend classes.

Among other things, he was now virtually out of the running for the 1992 Canadian Show Jumping Championship, an award presented to the most successful rider in all four events in Section II of the Open Jumper Division. Up until that year Ian had represented Canada as its champion for seven of the past ten years, including a six-year run that began in 1986. He had always worn the title with a regal dignity.

Many, including several fellow riders, felt it was wrong to give Ian what was perceived to be a break on the punishment received. Spruce Meadows, more than any centre in the show jumping world, preached equality and fairness, yet now eased the punishment for Canada's favourite show jumping son.

If it had been any rider other than Ian Millar, some argued, the full suspension would have been upheld.

Ron did not shy away from a response. In a bold show of honesty, he agreed that was probably the case. He stressed, however, that the decision to reduce the penalty was in the best interest of the sport and promised that Spruce Meadows rules would be immediately reviewed to allow for discretionary punishment to fit the severity of the impropriety.

"But don't ever think the final penalty was not significant," Ron later explained.

There was the denial of the Canadian Championship to Ian, some $7,000 in entry fees, stabling and winnings to date by Winchester were forfeited, an estimated $15,000 that he could have won over the forty-eight hour suspension was lost, and another $15,000 in direct endorsements would never be seen. That's about $45,000, and that's a significant penalty in any sport.

It is not an incident that either man likes to talk about.

"In remembering it now I wouldn't call the incident a fight or confrontation because Ron showed tremendous class in the way he handled it," said Ian. "There were a lot of things that he could have said that he didn't say. And there were a lot of things that I could have said that I didn't say.

"I believe that what saved the day, if you can say the day was saved, was a mutual respect. I respected his position and I hope he respected mine. I believe we were both trying to do it well . . . handle a bad situation as well as we could without making it a whole lot worse," said Ian.

The following might help to put it all into perspective:

1. The case of rapping was minor and did not threaten the health or safety of that horse. But, if rapping is permitted under even the most minor of interpretations, one must also assume it could ultimately lead to abuse of horses under the guise of a training aid. No form of rapping, therefore, can be tolerated.

2. The penalty was costly to Ian Millar. His reputation was challenged, but not threatened.

3. The sport at Spruce Meadows, and throughout at least Canada, emerged a winner. Held high on a pedestal by a public that never suspected any improprieties, it faced the severe scrutiny of a challenging media for the first time. The public learned that Spruce Meadows would uphold the rules, although there was no doubt that in this case they were bent in favour of a high-profile personality. But there was no attempt at a cover-up.

4. If, as most riders acknowledged, some rapping is common, but is not seen as being out-of-place at some other tournaments, it was time others followed the lead of Spruce Meadows.

Most riders and officials publicly condemn rapping in any fashion. They will argue from a "zero tolerance" perspective. Privately, many of the same individuals will say it could be regulated in such a way that it would never endanger the horse, yet remain an effective training procedure.

One such individual who openly offers a contrary opinion on the subject is Charles Barrelet, a retired Captain in the Swiss Army and coach of the Swiss show jumping team.

His direct reference was toward the celebrated and widely-publicized rapping incidents in the eighties involving leading German trainers and riders. The incidents were condemned soundly by virtually everyone, and every official organization within the sport.

"It was a true example of how one should not have dealt with the issue," said Charles. "The Federation at that time should have come out and said rapping, properly done, is not a cruelty to the animal . . . but stressing it must be properly done."

As a young Lieutenant in the army he was "taught how to rap a horse properly", he continued. "In America you can still rap with a tiny bamboo pole that won't hurt the horse or anything, but makes them slightly more attentive."

He said it was not an issue he wanted to raise once again, but warned if the sport was not careful - particularly at the FEI (International Equestrian Federation), National Federations and individual Organizing Committee levels - reactive rather than proactive measures would only lead to more trouble.

"I think the sport must be extremely careful how it handles itself to make sure that the movement (animal protectionist groups) does not get out of control. We must be careful to defend the sport before it is really attacked. If we are only reactive we will lose the game."

> "I think the sport must be extremely careful how it handles itself to make sure that the movement (animal protectionist groups) does not get out of control."
>
> (Charles Barrelet)

A month after the incident at Spruce Meadows, just prior to the 1992 NORTH AMERICAN, a new policy which allowed for overriding discretionary power when penalties for all infractions are decided upon was released.

When applied to particular cases, stated the revised rule and equity statement, the current rules at Spruce Meadows frequently caused undue hardships or offended "notions of justice or morality."

In the development of Spruce Meadows rules, it was explained, equity needed to be added to allow room for interpretation in concert with reason.

"An unbridled equity poses the threat of an arbitrary, capricious and uncertain rules system. To guard against this threat, equitable principles must be governed by strict rules and principles," it stated.

Ron concluded that the process of changing penalties to better reflect the intent of rules would be difficult because that invited an endless array of pleas for equity.

"What are the differences of various types of drugging? What are the differences of various types of rapping . . . nails in poles, steel poles, bamboo poles and offset?

"Where will our Organizing Committee find the wisdom? I don't know, but we're going to try," said Ron.

In conceding the change would have come eventually anyway, Ron said that a tough Spruce Meadows rule system still had to be put down.

"Not because we want to, but because we believe in this facility and we believe in you. We also believe in structuring this sport."

French journalist Xavier Libbrecht suggested more tournaments around the world must follow the Spruce Meadows example, but warned that until that happens there will always be incidents of rapping and other forms of cheating.

It's ignored at most tournaments in Europe, he said, unless it is blatant abuse.

"It is obvious if a rider can do it on the last fence before entering the arena, he will try," said Xavier. "I mean if the rider is not confident he has the right horse, and since he knows most of the horses can jump better, he will try."

Spruce Meadows pioneered the concept of zero tolerance for those who stray from the rules for any and all reasons.

"As a journalist and as a great supporter of the sport, I believe it's the only way to handle the situation. Keep the rules clear and the game clean."

The only other rider incident which provoked intense emotion involved a decision taken in 1989 that resulted in a one year suspension of Canadian Mark Laskin, one of the most popular and competent riders on the North American circuit.

Mark, the closest thing this sport had to a Canadian super hero when he dominated competition in the eighties, was emotionally crushed by the suspension. It is unlikely that any other rider had spoken so highly of Spruce Meadows and the Southerns.

What happened?

The Edmonton-born Laskin arrived for the '89 MASTERS with an entourage that included one Intermediate horse. Although he moved to the United States in the mid-eighties and now rides out of Sante Fe, New Mexico for Pinon Farms, Mark still gets more out of any horse than ninety per cent of the circuit riders.

"The horse had hurt himself a couple of weeks before we got to Spruce Meadows. The injury was best treated with a particular analgesic anti-inflammatory, and we went to the CEF veterinarian before competition to make sure it was OK to use."

Mark says he was asked if the horse was competing in events governed by FEI rules, or CEF (Canadian Equestrian Federation) rules. FEI regulations are traditionally tougher than those enforced by national associations.

"I knew the FEI rules wouldn't allow use of the drug, and I wouldn't have even tried if the horse was entered in the International Division - the only division I was told that would be governed by the FEI rule book."

Acting on the information the drug would be fine for a horse in the Intermediate Division, Mark entered the horse in question and ended up winning the lion's share of cash in that division.

A month or so later he received a letter telling him the horse had tested positive. "I never tried to deny the drug was used," said Mark. "I argued that I was given the go ahead by the vet, but was told in return that it was still my responsibility to make certain I understood all of the rules."

Mark was fined $100 and had to return the prize money. He was also banned from competing at Spruce Meadows for one year, and that pain will never be forgotten.

"In my case there was no middle ground. I was disappointed, but I accepted the decision. But it cost me an important year and probably about $100,000 in lost prize money.

"I felt like I'd been sent down to the minors. Everything I do during the year is in preparation for the three Spruce Meadows tournaments."

(Mark Laskin)

"I felt like I'd been sent down to the minors. Everything I do during the year is in preparation for the three Spruce Meadows tournaments. That year I had to settle for Tulsa and Oklahoma City."

Ron was sensitive to that decision when he spoke to riders years later about a more discretionary approach to handing out penalties.

"Mark, I wish I could go back," he told the meeting.

Tom Gayford, now retired as Canadian Team coach, still isn't convinced about the motivation behind rule enforcement at Spruce Meadows.

"The only feeling that I get there is a feeling they'd like to hang you. It's the only show in the world I know where you get the feeling they'd like to catch you doing something," said Tom.

The veteran competitor-coach insisted that at other world-class events the stewards will tell you "Hey, be careful, don't do that."

"But Ron is absolutely by the book and black is black and there's no grey area at all. The man has strong rules and I know he also has strong morals. He's trying to be absolutely straight on the line and as fair as possible, but I think at times he oversteps that."

In conclusion, however, Tom is quick to add he believes Ron and others do a "wonderful job."

"And you know exactly where you stand, so you play the game."

On the other hand, Ron and Marg are frequently told by riders not to give in or become as lenient as most other Organizing Committees.

They say Spruce Meadows is the one place in the sport that gives them a standard.

"A lot of riders see him (Ron) as a hard person to get along with, or that he deliberately sets out to find conflict," suggested daughter Linda.

"Unfortunately, I also believe that a lot of athletes throughout all sports have to cheat in order to win and achieve. Look at the bottom line of the Dubbin Inquiry (trial of Canadian sprinter Ben Johnson). In essence it told us that if you don't cheat, you can't win."

Within the sport of show jumping, riders now know it is different at Spruce Meadows. They won't be able to beat the system here, so they won't even try.

Marg Southern offered this final insight into her husband's passion for playing by the rules.

"Ron can't even stand somebody golfing and not counting every stroke. It doesn't mean anything to me. I don't care if they beat me, but why would they cheat?"

A triumphant Mark Laskin after winning the 1991 Chrysler Classic.

"Yes," conceded Ron. "I've always been intense in that respect. I don't believe there is another place in our sport with the same attitude of good sportsmanship."

Day One Continued:

Today's Riders' Meeting is quite uneventful by comparison with those of the past, but Ron's brief reference to the rules still has sting.

Alluding to recent world incidents alleging the killing of show horses for insurance premiums, Ron speaks of the shame it has brought to the sport.

He stresses it is not just in show jumping where rules are broken, but added this sport is not policing itself as well as some of the others.

"Yet," he tells the riders, "I firmly believe show jumping is a better sport than all of them. It's a better sport for the family, it's a better sport for the fans, and it requires more athletic ability on your part.

"We, at this facility, cannot have anything go wrong here. Our sport cannot afford that disappointment. I have seen people with the worst reputations come here and be nothing but supportive and a great credit to the sport.

"I ask the same of all of you now because it would be intolerable to look into the future to find that anything went wrong here."

Tomorrow the Spruce Meadows MASTERS begins.

Day Two
The Competition

Although it is not yet 8 a.m., Spruce Meadows is very much alive. Like a child groomed for a special occasion, the facility has been scrubbed and shined to reflect the freshness of a beautiful day.

The Southerns fondly refer to Spruce Meadows as "Camelot", and the claim is not a boastful wish. It has become an oasis of greenery on the edge of a concrete metropolis, and a majestic stepping stone to the Canadian Rockies that beckon beneath a wisp of cloud to the west.

The grounds have begun to rival England's Hickstead in terms of natural beauty. At Hickstead, however, the lushness is simply a continuation of a countryside decorated so generously by nature in a thousand tones of green. Spruce Meadows, meanwhile, shimmers as an island in eternal conflict with the burned-out prairie that laps at its shores.

Remembering what the land supported only two decades before, Spruce Meadows now presents visitors a vastly improved alternative.

The growth of Calgary, however, eats toward its boundaries at an alarming rate. The Southerns are hopeful City Fathers will ultimately see the wisdom in creating some form of green belt around the city, similar to what is done throughout Europe.

It would be a travesty if busy neighbourhoods, and the human pollution that inevitably follows, are allowed to smother the tranquillity of a setting so creatively perfect as Spruce Meadows.

Excitement strokes the facility as the tournament's first competition is under way on the All Canada course. Although five grass rings are available, only the top three will be used for this year's tournament.

As you approach from the highway, Spruce Meadows beckons in the distance like a fairy tale castle that has been hung in a shallow sky. Flags, hundreds of them, line every pathway and poke playfully into the air from the peaks of every building. Banners of every competing nation and the corporate insignias of every sponsor fly high.

Typical of the goodwill that exists between Spruce Meadows and various municipal and provincial authorities, arrangements have been made allowing vehicles to be parked on the extra-wide median of Highway 22X, the primary access road into the facility. Fans are transported several hundred yards to the main gate by buses. They only recently replaced a shuttle train originally resurrected from Expo 67 in Montreal.

Parking, once a huge problem, has now been brought under control and remains free for the up to twenty thousand vehicles that will arrive on a weekend day.

From the outset, admission charges were never a serious priority with the Southerns. They sincerely wanted to give the people of Calgary something back, particularly those who could not afford family activities.

A day of skiing for a typical family of four will cost more than $200; so will a day at any amusement park. Even an afternoon matinee will run $30, and that's without the popcorn.

Admission to Spruce Meadows, if anyone pays at all, has not changed in twenty years: $5 per person and no charge for senior citizens and children under twelve.

Ninety per cent of the gate enters courtesy of promotional tickets given to them by event sponsors. Companies pay for these tickets as part of their sponsorship package, so in essence Spruce Meadows is receiving payment for all in attendance.

It's an arrangement that benefits everyone. Spruce Meadows fills its stands and that makes sponsors very happy. The fan may not pay directly for the ticket, but he knows there is value to it. And the ticket comes as a gift from the sponsor, and that is inexpensive, but excellent public relations.

Building A Reputation

In the late seventies one major sponsor carelessly set out tickets for the upcoming MASTERS on a public counter. No one monitored the situation and people were grabbing the tickets by the handful. Many of those tickets, in turn, were then just dumped into a nearby trash can. Marg Southern phoned and insisted they control distribution.

"Those tickets meant nothing to anyone," said Marg. "It cheapened the process, the sponsor and Spruce Meadows."

During a competition a couple of years later, Ron Southern received an urgent call from security. A guard asked him what he wanted done with individuals caught sneaking in from the parking lot without paying.

It is an avenue of grace and beauty visited by show jumping fans from every walk of life.

"Welcome them to Spruce Meadows," replied Ron. "If you had told me five years ago that people in Calgary would be sneaking into a horse show I would have said you were nuts."

Mind you they still weren't sneaking into a "show". They were about to enter the show grounds of a world-class show jumping tournament.

Monitor the gate at a Spruce Meadows tournament today and you will see as many as ten different passes being handed in. Anybody with even a hint of grey hair is welcomed as a senior, and if a family arrives in a vehicle older than the children within, they are usually welcomed as special guests.

Traditionally, every seat at Spruce Meadows is available to all for the same admission price. There is no class distinction, and while sponsors are given priority treatment in pavilions, it is done as unobtrusively as possible to avoid any feeling of elitism. The best seats in the house are still those available to the general public.

By the early nineties enough patrons were demanding some form of reserved seating that the Southerns relented somewhat on their open seating policy. Seats can now be reserved in the main grandstand for $20 and are usually booked months ahead by the regulars. The best seats within all three rings, however, are still the grass banks.

Mexico's Alfonso Romo is one of the few to adopt the Spruce Meadows ticket policy. At his show jumping complex in Monterrey he has gone a step further by issuing a free invitation to the entire population of Monterrey, and then sweetens the proposal by providing a gratis carnival for the children.

"We have learned many things from the Southerns," said Alfonso, Chairman and Chief Executive Officer of conglomerate Pulsar Internacional. "Before building our centre in Monterrey my people spent a great deal of time at Spruce Meadows to see how things are done correctly," said Alfonso, who also rides with the Mexican national show jumping team.

By comparison with other great show jumping centres, Spruce Meadows ticket prices are the best bargain in all of sport.

In 1994 Hickstead was charging the equivalent of $10 per adult and $5 for children plus another $4 for parking. There are three main grandstands surrounding the main show ring, one of which is free but has no roof. The second adds $2 to the price of an admission, but it does keep you dry.

The most attractive deal at Hickstead is a membership pass which provides access to the best grandstand all year, as well as entrance to three area horse racing parks.

Prices at Aachen are a little steeper. Parking is a huge problem and even if you have

> ## "If you had told me five years ago that people in Calgary would be sneaking into a horse show I would have said you were nuts."
>
> (Ron Southern)

a pass, unless you get their very early, it won't do you much good.

As one incensed reporter argued, it made very little sense from a public relations standpoint to turn away working media simply because that designated lot happens to be jammed. Particularly when the brusque young man in charge offered the scribe no alternative other than to leave the grounds and come back by bus or taxi. The attendant, said the reporter, wouldn't even acknowledge the half-full adjacent lots reserved for VIPs.

Management at Aachen is very much by committee. Unlike Spruce Meadows and Hickstead, which are privately-held facilities, the Aachen Tournament is run by the Aachen-Laurensberger Rennverein E.V. Committee. This partially explains why you won't win any arguments there. They have more people with badges than a Boy Scout convention, and all of them have their orders which they will not compromise.

The least expensive ticket at Aachen, standing room only on the opening Tuesday, costs the equivalent of $5. That jumps to about $13 by Sunday, and nobody seems to mind standing for hours in tight proximity to their neighbours. The best perch in the stadium is in the Mercedes Benz grandstand where tickets start at $25 and increase to almost $250 for a weekend pass. Tickets for the weekend are traditionally gone weeks, sometimes even months before. It is refreshing for those who must struggle to attract crowds to see people scalping show jumping tickets with the same fervour, but not quite the same margin of profit, as a Stanley Cup or World Series playoff game.

Rooms are booked at least a year in advance at Aachen, and the production is worthy of its advanced billing as the "best venue in show jumping" as determined each year by a poll of global riders, media and show jumping officials. Spruce Meadows, at a slight disadvantage in the voting procedure because of its limited exposure compared with some of the European facilities, has been closing steadily on Aachen and in 1994 closed to a threatening second.

Hickstead will attract upwards of thirty thousand to its famed Derby, but otherwise attracts between ten and fifteen thousand to major Grand Prix presentations. Aachen will consistently pack in forty thousand for presentations at its major tournament each June.

Patrons at Hickstead, if they are lucky, can recoup entrance costs by shrewdly placing a bet on the outcome of that day's event. It's all legal and bookies provide some very interesting spreads on the different riders. Favourites like the Whitakers will get you $10 to $15 back on a $2 wager, while the return on an unknown rider can go as high as 100 to 1.

"It's not a big thing," said Nick Skelton. "Riders aren't suppose to bet, but it's been known to happen. Never big money, though. There are too many good riders and horses to ever suggest there is a sure thing."

Comparisons of the major rings of Hickstead, Aachen and Spruce Meadows is difficult because each is so distinctive. In the case of Spruce Meadows, the look of the International Ring changes almost annually as improvements are made, pavilions are added and grandstands expanded or covered.

Because there was no master plan from the outset for Spruce Meadows, it is amazing today that there is so much organization and symmetry to its design after years of constant construction.

Day Two Continued:
The Facility

The tranquility of a cascading fountain adds to "Camelot" image.

(photo by Al Savage)

Think of the three main rings - the International, the All Canada and Meadows On The Green - as the petals of a giant three-leaf clover. Tying them all together, like the veins of that leaf, are the paved roadways and pathways that also support the myriad of treasures and exhibits found along the way.

The stem, also its main artery, begins in the north-east corner of the property and gently follows the shores of a large pond. An erupting fountain visually serenades you upon arrival, and not surprisingly, some visitors take hours to get much further.

The pond, which was stocked with rainbow trout for a couple of years, gives way to Amoco Park, a sanctuary of red shale walking paths and picnic areas, as well as horseshoe pits and a play area for the youngsters that includes the replica of a stagecoach.

It is here that some parents, burned out by a tough week of work, simply pull up to the trunk of a tree and spend the day reading and napping while the rest of the family enjoys a full slate of activities.

Continuing along the main road you split the International and All Canada Rings, stopping to marvel at the archway of greenery provided by an assortment of spruce and poplar trees. Nineteen years ago there wasn't a tree in sight.

Although pavement is a necessary evil, it has been kept to a minimum at Spruce Meadows. Instead the grounds are crowned by a carpet of grass pinned to the earth by stalwart trees, manicured rows of hedge, and flower gardens alive in colour.

This is Marg Southern's legacy. As Ron tore away great chunks for necessary expansion, Marg put it back together with the loving touch of Mother Nature herself.

The name Spruce Meadows came out of a family strategy session and members now agree it was "probably Linda" that came up with "Spruce" and the rest instantly linked it with Meadows. There is nothing, however, secretly significant about the name.

Marg planted eighty or ninety trees that first year, but only a dozen or so survived the first two years due to a water shortage. It is somewhat ironic that only three or four miles west of Spruce Meadows the land is dense with spruce trees nurtured by a higher altitude, softer climate, and better soil.

A lack of water remained a problem for years at Spruce Meadows, and wasn't overcome until unlimited access to the City of Calgary water system was negotiated.

Marg now estimates that more than thirteen hundred trees have been planted at Spruce Meadows and she now confidently places their future in the hands of professional groundskeeper Martin Parry.

Not one square inch of soil is sacrificed to construction unless it has come under her close scrutiny. When workers began stealing land from a hedge garden to widen the paved traffic circle around the Riding Hall courtyard, Marg was furious. She made them tear out what had been done and return the land to the garden.

Marg Southern is from Dutch heritage - Ron affectionately refers to her as "the Flying Dutchman" - and one of her most memorable moments came on May 14, 1988 when Her Highness Queen Beatrix of the Netherlands visited Spruce Meadows.

A commemorative plaque marking the occasion was unveiled that afternoon. It has become the garden plot of the Spruce Meadows Tulip, a shock-white hybrid developed in the Netherlands in celebration of the visit and the continuing close ties enjoyed with Spruce Meadows.

Strong relationships have been forged between Spruce Meadows and the bodies commerce, politic and sport of many nations. Among the most noteworthy are those fostered with Great Britain, Holland, Germany and Mexico.

Each of these nations has taken special steps to assist Spruce Meadows over the years: Germany in aiding the breeding program, Great Britain in helping to attract international riders and Mexico in the development of strong new cultural and business links.

Holland, however, still remains singular. It is the Government of the Netherlands that since the outset has brought an unparalleled brightness to many a bleak September day at the Spruce Meadows MASTERS.

If there is a table anywhere at Spruce Meadows, it will be dressed in a bouquet of flowers. Almost every jump in every class is stroked by the beauty of flowers. Every sponsor and every special guest graciously accepts a bouquet of flowers. Little wooden shoes filled with flowers were even sent to radio disc jockeys.

On the final day of competition fans rush the jumps following the completion of closing ceremonies. They gather huge bouquets of flowers that then find their way into homes, hospitals and nursing homes throughout Calgary.

Another pocket of nature's beauty is the site commemorating 1988 visit by Her Highness Queen Beatrix of the Netherlands.

Dutch/Canadian Choir performs during "Holland Day" ceremonies.

Four to five tonnes of fresh flowers, enough to stuff the massive cargo belly of the Boeing 747 chartered to transport the European horses, are sent from Holland. Babysitting the precious cargo is Helen Valstaar, a specialist gifted in the art of floral design. She and her talented team work from dawn to dusk preparing the next day's banquet of visual splendour.

It is impossible to put a price on such a gift. The Southerns show appreciation by declaring one weekend day of each MASTERS "Holland Day", and the colourful opening ceremonies traditionally attract top-ranked government and business leaders from both nations.

The "greening of Spruce Meadows" has taken on a greater significance to all staff and volunteers in recent years. It is now vividly apparent just how powerful and positive nature can impact people.

Nothing in the world can challenge the beauty of nature's landscape, nor have a more calming influence upon a harried mankind. This has become a monumental strength of Spruce Meadows, and to preserve it for the future, all expansion is designed to retain the delicate balance between man and nature.

Is this greening philosophy, then, in vile contradiction to the sea of signage that slaps at your senses upon arrival at Spruce Meadows? Some say it is.

At Hickstead all signs, and they are very limited and small

in size, have been placed to blend into the facility's natural surroundings. The result, not surprisingly, is that you barely notice them.

That may be a moral victory for ecologists and the BBC which frowns on any advertising, but it's not great for the sponsor. Aachen's signs are a bit larger, but certainly don't come close to dominating its environment.

Tournaments throughout the United States offer a mixed bag approach. Some offer no recognition what so ever to sponsors, while others have bold signs

throughout. The best use of signs seen in recent years within the U.S. was at the 1992 World Cup held in Del Mar, California - but that's assuming your interpretation of best is a preponderance of signs.

Nothing matches Spruce Meadows. It has more signs than most countries.

No one, however, has ever seriously protested their presence as being garish or visually distracting . . . somewhat amazing since on a typical day there will be several hundred major signs daringly on display throughout the grounds.

One must also remember, however, that when you talk signs at Spruce Meadows, you aren't talking about normal, everyday, run-of-the-mill signs.

The smallest are 4' square while the largest are an imposing 8' by 102'. In the case of the latter, that's three times the length of most outdoor billboards.

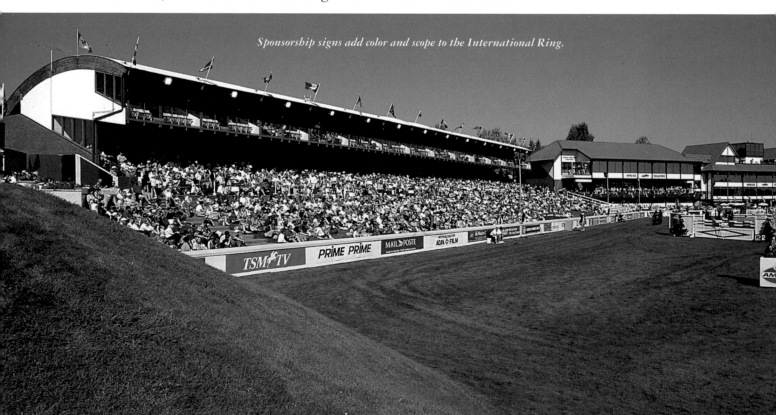
Sponsorship signs add color and scope to the International Ring.

Somehow it all comes together in an electrifying image of great sport at an exceptional facility.

It is not possible to put an 8' by 102' sign into a beautifully groomed arena of grass and expect no one to notice it. So imagine the sight created by fifty to sixty prime sign locations within the International Ring, and now try and convince someone who hasn't been there that it really looks great.

But as the cliche goes . . . you have to be there.

Andy Hordos, the Calgary graphic artist responsible for design work at Spruce Meadows, is a man sensitive to his surroundings.

"If I had not seen it at every tournament for nineteen years, I would have said no, it's impossible to pull off. No matter what you do it will look junky," said Andy.

"But somehow it works here and I believe it has something to do with the open space, the design of the buildings, and the fact the frames of the signs are well designed and engineered.

"Ron," he added, "is always pushing to the absolute edge by asking for just one more sign, or one just a little larger.

"I used to have nightmares that the addition of the next sign would destroy it all, but somehow that never happens. It's crisp, it's fresh, the colours are perfect, and by the time you work in the trees and flowers it has all come together," said Andy.

Sponsors, of course, love it. Being able to read your company's name while still half-a-mile away is a wonderful bonus. Few, however, understand the enervating strategy that goes into determining locations for the signs.

Don Stalman was responsible for signs for almost a decade at Spruce Meadows. He would spend hours into the early mornings with Ron creating the perfect pattern for each class, for each day, and for each tournament.

He also has strong feelings about their importance.

"Signs are the foundation of sponsorship at Spruce Meadows," began Don. "Without them, we wouldn't have sponsors. It's this incredible importance of a person hearing his company's name, or seeing it on an 8' by 48' sign. That brings pride and the sense of being involved. Take away the signs and what do you have left for the sponsors?"

He remembers fielding a radio call from Ron about the impending arrival of a major sponsor. 'Yes', Don replied, the usual signs would greet him on arrival.

An alert security official interjected to say the official in question had indeed arrived but was heading for a back parking lot instead of the traditional VIP designate.

"Then make sure we have his company sign somewhere along his route," ordered Ron. "We can't have him walking halfway through Spruce Meadows without seeing one of his signs."

Don managed to make it the edge of the lot just seconds before the official arrived. He casually leaned against the fence, pinning the new sign between himself and the fence to hold it in place. The sponsor, he said, did notice the sign.

The world is reflected by huge "facias" scattered throughout the grounds.

(photo by Tish Quirk)

Sometimes, as in the following incident involving Xerox, a bevy of sponsorship signs can appear unexpectedly.

Kevin Francis, Vice-President and General Manager of Xerox Canada, asked the Southerns one year if it would be possible to hold his Western Regional Sales Conference at Spruce Meadows in the off-season.

Asking for nothing special, he was dumbfounded upon arriving the morning of the conference to see Xerox signs everywhere.

"It was unbelievable. We never even raised signs as a question with them in preparing for the meeting. But that's the Midas touch they have. That's the subtlety of the meticulous attention given to detail at Spruce Meadows."

The same individual who made the first Spruce Meadows sign, is still at it two decades later. Not many would recognize the name of Terry Christensen, a quiet,  unassuming genius who conquers the impossible as routinely as sunrises at Spruce Meadows.

Terry is owner and sole employee of this company, and it would appear that its size is misleading since no demand is beyond its amazing capabilities.

"I'll tell you about this man's commitment," said Don Stalman.

"During one traditional late evening meeting with Ron we suddenly realized the next day was Great Britain Day and we didn't have the necessary signage."

Don called Terry at home to inform him that by the next morning he needed two signs, one 8' x 48' and the other 4' x 48'.

"And this wasn't just a sign saying Great Britain. It had to be the entire British flag as well as wording. But I couldn't be any more specific than that."

Terry calmly replied that he would see what he could do.

"I came in at 6 a.m. and leaning against a wall, still slightly wet, were these two huge British signs. To this day I have no idea how he pulled that off by himself."

Nobody is sure of just how many signs there are. Terry has calculated that from Day One he has used a pile of quarter-inch coroplast equal to the height of a fourteen-story building. Placed end-to-end they would produce the world's most colourful walkway extending far beyond what most men could walk in a day. If somehow all of the signs were destroyed, replacement costs would exceed $1 million.

Not all signs are commercial. The most impressive, in fact, are scenes of picturesque landmarks from around the world - including the Golden Gate Bridge, the great castles of Europe, fields of tulips in Holland, British Parliament Buildings and Japan's Imperial Palace.

To be historically correct, they are not signs at all, but vinyl facias of photographs blown up to billboard size (16' high and 30' long). Thirteen of them present the world's most unique photo gallery to passing motorists, mostly on roadways leading into Spruce Meadows. No words, just this giant photo of a scene that lightens the seriousness of any traffic jam.

Ron had seen the concept used in the foyer of the Calgary Tower, and immediately sent Don in pursuit of the concept for application at Spruce Meadows. Each picture costs roughly $1,500 to produce, but that is minor compared to the installation costs of the concrete footings and steel frames that keep them in place.

"This was state of the art technology involving a California company. But they were equally impressed when they found out what we were doing with their work. They asked for pictures and put out a major promotional video focusing on our unique use."

> "I don't know if I would stand in line to see Ian (Ian Millar), but this is Big Ben. I'll wait as long as I have to."
>
> (Big Ben fan from Moose Jaw, Saskatchewan)

(photo by Cansport)

Ian Millar joins artist Fred Stone in autographing special commemorative prints of Big Ben.

Even in retirement, Big Ben can draw a crowd.

Day Two Continued:
A Special Tour

This morning there is a different kind of video attracting a great deal of attention at a special celebrity tent set on the edge of the All Canada Ring.

It's not yet 9 a.m. and the guest of honour, star of this particular video, won't be arriving for almost an hour. Already, however, there is a lengthy lineup. This is a major stop in the retirement tour of the brilliant Big Ben, by far Canada's most successful show jumper and one of the nation's most popular sport personalities, and not just among horses.

"I don't know if I would stand in line to see Ian (Ian Millar)," confided an elderly woman from Moose Jaw, Saskatchewan. "But this is Big Ben. I'll wait as long as I have to."

By the time she left she had her picture taken with Ben ($7.95), bought a book about his conquests ($12.95), a cap with his picture for a grandson ($9.95) and the video produced by Spruce Meadows Television together with a Big Ben commemorative print by famed American equine artist Fred Stone ($25 for the two). She passed on the Big Ben coin ($49), the Big Ben T-shirt ($12.95) and the Big Ben sweatshirt ($29.95).

Ian Millar & Big Ben . . . A partnership of unparallelled talent and class.

Profits from her purchase, as well as from thousands of others across Canada in 1994, were being directed by Ian to the Canadian Therapeutic Riding Association and the Canadian Equestrian Team.

As he had shown throughout his competitive life, Ben was going out in style.

Ian And Big Ben

The magnificent chestnut had reached eighteen, and that meant mandatory retirement from events sanctioned by the sport's international governing body. If he couldn't compete in the major events, it would have been humiliating to enter him in the others. Big Ben would have known the difference.

His retirement tour would take Ben to eight Canadian locales, climaxing in late November at the Royal Agricultural Winter Fair in Toronto.

With more than forty Grand Prix victories and two World Cup Finals, Big Ben rose to be ranked among the best three horses in the world. It was at Spruce Meadows however, that this horse with the winning character stood far taller than his massive 17.3 hands frame.

Ian Millar, anchor of the Canadian Show Jumping Team for more than a decade, was introduced to Big Ben in 1983 at the farm of Dutch national team member, Emile Hendrix. In his book "Riding High", Ian recalled that initial meeting:

"He had on a saddle and an ugly halter. We looked at him, and he looked at us . . . a little belligerently I thought. A tall, raw-boned horse, he was slim and his head stuck up in the air. He failed to make a good impression, but I liked his arrogance. I asked the other horsemen who were with us, 'Anybody have an interest in buying this horse?' 'Too big, too ugly,'" said one.

Ian, backed by a syndicate of almost fifty, paid $45,000 for Big Ben and over the next decade would turn down several offers of more than $1 million. "I could never have sold him. He had become a national treasure," insisted Ian, the most successful competitor in the history of Canadian show jumping.

In a mid-eighties poll of Canadians, Big Ben ranked second only to Wayne Gretzky in terms of recognizable sport personalities in Canada.

Big Ben won nineteen major events and more than $675,000 in prize money at Spruce Meadows between 1984 and his retirement a decade later. He virtually owned the Spruce Meadows NATIONAL for those ten years.

"Spruce Meadows," said Ian, "was definitely Ben's favourite venue. He wanted to get into that International Ring so badly he automatically headed for the clock tower as soon as I got on him in the warm-up ring."

That same determination was evident during presentation ceremonies.

"I didn't always manage to earn our way to the head of the line, but with Ben it didn't matter. He was gone whether there were other riders or an honour guard ahead of us or not . . . and it took a lot to turn him away and wait our turn."

Ian describes Ben as a "big occasion" horse that could sense the importance of an event by the size of the crowd.

He remembers watching video of the 1993 Shell Cup at the MASTERS. Ben was one of the few to beat the treacherous Devil's Dyke and the crowd rewarded the feat with a deafening cheer.

"The louder they cheered, the higher Ben would jump. You could see it on the video. He didn't get harder to ride or anything. There was no negative reaction at all. He'd get up to the jump and there would be this extra punch off the ground that you could actually see on the tape.

"I mean this horse was jumping a foot over the planks for no good reason. He knows how high the planks are and he knows very well he should jump only two inches above them.

"But that's what I mean about a big occasion horse. He knew that the fans at Spruce Meadows had a home in their hearts for him. He knew their reaction and he just got up for them, any time and any way he can," said Ian, his face breaking into a broad trademark grin.

Big Ben's memorable Spruce Meadows moments are numerous, but none reflected the magnificence of this athlete more than his performance at the 1992 Spruce Meadows NATIONAL.

Ben is a fighter. In 1990 and then again in 1991 he underwent abdominal surgery for colic. He defied the odds both times by surviving. He then confounded all by coming back stronger then ever.

No one, however, could have predicted the outcome of his performance June 3, opening night of the '92 NATIONAL.

Just two weeks before, Ben's van was involved in a horrific road accident just outside of Saskatoon, Saskatchewan. Together with five other horses, two owned by Ian, Ben was on his way west for team selection trials at Edmonton and Spruce Meadows for the upcoming '92 Olympics.

Actually Ben was really only along for the ride and the fun of competing in his favourite ring. He had already been rightly granted a bye onto the team.

The van collided head on with another vehicle, and the seventeen-year-old driver of that car died instantly. No one would ever deny that the tragedy of that young man's death far out-weighed all concern about what may have happened to the horses.

> It was undoubtedly one of the most awesome demonstrations of show jumping prowess ever seen at Spruce Meadows, or anywhere else.

Nevertheless, an anxious nation awaited word on the condition of Big Ben who had to be cut from the van by emergency workers. The big horse had actually smashed a hole through the trailer with his head in attempts to reach freedom. One horse was also dead.

The surviving jumpers spent a week being patched up at a clinic in Saskatoon. Ian's other horses would be non-starters at Spruce Meadows, and in fact never would fully recover mentally from the terror of the accident. He decided to play it day-by-day with Big Ben, although he was not optimistic about the outcome.

Because it was a Wednesday night (at the 1992 NATIONAL) there wasn't a large crowd at Spruce Meadows to welcome Ben back to competition. He still displayed fresh scars, but did not appear nervous in any other sense.

His pace was even, his presence even cocky during the first round of the competition. He didn't even threaten a rail.

Although he advanced to the jump-off, no one expected Ian to push his partner. Most felt it would be best to bring him back gradually through the five exhausting days of competition. Ian, however, knew that with Ben there was no halfway. He let him go and Ben grabbed the moment as if a gold medal depended on the outcome of the ride.

No one else was close. Ron Southern, addressing the few who had witnessed the magic, said:

"What an amazing animal, and what an amazing rider on top of him. It was a wonderful moment that I will always remember. Some day there will come a time when Ian Millar and Big Ben won't be in the winner's circle any more. But I will always remember today. It was one of my proudest moments and one of the sport's most remarkable."

During the victory ride Big Ben kicked up his heels in two uncharacteristic bucks. It was as if he was telling his fans "Hey, I'm back. It takes more than that to put me away."

As glorious as that moment was, the next day brought deep despair for Ian Millar. As detailed in Chapter One, that was the day Ian was suspended from competition because of a rapping infraction.

Due to Ian's forty-eight hour suspension, the partnership did not compete for two nights, but was back for the Royal Bank World Cup on Saturday and the Shell Cup Derby that Sunday.

It didn't really surprise anyone that Ian and Big Ben won both of them, two of the toughest tests in show jumping.

It was undoubtedly one of the most awesome demonstrations of show jumping prowess ever seen at Spruce Meadows, or anywhere else. It confirmed the singular talent of this amazing horse, and the riding grace and talent of Ian. Many believed that if it had not been for the suspension, Ian and Ben would have swept every class of the '92 NATIONAL.

Day Two Continued:

It was performances such as those that flood the memories of the thousands who are stopping by to say farewell this week. Saturday holds the promise of being a wonderful day. Ben will make his final ceremonial appearance in the International Ring. Emotion will run high.

A surprisingly large crowd is building early this Wednesday morning. Two buses edge by and stop just outside the main tournament office.

For the Southerns, each contains very special and precious passengers - seniors from Calgary and area lodges. Twenty years earlier, when finding fans was almost as difficult as finding international competitors, it was the seniors who could always be counted upon to show up for every competition.

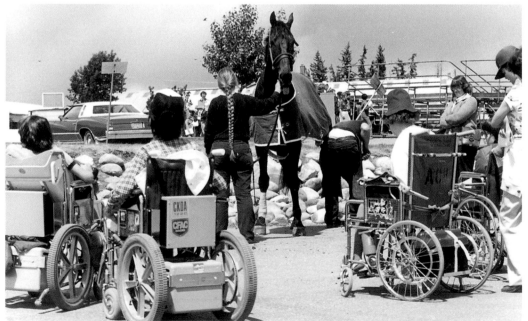

The power of the horse reaches out to all fans . . . as does its gentle disposition.

70   The Spruce Meadows Story

photo by Tish Quirk)

Tournaments remain a family destination with appeal to all ages.

The family unit is of vital importance to Marg and Ron, and they demonstrate a huge respect toward the elderly. They will often stop on any busy day to spend time with those confined to wheelchairs. Wheelchair viewing areas at Spruce Meadows are among the best of any entertainment facility in the city.

Similarly, mothers with young children evoke special attention. The Southerns appreciate the extra effort taken by these young women in wrapping up their infants and then struggling through large crowds all day in support of show jumping at Spruce Meadows.

One afternoon, and without warning, Ron asked the show photographer to go out and take pictures of every mother pushing a baby carriage. He then had the picture mailed to each of them.

Seen mixing with the seniors this morning are hundreds of school children, again a legacy of the family ambience which permeates Spruce Meadows. Since 1977, Spruce

Meadows has invited thousands of ten-to twelve-year-olds to a special School Tours program conducted on site by Spruce Meadows staff.

Content, approved by participating school boards in the city, delicately covers virtually every facet of horse husbandry as well as insight into show jumping. It is amazing how many adults now approach the Southerns to tell them of their interest and support of the sport, an interest they confess was spawned many years ago when as a twelve-year-old they were taken on a field trip to Spruce Meadows. Surveys now show that fully fifty per cent of those returning to Spruce Meadows to watch show jumping had their first exposure during School Tours.

For many fans, their first exposure to the sport came during a school tour of Spruce Meadows.

The support structures bordering the International Ring are a far cry from that single ATCO trailer that in 1976 somehow served as show office, official's office, judge's office and anybody else's office that didn't require more than four square feet. If someone did require more room, of course, they were simply out of luck.

Only one reporter showed up at that inaugural competition. With portable typewriter in tow, he asked for directions to the press room and was shown to a corner of that same trailer where he was given two boxes of programs for a desk, and a third box for a chair.

Today's press room is equipped with all of the latest electronic gadgetry to provide instant results, constant updates and international links for as many as two hundred visiting media. Media Co-ordinator Sheryl Dalik, together with a veteran volunteer staff that has included her mother the past fifteen years, isn't often stumped by the probing questions of reporters.

Nor is Tournament Secretary Joanne Nimitz who shares the spacious bottom floor of Meadowview, the second building to be constructed at Spruce Meadows. The upper floor lounge offers exceptional viewing for owners, volunteers and other special guests while the top deck handles accommodation for announcers, Central Communication and judges.

The press room, which saw a state-of-the-art television production studio added in 1994, faces directly onto the International Ring and sits beneath a covered viewing area utilized mainly by the general public and the handicapped.

One of the best seats in the house . . . journalists pack the Media Centre.

On special occasions, such as the June 29, 1990 visitation of Her Majesty Queen Elizabeth II, the viewing area is transformed into a Royal Box.

A second story was added in 1992 for badly-needed office space. Ron was the first to tear the design apart, actually within minutes of its presentation. His office was precisely what he didn't want, luxurious, private and in a quiet location.

Today, if you are looking for the desk of Ron Southern, it's one of several pedestrian-looking pieces of furniture sharing a large operations room. If you didn't know him by sight, he could be any one of the four or five men working in the room at any given time.

Known to all as SOC (Strategic Operations Centre), the work area is one of the truly remarkable sights at Spruce Meadows. Every inch of wall is covered in paper detailing every facet of competition and entertainment of the current tournament. If it is going to happen at the tournament, one of these walls will reveal how, why, where, and when.

Every second of every tournament day is accounted for somewhere on this wall in SOC (Strategic Operations Centre).

It reflects Ron's penchant for detail and must surely be reminiscent of the war maps which papered the walls of allied headquarters in Europe. He can sit back and strategically relocate sponsor signs along the walls of a jumping ring as adroitly as a general moving tanks around a war zone. Nothing is done without purpose and design, and nothing gets on those walls until it has been put to the test of probing minds.

During the winter months Marg and Ron escape to Hawaii for five weeks and the walls of their rented Maui condo take on a similar appearance. Because of the time difference he is up by 5 a.m. each morning to speak with sponsors. The remainder of the day is usually spent plotting next year's tournaments, right down to parade orders. Marg at last finds some time for golf, and towards the end of the holiday Ron will usually join her.

Day Two Continued:

As usual, fans are taking great delight this morning in photographing the various honour guards on duty throughout the grounds. Mainstays of the troops are members of the Lord Strathcona's Horse "Royal Canadians", always resplendent in their scarlet tunics, and ramrod-straight on meticulously groomed horses.

In contrast, attired in stained deerskins and leather, are members of the Sam Steele's Scouts. They are a tattered collection of history buffs who sling their good-life frames aboard pot-bellied horses. This commemorative troop truly reflects the image of the rugged ranchers, trappers and cowboys assembled in 1881 by North West Mounted Police sergeant

Sam Steele to help control the boisterous antics of four thousand men stretching the Canadian Pacific Rail Line across nine hundred miles of pristine prairie.

The two Canadian contingents are joined by members of the Lifeguards of the Household Cavalry, Royal Bodyguard to the Sovereign and senior regiment of the British Army. Members have been flown to Canada by the Southerns together with members of the King's Troop, Royal Horse Artillery, also British Army. It is a rare honour that the commanders of either regiment would allow visitation outside of England.

Years ago Ron had replica uniforms of soldiers from ancient European military units flown to Spruce Meadows. He then had grooms and other competent young male riders from the area doff the garb and take position on guard duty throughout the grounds. It all looked so very real until one of the young men predictably hollered over to a local buddy.

He went one step beyond that in the mid-eighties by flying over the entire fan club of Austrian superstar Hugo Simon. The German-born Simon, gold medallist in the 1980 Olympics, couldn't believe it. When he appeared on course for the first event at Spruce Meadows, there they were - six voluptuous and very vocal young ladies, appropriately tagged as the "Swedish Cheerleaders". They spent the day handing out Austrian and Canadian flags to somewhat startled patrons, as well as leading cheers for

(photo by Cansport)

Pageantry is important at Spruce Meadows. Shown here are members of the King's Troop, Royal Horse Artillery and Lifeguards of the Household Cavalry.

A touch of the past . . . Sam Steele's Scouts on parade.

their beloved Hugo. It is unlikely that cheerleaders will ever again appear at Spruce Meadows, but give them credit, they brought a difference to the facility and they did successfully conduct the first "wave".

The bowl of the International Ring boasts approximately thirty-eight thousand seats, and twenty thousand of them are now under cover. The initial seating for about six hundred was portable bleachers and there was some question in those early years if they would ever be filled.

No such doubt existed in Ron Southern's mind however. Following the first tournament, he confidently stated that someday more than ten thousand people would attend a Spruce Meadows tournament. He could have said a million and it wouldn't have increased the degree of scepticism.

His prediction became reality in just four years, launching a growth that finally surpassed the fifty thousand mark during the 1995 MASTERS. If parking and seating were doubled, and access routes somehow tripled, some believe a single-day crowd of one hundred thousand could be in the not-too-distant future.

Rapid transit, which in 1994 stopped a dozen kilometres short of Spruce Meadows, might be the answer to future transportation concerns. As the city expands to the south, rapid transit will eventually be at the doorstep of Spruce Meadows.

In 1988 corporate skyboxes were built atop the main grandstand. Each of the thirteen units offers approximately seven hundred square feet of luxury. Outdoor, veranda seating for thirty guests provides a premium view of competition on the International course.

Although the boxes are somewhat in contradiction to the common-man philosophy of Spruce Meadows, the Southerns accepted the fact that when a corporate sponsor puts up several hundreds of thousands of dollars, it had the right to also expect, if so desired, access to a private setting.

"There are a few spaces where the sponsors have hosting venues," said Ron, " but overall it is minor compared with the public area. It is the public space," he promised, "that will continue to grow."

The boxes are leased by sponsors for each of the three major tournaments, and invitations are in huge demand. Although some are used exclusively by corporate executives, invitations are utilized by others as incentives for good work.

Fans and riders hunt for unique items at the "Jumpers" Boutique.

In addition to the skyboxes, Spruce Meadows has two large on-course pavilions that will each comfortably accommodate several hundred people. Major sponsors utilize the pavilions on the afternoons of their competition, often combining that opportunity with a company picnic or performance reward celebration.

For years the ground level of the main grandstand was used for jump storage, a small first-aid room, some rudimentary commercial outlets and anything else that required dark and dingy storage space.

Recognizing its potential, the area was transformed almost like magic into one of the city's most distinctive retail outlets featuring exclusive riding apparel and some very unique gifts as they relate to the horse. When given the opportunity, Marg, together with her good friend and tournament deputy, Anne French, prowl the markets of Europe in search of distinctive items to sell at "Jumpers". It is open primarily during the fifteen tournament days each year.

Equally impressive is the Trophy Room, a glassed-in area capped with a plush carpet. Every trophy from the three tournaments is proudly on display, as are samples of the various medals and plaques handed out over the past years.

Not all are competitive trophies. The "Volunteer of the Year" trophy, donated by Dr. John and Chris Wood, is one of the most imposing and truly reflects the spirit of the volunteers at Spruce Meadows.

One of the first trophies ever awarded at Spruce Meadows came on loan from Calgary's

Volunteer of the Year Trophy - Ron Southern, Chris Wood, Wonneetta Hamilton, Dr. John Wood and Marg Southern. Wonneetta was the first recipient of the beautiful glass trophy donated by the Woods.

Glenbow Museum. A beautiful bronze, the "Trophy Of The Brave" depicts an Indian brave grasping the deadly talons of an eagle in its eternal struggle for freedom.

The trophy, awarded to the winning team in the Bank of Montreal Nations' Cup, was first presented by William Mulholland in 1977 to Germany. It is generally accepted as tradition that when a major cup is won three years in succession, it is given over permanently to the triumphant individual or team.

That seldom happens, of course. But nobody counted on the power-house Brits in those early Spruce Meadows years when Ronnie Massarella coached his squad to three quick Bank of Montreal wins . . . 1978, 1979 and again in 1980.

The Southerns found themselves perched uncomfortably upon the horns of the proverbial dilemma. They couldn't give the trophy over to the Brits, simply because it belonged not to them, but in perpetuity to the people of Alberta.

The British team - comprised of Graham Fletcher, Malcolm Pyrah, Jean Germany and John Whitaker - weren't making any demands, mind you, but something special to mark the occasion would still be nice. They didn't, however, expect the compromise. The Southerns flew the team members and their families to Hawaii for Christmas. Much better, agreed the Brits, than having possession of another trophy to dust for three months of the year.

Day Two Continued:

Because today is only Wednesday, the plaza and other special event locations are not yet at full throttle. It makes sense, therefore, to wait until later in the week to visit when the diverse value of each of them becomes more visible.

Instead the trail of one of the school groups is picked up as it heads toward the mares and foals barn. During each NORTH AMERICAN Tournament the year's crop of youngsters is introduced to a packed house. The foals are named in a contest attracting hundreds of entries from show jumping fans around the world. Winners, far prouder than most parents, get their names on the offspring's stall, as well as a Spruce Meadows jacket embroidered with the foal's name.

Breeding

Ron doesn't have a Parade of Mares and Foals during every tournament any more, and most agree that is unfortunate. The pressures of television and other production time constraints often makes it impossible.

When it does happen, it's true magic and brings out the very best of this man's pure love for the horse. He begins by introducing the Spruce Meadows stallions, and then calls on grooms to enter the ring with mares and foals. The foals are a delight as they dart mischievously among the jumps and other mares.

A special moment for Co-chairman Southern.

Throughout it all Ron speaks of their conformation, their temperament and that one special foal that could someday make it back into this International Ring as a competitor.

He speaks of the horse's binding powers with the family, its extraordinary relationships with young girls, and its need for love and care. He warns youngsters against startling a horse, and then demonstrates the proper way to call a young foal by sinking to his knees on a mud-stained course so that he is lower, and therefore less imposing to the young animal.

He marvels openly at the power of these animals as if it was his first acquaintance with them, and he openly shares that wonderment with a spell-bound audience. He is not aware of the fact he sometimes stops half-way through his talk to watch two foals playing off to one side. For those precious seconds he has forgotten about the crowd and his responsibility to them. The sight of those foals is truly overwhelming.

He sometimes wonders if after twenty-plus years crowds haven't tired of his mares and foals presentation. But then he remembers the advice of German author and sport announcer Hans Isenbart who was so moved the first time he saw it that he implored Ron to "never stop talking to the people."

"One of the toughest things I have to do is break in and tell him the course must be cleared," said Special Features Manager Randy Fedorak. "But if I didn't he would stay there for hours . . . and you know, I doubt if anyone in the crowd would object."

When Spruce Meadows was first introduced to the public in 1975, it was described as an equestrian facility committed to three distinctive pursuits: as a training centre for young horses and young riders, as a breeding centre of reasonably-priced show jumping horses and as a centre for world-class show jumping competition.

To this day, riding scholarships are handed out to at least six young riders every year. The scholarship allows for the boarding of horses as well as lessons under the guidance of Riding Master Albert Kley or trainer Dayton Gorsline. Many of those winners are now competing nationally for Canada or the United States.

The breeding program has been far more complex, and some of the success stories are impressive.

Within Canada, show jumping horses, particularly at the junior and amateur level, were traditionally Thoroughbred rejects from the race track. They were predictably hot-tempered and injury-riddled three- and four-year-olds that had neither the talent nor the desire to be among the best.

To buy one was a long-shot gamble and unfortunately, more often than not, the resulting bad experiences soured the aspirations and dreams of some very promising young riders.

On occasion it would work, as in the case of Bo Mearns of Victoria, British Columbia. Bo rescued her great mare The Flying Nun from a guaranteed destiny as dog food. She paid only $400 and turned The Flying Nun, winner of the first-ever Grand Prix at Spruce Meadows, into a national team competitor during the early eighties. Her story, however, is the exception.

In Europe it had always been different, particularly in nations like Germany, France, Ireland and Holland where literally thousands of mares are producing potential jumpers.

As a youngster, working for his horse-trading uncle, British coach Ronnie Massarella remembered one year buying more than one thousand horses in Ireland and bringing them into England ". . . and sold every one of them as a prospect."

In searching the world for a model to pattern the Spruce Meadows breeding program after, the Southerns felt Germany's was by far the best.

Joe Selinger of St. George's Stables had introduced the Southerns to the Hanoverian and through Joe's knowledge and love of the horse, he instilled a strong interest in Ron.

As a student of history, and one who deeply admires the strategies of successes that endure through centuries, Ron was immediately drawn to the German Hanoverian. Here was a breed that has enjoyed more Olympic successes then all other breeds put together, and it didn't come about by good luck.

The Hanoverian is traced back more than two hundred and sixty years to the early 1730's and the reign of the Duke of Hannover, King of England. At that time the area of Germany was known as Lower Saxony and the king spent a great deal of his time in the region. Horse racing was already a great favourite of the gentry and once a year he brought his beloved stallions with him from England to breed with the heavier, and immensely stronger German mares.

In 1735 he established the Hanoverian State Stud Farm, a government institution that continues to endure and prosper. Two hundred and forty years later, a branch office was opened in Calgary, Alberta, Canada.

The Southerns visited the State Stud Farm on several occasions developing warm personal relationships with Landstallmeister (Director) Dr. Bouchard Bade, and 1 Hauptsattelmeister (First Riding Master) Manfred Lopp, who officially retired in 1994.

It was most unusual for the State Stud to give up promising young stallions to other countries, but after scrutinizing both the facility and the intent of the Spruce Meadows program, a deal was struck.

(photo by Cansport)

1 Hauptsattelmeister Manfred Lopp.

Spruce Meadows breeds its heavier Hanoverian mares to Thoroughbred stallions, and the finer-boned Thoroughbred mares to Hanoverian stallions. The result, hopefully, would be progeny with the best characteristics of each . . . the quickness and athletic agility of the Thoroughbred, and the power and soft temperament of the Hanoverian.

Two foundation stallions were obtained. One was the extraordinary Hanoverian, Wodka, known during his competitive years as Young Wolfsburg. It is amazing the State Stud Farm let him go as he had finished fourth in the stallion licensing that year among all Hanoverian stallions of the same age. He also demonstrated startling jumping ability.

The Thoroughbred stallion, sleek and beautiful, was Anforan. Although he never raced, his credentials were equally brilliant and he came to Spruce Meadows in a trade with local race horse breeder Fred Mannix. Anforan was by Four-and-Twenty out of Tanbye by Flutterby – all very successful on the track.

Mares were purchased through either the famed Verden Auction in Germany, or from farmers in that region.

Albert Kley, who rode as a young man at the auction, still jokes about the entourage of Canadians, as many as four or five vehicles, which plied the Germany countryside in search of horse bargains.

"Mr. Southern insisted on renting the biggest Mercedes and as soon as the farmer saw what was coming down his driveway the price of the horse doubled." Ron's choice of vehicle at home is a Chrysler van or a twenty-year-old white Volkswagen "Bug" convertible.

Manfred Lopp, acknowledged worldwide for his uncanny ability to pick out exceptional horses, said that on average there are one hundred and eighty stallions standing at stud in Celle servicing eighteen hundred mares in the Lower Saxony region of Germany. Each year one hundred of the most promising young stallions are subjected to a stringent one hundred day testing program. The top forty or fifty then join the State Stud Farm, assuring a constant turnover for breeders who are mainly the farmers of the region.

The program has been under the direction of the German Department of Agriculture for more than two centuries, and although horses for sport are now its primary objective, that wasn't always the case.

Wodka (Young Wolfsburg) as a three-year-old.

Anforan as a three-year-old.

Good temperament and strength, said Manfred, were essential, since the Hanoverian was initially needed for farm work and the cavalry. The horse couldn't be too heavy or awkward as it would also need great agility and exceptional speed to perform in battle.

The program was threatened by the mechanical revolution and it was then that all efforts switched to producing a sport horse. Hannover was the first region to make the transition, using both Thoroughbreds and the Trakehner to put some fineness into the breed.

Although the Hanoverian continues to excel in all disciplines, the breed is now enjoying the most success in the dressage ring, followed closely by triumphs in the show jumping arenas.

One of the most beautiful sights in sport is the precision quadrille performance of the Celle Stallions, led before his retirement by Manfred Lopp. Spruce Meadows is one of a select few, non-European venues at which these majestic dressage stallions have performed, and they have been here several times.

Canadian foals can receive the distinctive Hanoverian brand, but only if they are born to registered mares that have passed inspection by a Celle State Stud Farm representative. Spruce Meadows Riding Master Albert Kley is one of only two Canadians authorized to make that determination. These special branding privileges are only extended to the Breeders' Club founded by Albert and the French and Southern families.

Initially there was some disappointment because the breeding program didn't produce World Champions in those first few years, which in reflection would have been most unusual. But young horses were being born that would later provide juniors and amateurs with a strong, reliable and competitive partner for a sum far less than what it would have cost them overseas.

The Southerns recently reviewed the breeding program at Spruce Meadows and after agreeing it had slipped away from some earlier commitments, have decided it would once again become a prime objective.

"I must confess that I lost some interest," said Ron, "but we do have some lovely mares once again and a terrific stallion in Wagner."

Wagner sired several prized youngsters in Germany before

coming to Spruce Meadows, including Wanderer (1980), now a top breeding stallion at Celle.

The latest additions to the Spruce Meadows stallion line-up are Evergreen by Eiger and most recently, the talented dressage stallion, Mister A by Matcho AA.

There aren't many stables in North America that can afford the luxury of keeping a horse in training for upwards of eight years before putting them on the market, or entering them into serious competition.

"A show jumping horse probably reaches its premium value at eight, and hopefully we will be keeping about ten per cent of our horses until that age," said Ron. By doing

(photo by Garth Pritchard)

A rare North American appearance by famed Celle stallions of Germany.

that, the number of horses in training will probably double over the years, but revenue from those horses will triple over what it was in the early to mid-nineties.

There's no issue as to whether or not the program can or can't provide quality horses. What must be settled on is a precise definition of quality.

If one is talking about the Grand Prix winner of a du Maurier International, then it's probably unlikely. There are very few that can be the best. When you compare the number of show jumping mares and stallions in the Calgary area with those of Europe, you can see why the odds of breeding a Dollar Girl, Milton or Big Ben here are unlikely.

"But if you are asking me if we can provide a quality horse that will do well, perhaps even become a local champion, then my answer is yes.

"Breeding," added Ron, "is a marvellous aspect of being involved with horses.

"There is something about a new foal every year that is like life itself. They represent new hopes and aspirations. I think that is one of the main reasons people have children."

For the serious-minded breeder it represents a great challenge because no matter how much you think you know about the sire and dam, their progeny will always surprise you.

"We started out to create an economically-priced sport horse for North America," said Ron. "We have always kept the number of broodmares around ten and people wonder why we don't at least double that on the theory it would also double the chances of producing better offspring. But that won't work. We are better off getting, and

Wagner

keeping, the best ten we can get our hands on."

The average price initially obtained for horses bred at Spruce Meadows was about $18,000 Canadian (about $13,000 U.S. at the time), ranging from lows of $2,000 up to as much as $60,000. By 1994 these averages had increased just slightly.

Wanderer (by Wagner) during his stallion performance test in Adelheidsdorf.

"You couldn't get anything out of Europe for those kind of prices. It costs $8,000 ($5,500 U.S.) just to ship a horse here. So in that sense, on a modest scale, it has been successful," said Ron.

Spruce Meadows has also pioneered the breeding of European horses, and encouraged others to follow. The Southerns persuaded many of their friends and surrounding farm and acreage owners to purchase mares. They have all enjoyed the rewards of raising a young sport horse.

Some, like Bas and Anne French, savoured great successes and from a financial standpoint, most have made more money raising horses then cattle.

Hanoverians and other warmblood horses are now being bred throughout North America, all directed to the sport horse market: show jumping, dressage and eventing.

"Today, at least in North America, most people want a warmblood horse - French, Dutch, Irish or German - with Thoroughbred blood in it," said Ron.

As a result, the horses are finer than purebred Hanoverians, but still much larger than Thoroughbreds. The better examples of this breeding have very good temperament, tremendous athletic ability, and they are easier to ride.

The Spruce Meadows breeding program has produced a few exceptional performers at the world level, as well as many local stars. Among them are two of Wolfsburg's offspring, a gelding called Concorde that United States Olympic Team rider Chris Kappler took to Show Jumper of the Year honours within the United States and a mare named Bavaria who became a Champion Hunter in the U.S.

Linda Southern-Heathcott is now in control of the breeding program at Spruce Meadows, but doesn't anticipate expanding it significantly beyond where it presently is.

"Unless you have at least two thousand mares and one hundred and fifty stallions, you can't succeed if your objective is solely to produce champions of the world," said Linda. "But you can breed a nice sport horse here at Spruce Meadows, and you can do it economically. Maybe, if you're real lucky, you'll get a great horse."

Linda suffers from no delusions when it comes to the horse. She is forthright and sometimes painfully honest when discussing all aspects of Spruce Meadows and her present and future relationship with it.

"I don't love horses in the same way I have affection for my dogs," explained Linda. "I admire their versatility and I have a sincere sense of gratitude for what they have given mankind."

But, Linda adds, she does look at the horse somewhat differently than many others.

"As a rider, they're the tools of my trade. I have a lot of respect for them and I have a lot of understanding about them, but I wouldn't classify it as love."

Comparisons between the two sisters have always been inevitable. Their relationship, however, leaves no room for bitterness as each holds the other in very high esteem.

Their parents extol the distinct virtues of each daughter equally and, as is their nature, focus only on their many strengths.

Spruce Meadows' Albert Kley knows the riding attributes of Nancy and Linda far better than anyone else. He also knows them as his very close friends and would defend either as one of his own.

Nancy and Jonathan with children in 1995 family portrait - Kelly (11), Ben (2) and Kyle (8)

> If the Southerns believed the game should be played that way, they could afford to go out and buy Linda the finest horse in the world . . . a proven champion, that with Linda's natural ability, would continue to win and even improve.

Nancy's early riding career was experimental in many respects. She was mounted on huge horses from Europe in her early teens and placed in Open Divisions against far more seasoned riders and horses.

Her determination and courage were legend, and she upset the favourites often enough to push aside any criticisms. But she also suffered some horrifying crashes that left others shaking their heads.

"Nancy had to work hard at her riding. She would never give up, but it didn't come easy," said Albert.

Linda, however, is very much a "natural rider".

"With Linda you can put her on a strange horse and she right away feels the horse and understands it," added Albert.

He said it is difficult to measure Linda's ultimate potential because she hasn't yet found that special horse.

"She is as good as anyone in Canada, and she has had a lot of successes on lots of horses. But unlike a Lisa Carlsen or Beth Underhill (Canadian National Team riders) or Gail Greenough (first Canadian and first woman to ever win a World Championship – 1986), she hasn't yet been lucky enough to have a great horse," said Albert.

If the Southerns believed the game should be played that way, they could afford to go out and buy Linda the finest horse in the world . . . a proven champion, that with Linda's natural ability, would continue to win and even improve.

More than anything else, however, that would only prove the extent of their wealth, not the depth of their daughter's ability.

Instead, with Linda's guidance, they search for young horses with strong potential. The result is development of a respect between horse and rider that matures gently over time. Ultimately that horse will give its best, and no one can ask for more.

The late Wilmat Tennyson came to Spruce Meadows as a sponsor in 1981, and stayed as a friend until his death in 1995. The retired President and Chief Operating Officer of Imperial Tobacco, sponsor of the prestigious du Maurier International, knew the Southern family well and had a great deal of empathy toward Linda's situation.

"Others look at Linda and assume she is on good horses only because her father's rich," said Wilmat. "Linda can never be a rider on her own. She's always Southern's daughter. It's a hell of a burden for that kid to carry and still love the sport."

Linda with husband Tom and children Patrick (10) and Ronnie (8 months) and "Casey" at Christmas - 1995.

Although Linda has never enjoyed wild successes as a rider at Spruce Meadows, she is probably one of the venue's most consistent performers. No one, it seems, has more single-knock-down rides at Spruce Meadows. That keeps her in the top ten, but not the medal positions.

She has also had some nasty falls on her home turf, one of which was played back for her under unusual circumstances.

After competing in the Spruce Meadows NORTH AMERICAN one year, Linda and husband Tom escaped for a quick camping trip into the British Columbia wilderness. She did, however, want to see the tape-delay presentation of the Chrysler Derby, so they stopped at a tough-looking bar in a two-blink town deep in the interior that advertised satellite television.

"There were a couple of guys at the bar, and I mean big, huge, burly men. I hesitated to ask the bartender to put Spruce Meadows on, figuring they'd be into wrestling or something else," but Linda did ask and the bartender didn't hesitate.

"It was amazing. No sooner had we switched it over when this trucker walked in and said: 'Oh, great. Spruce Meadows is on. I watch it all the time.'"

It was remarkable said Linda. The ladies sitting behind her referred to the riders by name and knew many of the horses.

Linda had taken one of her nastiest falls during that particular Chrysler Derby and really wanted to see how it had happened. She cringed, as did everyone else in the bar, when the crash - which left her unconscious and bruised but not seriously injured - was shown.

"Nobody knew me, but when I fell off my second horse in that same class, people were starting to stare. I grabbed Tom and said it was time to go.

"Anyway, that to me shows success . . . the fact that in a small remote town so many people knew all about Spruce Meadows and show jumping."

Linda is committed to her profession, but not at all costs. There are, she confesses, other more important considerations in her life, particularly her family.

"Maybe I haven't been able to be the best show jumper because I haven't been able to focus solely on being an athlete," explained Linda.

"I know people that can do that, and many are more successful than me. But I don't like what winning at all costs does to them as people, and I don't want to become one of them."

In 1983 at the age of nineteen, Linda took a bold step by announcing her intention to turn professional, the first rider in North America to do so. It immediately scrubbed her life-long dream of riding for Canada at the Olympics, although regulations have since been relaxed so much that virtually any professional can now compete.

"Turning professional has been a hard thing for me to learn to deal with," said Linda, "but I will never say it was a bad decision to make."

She agrees with her father who told her at the time the move would give her pride in what she did because it would be hers. But, she quickly learned, what was hers also belonged in part to her sponsorship family - AGFA Film, Canada Post, Canadian Airlines International, Chrysler Canada, Evian, Fletcher Challenge, NORTEL, Pepsi, TransCanada PipeLines and Xerox.

"I've finally learned to deal with my sponsors on a personal basis. I know now how much I can give of myself, and how much to keep back in order to compete. That's taken me more than ten years to fully understand, and I should have maybe learned it before taking the step.

"The most stabilizing force in my career now is Tom (husband Tom Heathcott). Because he's not involved in Spruce Meadows, he sees all of the things that would distract me. They are meaningful things to Spruce Meadows, but things I can't deal with and still focus on competition. He keeps me clear of them, or takes them on himself."

She also accepts the fact her career could be shortened due to increasing responsibilities at Spruce Meadows, responsibilities that ultimately will see her in full control of the complex.

Is she ready? You bet she is.

"I look forward to it because Spruce Meadows truly is a dynamic place. But I am also slightly frightened by the prospect. I have huge shoes to fill."

The thing she appreciates most is that the decision regarding her management future was taken at a time when both her mother and father enjoy good health with the promise of many strong years still ahead of them.

"It's important for both Nancy and I to have this time with our parents now . . . to continue to observe how they have made Spruce Meadows great and to absorb their philosophies and goals."

> "It's important for both Nancy and I to have this time with our parents now . . . to continue to observe how they have made Spruce Meadows great and to absorb their philosophies and goals."
>
> (Linda Southern-Heathcott)

Linda is adamant the primary reason Spruce Meadows is so successful is because of the unique working partnership forged between her parents.

"Working together has made both of them that much stronger. I believe that will also work for Nancy and me."

Somewhat in awe of her parents' global reputation, Linda understands fully there will be times when she will be directly measured against their monumental accomplishments.

"Especially when mistakes are made. People will come back and suggest that my Mom or Dad would have done it differently. But, you know everybody lives with that. It will be a bit more magnified for Nancy and me, but they've taught us well. Including a belief that if you keep it simple and don't get caught up by unnecessary emotion, anything is achievable.

"I know it will be difficult, but I also believe that maybe in the end it will be just as good and maybe even better. That's how you have to look at it.

"In the beginning," Linda continued, "I heard a great deal from people as to how lucky Nancy and I have been all of our lives. And they're right. We have been fortunate. But we also have a big commitment to uphold and that's a pretty intimidating realization. But it's also a wonderful challenge and opportunity for both of us. Our parents may have given us the playing field, but now it's up to us to make certain points are still scored.

"That may be hard, and yes, on occasion I have wished that I was anyone other than this person. But on the other hand, what great opportunities await. Sure it will be a bumpy road, but I bet it will also be a real fun ride."

Day Two Continued:
Competition Begins

Linda doesn't have a great opening day, but she does a lot better than most of the Germans. Already people are asking what happened to the "best in the world".

Mexican Jaime Guerra wins the first event, the $15,000 Canadian Utilities Cup. Two Canadians, Eric Lamaze and Jill Henselwood, ignite the crowd by placing second and fifth respectively. The top German is ninth.

In the Section II event, the $25,000 Laidlaw Cup, Ireland's Peter Charles is beyond reach and one has to search down to eighteenth place to find a German competitor.

Later in the day the personable Charles tells reporters that he started the MASTERS the same way two years earlier and then failed to get another decent round out of his horse. He hopes history will not be repeated.

No one in the German camp expresses concern over first day results, and probably for good reason. Performances at opening day competition of this calibre seldom reflect the tone of those still to come.

Course designer Paul Duffy of Ireland would never threaten a horse by over-matching it with difficult fences the first day out. Most of these animals have travelled vast distances to be here, and need time to adjust to the surroundings and the course.

By tomorrow he will build some difficulties into his tracks, and by Saturday they will match the intensity of any faced in the world this year, and that includes at The Hague and the World Equestrian Games.

But it is a great opening day for the MASTERS. Bathed in constant sunshine, a record crowd of just slightly more than fifteen thousand is in attendance.

When Ron Southern predicted that someday a crowd of ten thousand would attend a day of show jumping at Spruce Meadows, not even he believed it would ever be on a Wednesday.

Member of the Lord Strathcona's Horse (Royal Canadians) Mounted Troop.

SPRUCE

Day Three
Riding with the Best

It's the unforeseen things that make this sport and facility so intriguing.

As the rising sun singes a path across a blue prairie sky, hundreds of people wander aimlessly behind the Riding Hall. Soaked in glorious sunshine, none are expecting, or searching, for anything that might threaten the comfort of this unblemished Thursday morning.

A dozen or so riders are already in the sand ring testing the temperament of their horses in preparation for major competition later in the day.

At this precise moment the most recognizable include England's John Whitaker, Canada's Mark Laskin, Ireland's Eddie Macken and Franke Sloothaak of Germany. George Morris, U.S. riding legend, and Ronnie Massarella, veteran British coach, are among the few spectators looking on intently.

It is somewhat amazing that aspiring young riders aren't stacked ten deep around the rail.

So much can be learned just by watching these masters as they prepare horses for competition. Observe the quiet hands of Macken, even in a casual walk. Listen in as Laskin, always in search of knowledge, asks others about any perceived weaknesses to today's courses.

Parents spend thousands of dollars on riding lessons for their children. Yet today, and every day of a Spruce Meadows tournament, post graduate classes are being offered free of charge by the best riders and coaches in the world.

Leaving the international barn area, it is interesting to trace the steps followed by riders to the main arena.

Particularly if, as is the case this morning, you are walking behind one of the truly great performers in show jumping, Nelson Pessoa of Brazil.

Nelson, aboard a beautifully-created chestnut mare, is out for a casual walk when the young horse balks abruptly at a small water ditch. The dry cut is no more than two feet across, but something about it concerns the horse.

Always an opportunist in search of a lesson to teach, the former European Champion calmly talks to his horse, urging him across the ditch and then spends the next ten minutes repeating the move until the horse shows absolutely no hesitation.

Satisfied with the results, Nelson then spends several minutes talking with some young fans, allowing them to lovingly stroke the neck of his horse.

And that is one of the lesser-known treasures of Spruce Meadows - the freedom of movement for all. Unlike at Aachen, where it seems a strong hand is constantly pulling at your shoulder because you have wandered into restricted space, there are few off-limit areas at Spruce Meadows.

Every warm-up ring is accessible to fans, and even during the MASTERS, only the international barns are out-of-bounds.

(photo by Al Savage)

Invaluable lessons can be learned by watching international riders and grooms schooling the world's best horses.

Anything goes in the unique AGT "Battle of the Breeds".

It's still early in the morning but the new Meadows On The Green course is already being tested, not by the expected sleek jumpers but by an odd representation of breeds from ponies to heavy horses. Each is harnessed to a spit-clean buggy that will tackle an obstacle course of routine dimensions to some, terrifying to others. It is part of the Battle of the Breeds competition, a five-day event sponsored by AGT.

This novel presentation is another example of a MASTERS feature that has taken on a strong life of its own since its launch in the late eighties as part of the Alberta Breeds For The World exhibition. The intent was to create a fun event that would also determine the most versatile of the eleven breeds on display. The best of each breed strut their talents in five distinctive events that include jumping and dressage.

The competition became an instant hit with crowds and now offers more than $30,000 in prize money, while regularly attracting stacked houses of five thousand and more. The Arab, for the record, has shown to be the most versatile breed winning the title seventy five per cent of the time.

Meadows On The Green was not completed until the early summer of 1994 and is built on the former site of the Rocky Mountain Hunter Ring. That, however, is the only commonality between the two.

Hunter classes began fading in popularity in the mid-eighties after a decade of lofty successes at Spruce Meadows. Entries at the junior, amateur and open levels would often surpass those in jumper classes.

The Canadian Open Hunter Championship attracted riders from throughout Canada and the United States, and events within that championship division were the richest on the continent.

By 1991, however, entries in most hunter classes were down to only a handful, and almost all of those were highly-polished California riders. It had reached a point where a few very expensive horses had become so dominant that it was no longer worth spending the entry fee to ride against them.

Fortunately, the declining interest in hunters was more than offset by an explosive surge in jumping. As more and more riders entered the sport, and not all of them were juniors, demand for events catering to both young and amateur jumpers was overwhelming.

Some form of competition still had to be provided to make certain young horses with potential had an opportunity to develop at a challenging, but sheltered pace.

The solution was the 4/5 Year Old Jumper Championship introduced to the NORTH AMERICAN Tournament in 1993. The concept, unique to North America, was one that enjoys extraordinary success throughout Europe.

Jumps for four-year olds are restricted to 3'3", increasing to 3'6" for five-year olds. These heights are no greater than those previously allowed for first- and second-year green hunters. To stress control, rather than speed, faults are converted to fifty per cent of an entry's score while the remaining fifty per cent is based on style using the same criteria as used in judging hunters.

Experience has shown that graduates from this division are far better prepared for the senior jumping ring than those six-year olds facing the challenge directly from a hunter ring.

More important, talented young horses with raw but uncertain potential won't be frightened away from promising careers.

Nature and man combine in the striking beauty of the Meadows On The Green course, together with the Pulsar Internacional Gallery.

Day Three Continued:

The Meadows On The Green course is more of a masterful creation than the cold reality of a construction project. It is state-of-the-art technology with enough electrical outlets and power snaking through its domain to support a small town.

Walking toward the new course, one believes that ancient Roman baths must surely await to entice all those who venture behind these sculptured walls. A sweeping staircase lifts you to its rim where senses succumb in unison to the striking beauty of the course below. A huge fountain punctuates the mood.

The ring itself is mammoth. Its 360' x 360' bulk gives it the heavyweight title at Spruce Meadows, making it even more spectacular than the famed International Ring. And like the International, Meadows On The Green has all of the permanent obstacles offered in the sport, including a 12' high bank. Lawn chairs nestled beneath the lips of umbrella-crested tables offer the only synthetic seats. Otherwise you must drop tired bones onto the downy grass banks that frame two sides of the ring.

Ultimately the Meadows course will play a key role in all competitions, eventually surpassing the All Canada in hosting status.

As you drink in the man-made grandeur of the facilities surrounding you, a shudder is appropriate when one thinks it's all in support of a sport that sceptics doomed to failure twenty years earlier.

It also begs the question as to why the sport of show jumping is so popular in Calgary, yet fighting for survival in other areas of the world. A look at the sport's evolution, in Calgary and elsewhere, spins an engaging tale.

The Sport of Show Jumping

At the first tournament in Dublin, Ireland, three events were offered to the brave young men who ventured into the unknown. The first was a high jump of three poles, and the second a broad jump over hurdles. Winners in each of the two were awarded five pounds and the runner-up two pounds.

In the third event, riders jumped a stone wall and the victor was awarded a cup valued at ten pounds and a whip worth five.

The first international jumping trials were included in the Paris World Exhibition in 1900 and two years later one hundred and forty-seven riders from throughout Europe met in Turin. The Italians dominated that competition, led by a Federico Caprilli who set a high jump record of 2.08 metres (6' 10") and a long jump record of 7.40 metres (24' 3").

The modern high jump record, still standing, was set in 1949 by Capt. Alberto Larraguibel Morales of Chile who sent a horse called Huaso soaring 8' 1.6". The long jump record stands at 27' 3.6" set by a Spanish army officer, Col. Fernando Lopez Del Hierro on a horse called Amado Mio.

Scoring rules at the 1912 British National were intriguing. In the "Officers Competition" the following system applied: first refusal or bolting, one fault; second, two faults; third, dismissed; horse and rider falling, four faults; horse knocking down a fence with front legs, three faults; horse knocking down a fence with hind legs, two faults; a touch with front legs, one fault; a touch with hind leg, one-half fault. A judge stood beside each fence and eventually thin pieces of wood called a "slip fillet" were placed freely on the top elements of each fence to indicate more conclusively whether or not the rail had been touched.

The International Equestrian Federation was created in 1921, at which time refusals, knockdowns and falls were adapted as standard, four faults for a front knockdown, two for a hind, five faults for the first refusal or fall of horse or rider, ten faults for the second refusal.

This has since evolved into today's scoring which is four faults for all knockdowns, three faults for the first refusal, six for the second and dismissal for the third, time faults accrued at the rate of one-quarter time fault for each second over the time allowed on course, and dismissal when either horse or rider fall.

There are some within the sport, including Ron Southern, who would like to see some of the old penalty standards re-instated, particularly the one pertaining to refusals.

"A refusal is a more serious error than a knockdown, especially in North America where course designers are quite generous in their time allowed," said Ron.

A first refusal, he said, should be five faults instead of three, or keep it at three and drop faults for a knockdown down to two instead of four.

The sport thrived in Great Britain until the thirties. That was when a rule change, adopted by the Brits in 1921, finally succeeded in draining all interest in the sport. The rule, accepted by no other nation, allowed riders to take as long as they wanted to get around a course. It was too easy and far too boring. An entire generation of riders

> "A refusal is a more serious error than a knockdown, especially in North America where course designers are quite generous in their time allowed."
>
> (Ron Southern)

never learned how to take fences at anything but a crawl and it took years to relearn the process for British riders.

Surprisingly, Calgary was not far behind Europe in terms of the sport's development. By the turn of the century, and at the tender age of only six, the city was already attracting national attention as one of the country's leading competitive horse sport centres.

The first "horse show" in 1901 was strictly as the name implied, with a limited amount of equitation competition. By 1905, however, the sport was gaining in popularity, particularly the high jump. By 1908 evening events were featured and the Calgary Spring Horse Show was being touted as the town's premier social event.

Consider the somewhat prophetic message contained in this Calgary newspaper article:

About the horse:

"Alberta out-classes any other district in Canada for horses. There is no doubt, whatever, that this province carries off the honours, not only in Canada, but of America . . ."

And about a new building just constructed for show jumping in the city:

"I regard this structure, which is by far the largest and the best of its kind in Canada, as a monument to the energy and capability of . . . "

The comments could easily have been delivered at the April 13, 1975 opening of Spruce Meadows as testimony to Marg and Ron Southern.

The article, however, was written on April 11, 1912. The next paragraph confirmed the time warp.

"Senator Lougheed, who returned to town last night from Ottawa, was able to be present with Mrs. Lougheed who was entertaining a box party in honour of her guest, Miss Watson, daughter of Senator Watson of Portage la Prairie. Mrs. Lougheed wore an elaborate gown of cream duchesse satin with a cerise chiffon overdress and a white plumed picture hat. Miss Watson was in an effective gown . . . ."

The story appeared the day after the official opening of Victoria Arena, a building designed and structured specifically for the sport of show jumping. When hockey moved indoors several years later, the building also became home to top amateur and professional teams. It served the needs of both sports for more than thirty years.

On the second night of that initial competition in 1912, and before a crowd of more than 3,000 fans who had waited patiently well beyond midnight to watch its conclusion, history was set.

"Miss Walsh on Smokey, world's record breaker and winner of the lady amateur high jump of last year, captured first place again . . . but it was not without its spectacular and dangerous features," stated the newspaper article.

The story went on to suggest the horse appeared nervous at the start and eventually "ran away from the rider on three occasions during the course of the event."

"The first time he became uncontrollable, the spectators did not realize the danger until they heard the pretty daughter of a Millarville rancher cry, "He is running away!"

The "lives of the spectators at the end of the ring were in danger," concluded the writer, for it appeared Smokey would surely jump clear out of the ring and bolt from the building.

Smokey survived that episode and was back in the headlines a year later, this time with Percy Sutell in the saddle. Once again, we will allow the author of the era to create the image:

"When Smokey cleared the seven-foot jump on Saturday night, or rather in the small hours of Sunday morning, the dense mass of spectators who crowded the Horse Show building rose in one body and gave such a cheer that has probably never been heard in any building in Calgary before, making the rafters ring with the echo of the sound.

"Hats were sent flying through the air. Staid and proper persons stood on chairs and tables and waved their arms about like so many wild windmills, at the same time shouting at the highest pitches of their voices."

(Glenbow Musem archives photo)

Smokey, an old weather-beaten cow pony with a brave heart and a "spirit that couldn't be downed" had set another world high jump record. At the time he was seventeen and when stretched to his fullest, stood only 15.1 hands.

Unbelievable!

The high jump was abolished for almost twenty years at the Calgary

"Smokey" and rider Percy Sutell up, standing in front of the 7' high fence they cleared at the Calgary Horse Show (April 1913). Owner D.P. McDonald of Cochrane is holding "Smokey".

show. In 1920 officials declared the event placed "a terrible strain on horses and riders" and was also "cruel." It was replaced with "performance jumps" of obligatory heights of between 4' 6" and 5'6" ". . . high enough to provide thrills and to judge the jumping ability of horse and rider."

A puissance class has never been held at Spruce Meadows, and it is very unlikely it ever will. The Southerns are not in conflict with the sentiments expressed by those officials more than seventy years ago.

Until the mid-forties, show jumping offered the most sought-after sport ticket in town. The Calgary Herald reported that every show was packed from floor to ceiling and tickets were sold out immediately. Many offers of $4 and $5 were made to lucky holders of seats, but there were no takers.

Ironically, half a century later, $5 at Spruce Meadows will still buy you the best seat to the best show jumping - not just in town - but in the world.

Interest in show jumping began to wane following World War II, and by 1962 Calgary columnist Tom Primrose wrote:

"It's a crying shame that Calgarians and people from surrounding districts don't provide better support for horse shows. Here we are sitting in the midst of one of the greatest horse areas of the world, and what do we do about it? We let a show which many people would give their eye teeth to see, go without sufficient patronage to pay for the arena overhead it is held in."

Spruce Meadows, which dramatically heightened the interest of the sport locally, was unfortunately blamed by some for contributing to the demise of the Calgary Spring Horse Show in 1985.

In reality, however, the Spruce Meadows summer tournaments were never in competition with the indoor Calgary Show. The Southerns, through ATCO, were among its largest sponsors and continued this support even after Spruce Meadows opened.

The indoor show simply didn't react to change. It preferred instead to offer a presentation that couldn't, or didn't want to, shake its high society image. Society, as shown at Spruce Meadows, changed instead.

From the outset, a Spruce Meadows tournament was different from any other in the world. Fresh ideas openly challenged a status quo that had been grooved over decades of presentation.

The important rules of show jumping were never broken, but in fact were actually strengthened and then enforced. Those that couldn't stand the challenge of logic, particularly some of the unwritten "gentleman's understandings" of the past, were gone.

Bas French, Spruce Meadows' Competitions Manager and close confidant to the Southerns, recalled his reaction to the format followed at the first two Spruce Meadows tournaments in 1976.

Because it made sense at the time, the Spruce Meadows Organizing Committee was comprised primarily of the same old guard that ran all horse shows in the area - a very committed group - but one dominated by those who lived and died by policies formulated deep in the past.

Most of all, Bas resented the fact that the committee ran the Spruce Meadows tournaments with an iron fist.

"Nothing ran on time. Riders would have to wait around for an hour or two because no one attempted to keep the thing on schedule. That, I thought, was an insult to them and to the few fans who were in attendance."

(Bas French)

Not only did that kill the spirit of the occasion, he complained, he couldn't find even one among them who was at least willing to discuss some change. The Ringmaster did only what the book allowed, the stewards did the same, and no one dared to suggest otherwise.

"Nothing ran on time," said Bas. "Riders would have to wait around for an hour or two because no one attempted to keep the thing on schedule. That, I thought, was an insult to them and to the few fans who were in attendance."

He suggested to the Southerns that someday a Spruce Meadows tournament would be televised live and things would have to be on time ". . . so we might as well do it right now."

He followed this with one of his infamous "French notes" (several hand-written pages of suggestions on how to improve the presentation of the sport) and was promptly promoted to Competitions Manager.

Within North America, trainers traditionally set the pace of competition at all horse shows. If a student isn't ready to enter the ring, it is no problem delaying the competition for a few minutes, or at the very least, moving that entry to a later time slot.

Not at Spruce Meadows. The Southerns very much wanted to emulate the precision of European competition. Don't make it when called and you don't perform. If you were competing in a different ring at the time, then sorry, but that is a conflict that could have been avoided with proper planning by the rider.

As discovered by Hugh Graham in the early eighties, this rule had no exceptions. Not even for seasoned national team riders of the host nation.

As is tradition, each international squad is given a team vehicle for use at the MASTERS. On this occasion Hugh was the only Canadian rider facing an early morning class, and it was agreed the night before that he should take the car by himself the next morning. But teammate Jim Elder failed to provide Hugh with one important detail - where the car was parked.

"I had no choice but to grab a taxi and arrived at Spruce Meadows just in time to hear them calling my name for the class," said Hugh. "I saw Ron and desperately pleaded my case for a later start. You know what he said?"

"'No problem! These things happen. I'll get you another car, but you still can't go in the ring.'"

Spruce Meadows, by enforcing rules, stripped trainers of their controlling influences. Instead, the focal points of a Spruce Meadows competition became the sport, the rider, the sponsor and the fan. The transition was not always smooth, however, since most of the trainers were also the sport's top jumpers. Many, not surprisingly, were offended and deeply resented the intrusion.

(photo by Tish Quirk)

Bas and Anne French were called upon from the beginning to "share the dream."

Announcer Bill Kehler broke all of the rules.

Calgary radio personality Bill Kehler joined the Spruce Meadows team in 1978. Although he was a veteran of the announcing game, like most of the people at Spruce Meadows, he had only limited knowledge about the sport of show jumping. Today he is recognized as the best in the sport and many of his innovative approaches have been adopted throughout the show jumping world.

"Ron didn't give me a lot of early direction," recalled Bill, "but he let me know his idea was to give as much recognition as possible to the sponsors and to the athletes."

He was told to dig deep and educate himself as much as possible about the sport, and the riders. Equally important, he was directed to announce it in such a way that all people could easily understand. Take away the pretention and it's a very simple sport to follow.

Tradition came under full assault. At most tournaments around the world, announcers gave the name of the rider and horse at the start of the ride, and that was it. The crowd, taking its clue from the announcer, then settled into a reserved and hushed solitude.

Spruce Meadows sent out questionnaires to every rider, junior through international, seeking answers to questions which would ultimately unveil their innermost secrets to the sporting public.

What was your most embarrassing riding moment? Tell us about your fears and dangers. Who are your riding heroes and why? What superstitions do you have? Tell us how to improve Spruce Meadows. Tell us the one thing about your riding you don't want anyone else to know.

Suddenly, where silence once ruled, the voice of a chattering Bill Kehler now boomed across the ring. In the middle of a crucial Grand Prix ride, Bill was merrily telling the crowd either about Harvey Smith's hilarious wrestling career, Mark Laskin's long string of superstitions, or Michael Whitaker's lucky underwear.

When some of the riders - particularly the established stars - failed to return completed questionnaires, a note was placed in their welcome package stating that no prize money would be awarded until the questionnaire was completed and returned to the Media Office.

At the time Bill shared his announcing booth with the international judges, not all of whom liked what they were hearing.

"Frank Chapot (a judge at the tournament) told me to shut my mouth and that I would be told by the judges what to say and when to say it. Fortunately, Bas French came by and pointed us in different directions."

To this day, however, Bill insists that the only people concerned about his running dialogue are those not riding horses. "Most of the riders never hear a word, and those that do, usually enjoy it," said Bill.

"Harvey Smith asked how I could speak through most of his ride without repeating myself. He thought it was just a tremendous departure.

"Does it bother you?" Bill asked.

"No," replied the congenial Harvey. "The only thing I'm worried about is that if you are still talking when my ride is finished, I'll have to go back and start again."

Never one to ignore a challenge, Bill did precisely that on Harvey's next ride. As the burly rider cleared the finish line, Bill announced: "There, Harvey. I've done it and I'm still talking."

The good-natured Yorkshireman put his horse into a starting canter again and headed for the starting line. He drew up just short.

Through the years Bill has encouraged crowds to react loudly and with enthusiasm to any good effort, even if it was still in progress. Again, this was in stark contradiction to the reserved demeanor encouraged from most show jumping crowds. At Spruce Meadows, a horse and rider successfully negotiating the dreaded "Devil's Dyke" can expect 40,000 people to stand and erupt in a deafening cheer. It's like a winning goal or go-ahead basket. Great efforts deserve boisterous recognition, not silent approval.

"If you don't want people to enjoy a sport, don't invite them. You can't expect them to get excited and sit on their hands," reasoned Bill.

Things rarely come as a shock at Spruce Meadows. On any given day riders can expect a TV helicopter hovering just above the International Ring, a blustering aerobatic biplane firing over the main arena, skydivers tossed onto the ring from the heavens above, bands blaring from every corner, and now, even fountains dancing at centre ring.

The horse does not appear to be fazed in the least. He is far more likely to balk at a solitary child waving a balloon among a huge crowd.

Bill also remembers when the term "horse show" took on a different moniker at Spruce Meadows.

The Southerns, among others, felt the term "show" did not reflect the magnitude and seriousness of show jumping at the international level. The term "tournament" had a much more significant ring to it.

"The only reaction I got was from the jury box," said Bill. "'Since when did this become a tournament, Bill? And why are the riders all of a sudden athletes?"

"I told them they too would be quite comfortable using both terms in a very short time, and of course I was right."

When the Southerns began studying existing rule books in preparation for competition at Spruce Meadows, they concurred that some were simply "asinine."

"The truth is, at any tournament you went to, the organizers and the athletes were in absolute confrontation," Ron said. "The organizers hated the riders and the riders hated the organizers, or at the very least they were angry at each other."

American Chef d'Equipe George Morris and 1994 Bank of Montreal Nations' Cup victors - Darlene McMullen, Leslie Lenehan, Tim Grubb and Anne Kursinski.

> Canadian luminary Ian Millar remembers his first visit to Spruce Meadows as a "culture shock" since traditionally "riders had always been viewed by show management as customers."

Right from the beginning he was determined not to have it that way. It was made clear to the riders that Spruce Meadows' rules were not superficial and would be enforced. But it was also made clear the athletes would be the beneficiaries of these rules.

The rule governing the determination of ties was a prime example.

"We didn't think it was right there were so many ties. Yet the only reason it happened was because the rule called for judges to time only to the tenth of a second. We had equipment that timed to the thousandth of a second, so why not use it?" said Marg.

"We have never," she added, "broken any rule of substance."

George Morris, who helped the Americans to a team silver in the 1960 Olympics, said he finds Spruce Meadows tough ". . . but so what?

"I understand that because I have always gone by the rules in conducting my relationships, businesses and every department of my life," said the man who is seen as one of the best coaches in the sport.

While it's hard to deal with leaders, he suggested, it is through leadership that one is also led to excellence.

"That's the problem in this country (the U.S.) and throughout the world . . . lack of standards. People cut corners, lower ideals, and that's why I admire Spruce Meadows. Standards have been kept, maintained and probably improved. I'm always amazed that show managers in the United States don't go to Spruce Meadows and learn how to run a tournament," said the author of several books on the sport of show jumping.

Canadian luminary Ian Millar remembers his first visit to Spruce Meadows as a "culture shock" since traditionally "riders had always been viewed by show management as customers."

"We bring our horses, we bring our owners, clients and students . . . and we spend quite a bit of money to compete. We are the customer, and if they don't have us they don't have a competition."

Not surprisingly, therefore, since entry fees fund the entire competition, riders and trainers felt they should also be in control.

"But all of a sudden we get to Spruce Meadows and it's very different," said the soft-spoken Ian.

"There's a tremendous group of wonderful, supportive sponsors and there's a management group in place dedicated to giving value to those sponsors. They recognize that those sponsors are financially what makes it all happen.

"If the sponsors aren't there," he surmised, "there won't be a competition. If there's no competition there's no media. And if there's no media there's no sponsors.

"It's a chain that's only as strong as its weakest link," he said. "To confound things Spruce Meadows management is saying to us: 'Wait a minute. We are trying to deliver a very precise, co-ordinated, sport entertainment package to international media and very top-of-the-line sponsors. To do that, we have to get you people under control and channelled, on time, and dressed the right way.'

"It definitely," said Ian, "came as a huge "culture shock" the first time out."

In the early going, and again Ian stressed this is his interpretation, the approach to making it happen fell solely to the "big hammer" philosophy. That approach, he clarified, softened considerably in later years.

"Not a softening of the position, that was non-negotiable for sure. But I guess what happened is now there might be two or three taps from the tack hammer before going to the carpenter's hammer, before going to the big hammer."

As a group, Ian suggested that riders now know more about what Spruce Meadows is trying to accomplish with its presentation.

> " I can't think of anything that would ever get me there . . . and by the way . . . where is Spruce Meadows?"
>
> (David Broome - 1977)

"We've learned to deal with it, how to do it. The younger riders coming up have grown up in it. Now the athletes are much more knowledgeable, much more sensitive and reactive to what Spruce Meadows needs from all of us," he said.

As a result, riders freely mingle with sponsors, attend media conferences promptly, are always mounted for presentation, take time to visit cultural exhibits in the public areas, and genuinely thank those responsible for the richness of their sport.

One of the major difficulties faced by Spruce Meadows in the late seventies and early eighties was enticing international riders to even come to Calgary.

In 1977 David Broome, certainly the best rider in the world at the time, was asked what it would take to get him and others to make the trip.

"Why would we ever want to? I can't think of anything that would ever get me there," he said. "And by the way, where is Spruce Meadows?"

He was not being unkind. He was merely reflecting the sentiment of most international riders of that time. They simply could not fathom circumstances that would make a one-tournament trip to the wilds of Canada worth the effort.

They didn't, however, count on the persuasive abilities of the Southerns - Marg in particular.

The Brits did come in 1977, and as remembered by British journalist Alan Smith, "it was an immediate success."

"Once the teams came over and returned to tell everyone what it was like, everyone was keen to get here," he explained.

Veteran British coach Ronnie Massarella remembered being approached by Marg Southern at Aachen in 1977. Great Britain had already agreed to send a team to Spruce Meadows that fall and even though he wasn't slated to coach, Marg still invited him along.

British coach Ronnie Massarella - Spruce Meadows' ambassador throughout the show jumping world.

Ronnie said it was never his intention to take up the offer personally since four riders and a couple of the owners were already going ". . . and they certainly didn't need a second Chef d'Equipe."

Marg, however, called him the night before the tournament to tell him the tickets were still waiting at the airport, adding sincerely just how much she was looking forward to seeing him once again.

"Now I had no choice," said Ronnie. "I had to go, but I couldn't convince my wife. So I went alone.

"When I arrived they made a real fuss over me. They still do and I look forward to it every year. But I told Ron (Ron Southern) that one day for sure, I won't be coming any more."

Ron said: "Ronnie, when you finish up chefing, there is a free ticket and free hotel waiting for you. You will always be welcome at Spruce Meadows."

"He made tears come to my eyes actually," said Ronnie.

Within the decade, the power nations of show jumping were lined up for invitations to Spruce Meadows. David Broome, who competed several times at Spruce Meadows, became one of its most vocal and sincere advocates.

What is it about the sport of show jumping that, at least in the minds of those who follow it, makes it unique among all others? And secondly, what is its perfect format?

These were among the questions directed to more than one hundred of show jumping's leading riders, officials and sponsors around the world. Their answers were packed with compassion, warmth, controversy, and sometimes even anger.

Most people began by extolling the many qualities of the horse, and then transferred those specifics to the sport itself.

Canadian Coach Michel Vaillancourt chose Spruce Meadows for the 1996 Olympic Trials.

"What we've done," said Ian Millar, "is taken the horse that so many people just naturally love, and used it to create a top-of-the-line sport."

Nor can one ignore the fact there is a universal appeal to show jumping that covers the full spectrum of society in a way few other sports can.

"So," said Ian, "you can start with the person who just loves a rough and tumble football game, but has no great interest in animals, and take them to Spruce Meadows. Show them one of the speed classes when the ring becomes slick as the rain turns white. If they don't come away shaking their heads saying 'that was a serious brawl and damn good sport' then, they're not being honest."

But you must get the sceptics to the brim of the well. They must see for themselves that show jumping is just as tough and gruelling as any physical contact sport. As a test of nerve and mental strength, few others even come close.

For some fans, however, the competitive aspect of show jumping is secondary.

"They're just mesmerized by watching the grace, the power and the beauty of that animal," said Ian Millar. "They really don't care who wins or loses. To them it's not about competition, it's an opportunity to enjoy the beauty of the animal."

He identified others who must also be brought into the loop: the young people who want to be riders, people who ride themselves and just want to rub shoulders with the great athletes of the world, and older couples who come just because it's a wonderful way to spend a day.

"It's a great place to be for all levels and combinations of society, and goodness knows we all need something to transcend the pressures and hidden agendas of modern day life.

"When you come to a competition at Spruce Meadows and hang out with the horse for a day, it's like a vacation. It's a great thing," said Ian.

Canadian national team coach Michel Vaillancourt, put it in terms anyone can understand:

"Nobody could say, 'horses . . . yuck.'"

Considering the classical aspect of it ". . . the beauty, the pending danger and the talent involved . . . you can't help but enjoy show jumping," suggested the only Canadian to ever win an individual Olympic medal in show jumping - silver at the '76 Montreal Olympic Games.

"People don't realize how difficult it is," said Michel, who took control of the Canadian team in 1993. "It's not just a matter of training hard and building up muscles and gaining speed.

The stories they could tell . . . Canada's Hugh Graham, Kim Kirton and Jim Elder.

"You must remember that two athletes are involved - the horse and the rider. Two minds to be satisfied and one of them you have little or no control over."

Each is so very much dependent upon the other that even a minor flaw in judgement or command invites disastrous results. Yet when the magic of both talents flare as one, the result is an invigorating experience unequalled in sport.

The Dean of Canadian show jumpers, Jim Elder, would never suggest the sport is easy, but he does confess that sometimes it does appear boring because there are so many good riders and horses.

A four-fault ride, said the man who has won team gold at both the Olympic and Pan-American Games, is now regarded as a bad round. There was a time when one knockdown would still win a lot of classes.

Calgary's John Simpson on the magnificent Quarter Horse Texas.

"The horses are going so well now we should be looking to create something a little different," said Jim. "We once jumped the whole course backwards in the second round of one European Grand Prix, and I thought that was great."

John Simpson, former Canadian national team rider and Canadian Equestrian Federation executive, developed nerves of steel by jumping over chicken coops at his father's Cochrane ranch. The difference was that Jack Simpson, his father and one of the sport's most avid boosters, was lying across the coop at the time.

"Did I ever hit him? Are you crazy? He'd have killed me. I learned the value of riding carefully the hard way," said John.

John, who took his big Quarter Horse Texas to the top of the world's ranking charts in the early eighties, said show jumping is the hardest among

> "The sport is challenging because of this interface with another live animal rather than a tennis racket or baseball bat."
>
> (John Simpson)

those sports dealing with horses, with the possible exception of calf roping, where a third animal is introduced to the equation: the calf.

"The biggest variable is you never know what is going to happen to your partner," said John. "If you're on a pair of skis, they're either hot or not. You can't tune a horse like that. The sport is challenging because of this interface with another live animal rather than a tennis racket or baseball bat."

Hugh Graham, a calf roper turned show jumper, loves the longevity offered by show jumping.

"Think about it. How many baseball players are around after thirty-five; how many swimmers after twenty-five or gymnasts after eighteen? Then you see David Broome at fifty-five, and George Morris at sixty, jumping with the young guys and usually beating them. Put them on young horses and look out . . . young legs," said Hugh, who was first named to the Canadian team in 1971.

Eddie Macken, Ireland's most revered sports personality, likes what the sport does for families.

"It's a very healthy sport, and a very clean sport," said Eddie, a naturally gifted rider who is at his best when facing crippling pressure.

"It requires full-time involvement by the whole family, and that involvement helps avoid the problems and temptations that are available to today's youth."

Eddie, increasing the distinctive lilt in his voice, shared this story when asked to describe the ultimate dream of an international show jumper:

"If you could die and go to heaven, and sort of look out your bedroom window every morning to find five or six top Grand Prix horses in the field . . . all of them careful and uncomplicated to ride . . . that would be the ideal situation. Pay no entry fees, no stabling costs and a lot of prize money."

Irish veteran Comdt. Gerry Mullins said it amazes him how mentally and physically strong the best riders in the sport must be.

Day in and day out, week after week, and for at least eleven months of the year, the top riders must stay hungry, said Gerry. That doesn't happen in other sport where seasons last anywhere from three to four months, allowing participants most of the year to unplug both mentally and physically.

"In America they try to help by teaching riders a little about the mental approach to the sport. But for the likes of Nick Skelton and the Whitakers, it comes purely natural."

From a presentation standpoint, Gerry suggested there are two ways of making show jumping exciting. "A Grand Prix," he added, "is dramatic as long as there is a good jump-off, otherwise it's boring.

"One is to make the course small so that everyone gallops like lunatics. The second," he said, "is to develop personalities so that people associate the sport with them."

Given a choice, Comdt. Mullins would prefer the latter.

"The biggest problem with riding," he said "is that very few people can identify with it. It's not like golf where everyone can relate to a missed putt because we've all had a putter in our hands at least once.

"So how do you get it across to those watching exactly what it feels like to be a long way off a fence, or that feeling when you turn too tight and find yourself in big problems?

The du Maurier International changed the sport forever - in Canada and around the world.
Winner of the first du Maurier International, 1981 champion David Broome of England on Queen's Way Philco.

"And how do we share the euphoria of winning a Grand Prix against the best riders in the world? The elation is there, but oftentimes a rider won't show this which might be fine for the rider, but it's not good for the sport."

Britain's David Broome said "it is time more announcers got a little excited during the events. Give the audiences good information about the sport, the horse and the riders," remarked the man whose riding conquests have included six British and three European Championships. "It is," said David, "the power of the commentator that plays a big part in all sport.

"There's nothing wrong with the sport just the way it is," said David who called a halt to his brilliant career in 1994. "What we have to do is convey the sport from the show ring to the audience and the television public. Within Europe, only the French announcers make it exciting."

He criticized British announcers for not going beyond telling fans the rider's name and the horse's number.

"It's got to be a lot more than that to hold my attention for an hour and a half. About ten of those and one might fall off."

"Spruce Meadows announcer Bill Kehler is one of the best", said David, "and other show jumping announcers could learn a great deal from his style and approach."

When new concepts designed to bring more excitement to the sport are discussed, one in particular worries Ron Southern. He is disturbed by a North American trend which advocates building smaller courses as a way of easing pressure on horses, and thus allowing them to jump even more often. It is of even more concern if done under the guise of providing fan excitement.

"From that philosophy a cult has developed that preaches you need fifteen clears for a jump-off if there is to be excitement in the sport, and then these horses are raced over obstacles that don't test real athletic ability."

And even though most people would argue vehemently that is true, Ron said he still does not believe it. "This sport is very much about strength and jumping ability, not just flat-out speed." He also believes that while it is hard for a horse to jump big all of the time, it is even more difficult, particularly from a mental standpoint, to ask them to always jump and run.

"The best thing for a horse, if he's got real talent, is to jump big and not have to jump too often - it's not good for him to have to run every time he's on course."

It is for this reason, he concluded, that in countless cases good horses are brought from Europe ". . . burn like a meteor for a year, and then they're gone. Burned out."

Show jumping, added England's David Broome, is clean, healthy and "very spectacular."

"When you get into it," he continued, "it truly is exciting, especially that moment when you relate to your horse and together you put out a 99.9 per cent effort."

But sport is sport, said David, and sometimes there is bad show jumping just like there is bad football.

"And occasionally there's the perfection of a Torvill and Dean (World Figure Skating Pair Champions Jayne Torvill and Christopher Dean). If you have been lucky enough to see John Whitaker and Milton, you know what I mean. I tell you that's worth watching. Everybody should have a chance to see it at least once."

As close as one may ever get to perfection - John Whitaker of Great Britain and the legendary Milton.

Irish coach Ned Campion loves the "extra dimension" that is so critical to success in show jumping.

"I am talking of the combination and interaction between man and animal. I golf and it's a game that I love because it is fantastic to be able to participate. But it's nothing compared to the whole concept of having an animal and a human working in harmony and always trying to refine that harmony."

That, he said, is the extra dimension this sport has.

"When you see it you recognize it. It may not be the winning performance but it's something that happens now and then - sheer poetry in motion.

"I can remember a ride by Brazil's Nelson Pessoa at Hamburg on a horse called Vivaldi. He set up a pace before he went through the start, very fast, very steady, and he just didn't draw a rein or change anything all the way around this enormous course. Even those who weren't horsemen were conscious of the fact they had just seen a performance that was the equivalent of a prima ballerina."

Few see show jumping as an overly dangerous sport, yet there are very few riders who have been fortunate enough to escape serious injury. Incidents of death are fortunately rare.

It is the fact that two living beings, each with a vastly distinctive character, must jell at just the right time is the thing that excites Swiss coach Charles Barrelet most about the sport.

"How many times have we seen an average horse with a great rider not make it, or a great horse flop with an average rider? Even if you see a jump perfectly, and that takes great skill, there's no guarantee it's going to work. The rider must make sure his mate is going to co-operate and how can you rely on that?"

Jimmy Elder recalled that when he was a boy he would be teased about competing in a "sissy sport."

"I said fine, you come with me. First thing we're going to do is climb on a horse and then race him around a course at thirty miles per hour. And then ahead of us there will be a sixty pound pole suspended five feet in the air. You and I will then ask this half-ton of horse to jump the rail.

"Now if we make it that's great. But if that horse stops dead and you land flat on the ground, or worse still it lands on part of you, then you tell me if it doesn't take a little guts to get up and do it all again?"

> "I used to peek under my arm so that before I hit the ground I could see which way the horse was going to roll and then I could bail out the other way."
>
> (Jim Elder)

The funny thing, said Jim, none of his friends had ever thought of the sport in those terms before. Falling off that horse, he convinced them, isn't much different then jumping out of a car going thirty miles per hour.

He is, however, surprised there aren't more serious accidents.

"The worst seem to happen while trotting over little poles. At that speed the horse won't throw you far enough to escape danger, and you both sort of crumble in a heap. You have to be quick to scramble away before the horse lands on you.

"I used to peek under my arm so that before I hit the ground I could see which way the horse was going to roll and then I could bail out the other way."

One of the most graphic explanations of the emotion that spins this sport came unexpectedly, and totally unrehearsed, from Ron Southern.

He had just finished an on-course presentation and was walking back from the centre of the ring. He still had the microphone in his hand and turned it back on when he stopped at a huge vertical that was part of the next course. With neither an introduction nor an explanation, he began:

"This is a truly difficult sport, maybe even the most difficult."

People scanned the massive ring to try and find him. They then noticed him as he stretched an arm skyward toward the top rail of the jump. He asked the audience to think of themselves as runners approaching a hurdle. And when they arrived at this hurdle, he added, they would find it was far bigger then they ever imagined. If they came too close they would hit it on the way up, or if they took off too far away, they would land in the middle . . . probably hurting themselves, which, he explained, is why there are more spinal injuries in show jumping than any other sport.

"To clear this jump it will take perfect balance, nerves of steel and your ability to ignore gut-wrenching pressure. I wish you could see the riders when they come through that clock tower, sweat dripping from chins, and jackets wet right through from the tension of the explosive exercise they must go through to jump correctly.

(photo by Cansport)

Some days are simply best forgotten - Canada's Sarah Watt would love an ejection seat at this point.
Amazingly, both horse and rider escaped injury after this fall.

Calgary fans learned early about the dangers of a sport many had believed was only for the timid and the gentry.

"They know if they go down there's a fourteen hundred pound horse coming down with them, and that takes nerve. They are professionals."

Nancy Southern has climbed back aboard horses after falls that left her eyes so swollen she could barely see the next fence, but she is still not one to discount the value of the "danger" element in show jumping.

"Motor-car racing is very popular for masses of people, and why is that? There's thrill, there's expertise and skill, but there's also danger as well as challenges and challengers," said Nancy.

"Jumping horses has all of those, but it also has the horse - an intangible element. People are in awe of what these horses will do for riders, how dangerous it is, how temperamental the horse can be."

Most people, she suggested, don't know how you get a horse to jump, but the truth is most people don't know how to drive a car around a corner at two hundred miles per hour either.

"But we have a much better understanding of how to drive a car at such speeds then we do of how to ride a horse. There's a bit of a fantasy and mystique surrounding this sport that you don't get in any other.

"Since the outset of time, civilizations have dreamt of riding winged horses and, many will passionately argue, that's what show jumping is.

"There is nothing," mused Nancy, "that comes close to the joy of being in sync with your horse as it takes a huge course jump by jump.

"Galloping between the elements and then leaving the ground and being hung in the air. The heat from the horse when his shoulder comes up to meet your chest as you're going over a fence. The muscles quivering beneath your saddle, and the thought of all of that power. There's nothing like it."

What is Success?

Although the sport of show jumping prospers at Spruce Meadows, some see this as an anomaly that has bad influences as well as good.

The facility has set such high standards that others feel too intimidated to even try to match it, thus fewer new tournaments are created and existing ones disappear.

There are also many riders and trainers who feel their sport has been kidnapped from them by those adhering to what is perceived as the "Spruce Meadows Philosophy". This philosophy, they argue, focuses on fans, sponsors and riders, rather than the rider exclusively.

The traditional "club atmosphere" which dominated tournament grounds for decades, is now more difficult to maintain. More and more riders now believe the Spruce Meadows way is probably the only route to future growth and successes for the sport. Conflict between the two factions is more apparent in the United States and Canada than in Europe.

The misunderstanding erupts, however, when an improper interpretation is applied to that described as the "Spruce Meadows way". No one at Spruce Meadows, particularly the Southerns, suggest the primary measurement of success is the amount of prize money, or the size of investment in the facility.

In fact, both Marg and Ron constantly stress that success will follow any tournament that adheres to rules, treats sponsors and riders with equal respect, and offers fans a sports entertainment package that runs on time and at a fair price.

It is a benefits loop that has proven itself at all levels, whether it be the MASTERS or a one-day pony club rally.

Frank Chapot of the United States knows horses and horse competition as well as anyone in the world. The former Olympian does not hesitate to share that knowledge in a direct and often opinionated fashion.

He spoke highly of the Southerns and their accomplishments at Spruce Meadows, but said he "can't say one way or another" if its existence has helped American riders.

"It (Spruce Meadows) hasn't made it a better sport for the American team. I mean the U.S. Team has to pay its way there, unlike the Europeans," said Frank who took over the captainship of the American squad upon the retirement of legend Bill Steinkraus in 1972.

Host tournaments of sanctioned Nations' Cup competitions are responsible for transportation costs of visiting nations only to the border of the host country. Spruce

Meadows, in addition to flying as many as six European teams to the MASTERS, also brings other outstanding individual riders from Europe if space is available.

Although requested to do so, Spruce Meadows also refuses to pay appearance money to any rider.

Frank disagreed with those who argue big prize money is the prime motivation in a tournament's appeal package.

"I don't think prize money is what makes Spruce Meadows what it is. Those tournaments have good character and are simply wonderful competitions," said the man who was also a successful steeplechase rider.

The United States Equestrian Team came under heavy fire a couple of times in the late eighties and early nineties when some team members competing at the MASTERS entered their second-best horses in the Bank of Montreal Nations' Cup, one of the two premier events of competition at that tournament.

Although never admitted publicly, the ploy was obvious to any horseman. Those who pulled their Grand Prix horses, and it should be stressed that not all of the Americans did this, were saving their big jumpers for the next day's du Maurier International where prize money was considerably higher.

It reached an ugly climax in 1993 when the entire team comprised of Hap Hansen, Michael Endicott and Anne Kursinski, mounted on their best horses, withdrew from the second round of the Nations' Cup. Their fourth rider, Philip Cillis with Juniperus, did not compete as his horse was not sound. At the point of withdrawal the team probably couldn't have done much better, but thousands of Americans in the audience were deeply disappointed.

It was viewed as a huge insult to the Southerns, Spruce Meadows, sponsors and the sport in general.

Frank Chapot, not commenting on that incident specifically, said "it is tough on horses when you jump them in the Nations' Cup on a Saturday, and then ask them to come back for the Grand Prix the next day."

When asked what else could be done when the events are the anchor competitions of the MASTERS and rightly deserve the best fan exposure for their sponsors, Frank curtly replied:

"I would solve it by saying, look, money isn't everything. I'd tell one of them to take a hike if they want to."

Spectators may pay for the sport in Europe, he said, but that is not the case in North America.

"Here it's the exhibitors, and I'm not sure it will ever change; probably not. I don't think you're ever going to make money off spectators here."

Spruce Meadows, he conceded, might be the only exception.

"The Southerns have educated the fan. Just like it was done years ago in Aachen. They had kindergarten children come out of school and the place sounded like a chicken house. I think Ron has done that."

Spruce Meadows, he suggested, is a wonderful hobby for Ron Southern.

"I'm glad he likes it, it's very nice for the rest of us. It's wonderful we have people like Ron Southern to keep the sport going."

But if it can succeed at Spruce Meadows, why not elsewhere?

"What other things in Calgary do you have to do? It's not New York or L.A. where the public can choose from the best baseball, football, hockey, basketball - three or sometimes four teams in each.

"What I'm saying is you have the best of horse sport in Calgary, and it's the best in the world. Because of that it's sold very well."

In conclusion:

"I think we should be satisfied with what we have. There's enough money in the thing for these people to make a living, for the horseman and for the owner to enjoy," said Frank.

Larry Langer, Competitions Manager of the highly successful 1992 World Cup in Del Mar, California, described Spruce Meadows as an "aberration" and "an oasis in the desert."

"I would have expected," he said, "that twenty years after Spruce Meadows there would have been a number of other international events that would have sprung up in the area. I would have thought it would bring western Canada into the forefront and then the spin-off would have come to the western United States."

That hasn't happened, according to Larry.

He, in fact, charges that Ron Southern was "intensely jealous and intensely possessive" during the first years of Spruce Meadows. He accused him of not wanting to share his success with anyone.

Californian interests, said Larry, tried to strike deals with the Southerns that would have seen the European riders and horses competing at the MASTERS move directly across the border to California competition.

"I mean Ron made that so difficult, he absolutely didn't want those people to stay," said Larry.

Ron Southern recalled the negotiations in a different spirit.

"If a deal could have been struck whereby all associated costs were evenly split, I would have endorsed it with enthusiasm," said Ron.

Looking within California, particularly in the Del Mar region, there are new show jumping arenas springing up ". . . without regard to Spruce Meadows at all."

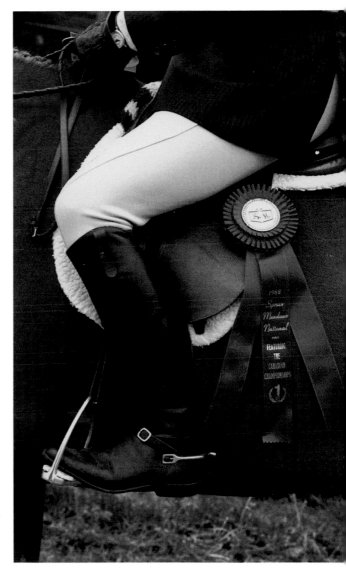

"That would be the only aspect of the facility that I think is sad. Now, if I turn the corner and say how wonderful Spruce Meadows is, I will agree with everything you're going to write," said Larry.

In conflict with some of his observations, however, are the comments of others who said the Del Mar complex and the World Cup it hosted incorporated more Spruce Meadows concepts then ever before seen in California, New York or Florida, the sport's supposed hotbed states.

"I've been working on this Del Mar World Cup Final for two years," Larry insisted, "and not once in any of our meetings did we ever mention Spruce Meadows, although some of the people went to Spruce Meadows just to look around."

He also disputed claims that California riders - always prominent in huge numbers at all three Spruce Meadows tournaments - wanted things done back home as they were at Spruce Meadows.

"In their brains they're treating it (Spruce Meadows) as an island. There's certainly no pressure on management around here to duplicate anything. And horse show organizers don't think about Spruce Meadows as something to aim for. It's too far out of the norm."

"If other people are reluctant to do what Spruce Meadows does, then I believe it can always stand on its own. That will simply make Spruce Meadows stronger and stronger."

(Nancy Southern)

The Spruce Meadows image, however, was not at all out of standard with what transpired at the World Cup at Del Mar. The Organizing Committee of that competition earned international accolades because it ran a tight ship, on time. The grounds were rife with sponsor signs, and jump equipment was delightfully imaginative. The Media Centre was exceptional, flowers were evident throughout the grounds and volunteers were plentiful. The competition had been designed to please the fans, and stands were packed most evenings. They also enjoyed the insights of the announcer, Spruce Meadows' Bill Kehler.

Spruce Meadows, it can confidently be said, is out of step with those American shows allowing riders to dictate the pace of the event. But that comment should not stand as a judgement of the success of such shows. At the California, Arizona and Florida competitions, riders are openly relaxed, very happy and quite in control of the destiny they have chosen. Parents love it because every trainer manages to watch every student's ride, even if half a dozen shuffles of the order-of-go are necessary. And, if at the last minute you want to enter another horse, go for it. That's another $20 for the organizers and that's the way these tournaments survive.

Others, of course, argue vehemently that Spruce Meadows has struck out on the only road that will ultimately strengthen, perhaps even save, the sport of show jumping.

"If other people are reluctant to do what Spruce Meadows does, then I believe it can always stand on its own," shrugged Nancy Southern. "That will simply make Spruce Meadows stronger and stronger."

Just like at Augusta, Georgia, where nobody knows how the invitation list is drawn up for the Masters Golf Tournament ". . . there are people who recognize that Spruce Meadows is doing things the right way and they want to capitalize on that," said Nancy.

Canada's Michel Vaillancourt said Canadians in general are proud of Spruce Meadows and what it has done for the sport in this country, particularly in the area of attracting major corporate sponsorship.

"It would be a lot better if we could duplicate Spruce Meadows across the country, but that would be almost next to impossible," said the boss man of Canada's show jumping team.

"If there is a negative point," Michel said, "it is that the standards of Spruce Meadows are so high others fear they will always be measured against them.

"When other shows in the province approached sponsors, they were always compared with Spruce Meadows. Nobody can compete against what is there, so it made it very difficult for other shows."

England's Ronnie Massarella, who throughout his career never accepted a dime for coaching the British team, said he doesn't have to look far in searching for the underlying reasons for success at Spruce Meadows.

"You know why? Because it's run professionally and very tough. People know they can't get out of hand because if they do they'll be taken to task, and I think that's good," said Ronnie.

He said that riders who go to Spruce Meadows have a deep respect for the people, and therefore will always give their best. "Sure it's ruled by an iron fist. But what's wrong with that? I know I keep in check."

And as tough as regulations may be, he said the softer side of Spruce Meadows is equally unique.

"Whenever you go to Spruce Meadows people remember your name," said Ronnie. "They make you feel like you're the last man on earth. That's what Spruce Meadows is like.

"I can walk around any other showground in the world and nobody goes out of their way to talk to me. But when I get to Spruce Meadows, everyone wants to meet you and spend some time with you. They want you to win, but even if you don't, they still talk to you."

Spruce Meadows, added Atlanta Olympic course designer Linda Allen, has set the example for all others to aspire to.

"No one has yet even come close. Not

(photo by Rick Maynard)

Atlanta Olympic course designer Linda Allen, riding on the American team at Spruce Meadows in 1978.

only at the MASTERS where they have the European riders, but through the other two tournaments as well."

Linda, who also designed the course for the Del Mar World Cup on her native California soil in 1992, said that no matter what meeting she attends, if the topic is new ideas and strategies for the sport, Spruce Meadows is always held up as a positive example.

"Technically, atmosphere-wise, facility-wise, no matter what subject you're talking about, this is what the comparison is," said Linda.

Every world-class competition has its own distinctive claim to fame, and while there are technical aspects that can be moved from venue to venue, the atmosphere of each is unique.

Henry Collins has been overseeing the production of show jumping in the United States through several evolutions, and says he is always amazed at the differences between them.

"The atmosphere at the National Horse Show, with the officials all in white ties, top hats and tails, probably has its place only in New York. Likewise, Olympia in London is a Christmas show that only plays in London.

"As much as you might want these shows in either Calgary or Los Angeles, they probably wouldn't work in either locale. The same goes for Spruce Meadows; it's unique to that part of the world. I don't think you can transport it literally to another part of the world and say it will work there too," said Henry.

Journalist John Quirk, however, will argue vehemently that Spruce Meadows has become a model of excellence for any tournament in the world.

"It is the paragon, and people come not to compare themselves with Spruce Meadows, but to find out how much of what they find they can borrow," said John.

The facility itself, added John, is "awesome", but it is its organization that most impressed the publisher of Horses Magazine.

"The combative control centre (SOC) is in some way the most remarkable thing about Spruce Meadows. The fact that everything goes off as though it's a combat exercise.

"When it comes to pure organization, timing and the way all things have been thought through in advance - Spruce Meadows is the epitome."

He doesn't remember who on the British team said it, but in asking for a description of Spruce Meadows he was told:

"Spruce Meadows is Hickstead the way God would have built it, if God could afford it."

John said Spruce Meadows had a huge impact on the California riding community as it became the "first opportunity for most of them to ride on the world scene."

The two major events which catapulted the sport on the west coast of the United States were the Olympics in Los Angeles, which created a new interest and Spruce Meadows, which gave riders the opportunity to compete.

"Before Spruce Meadows, the showing in California was provincial. It brought California into the international world. From its inception Spruce Meadows has been California's #1 tournament destination . . . even if it is seventeen hundred miles away.

"And now," concluded John, "Spruce Meadows sets the standard for the world."

Ronnie Freeman first hauled horses to a Spruce Meadows tournament from California in 1982, and while it was a costly trip, it was also very educational.

"I learned that year that if you come to Spruce Meadows hoping to win some money, then you better have some strong legs beneath you," said the personable veteran. "It's not the place to be without a top jumper."

Ronnie, an admitted professional at a time when others tried to hide it, waited three years before returning to a Spruce Meadows tournament, and true to his word, he came armed with talent. Aboard the young Dutch/Thoroughbred Mr. Ecker, he won the exhausting Texaco Derby at the 1985 INVITATIONAL (now the NORTH AMERICAN).

Hap Hansen of Encinitas helped direct the charge of the "California Connection".

An early portrait of the Spruce Meadows team . . . and most are still involved more than two decades later.

Spruce Meadows: *The Facility*

Calgary graphic artist and designer Andy Hordos came closer than most in trying to find a simple explanation of what Spruce Meadows is. It is, he said, a "living thing."

"Spruce Meadows is constantly changing, and while I think the focus is still the Riding Hall and the International Course, everything else seems to be constantly evolving."

Use of the word "incredible" has become a cliche in describing Spruce Meadows, suggested Andy, yet to be part of it ". . . now that truly is an incredible thing."

So what is the magic it creates?

"That is probably the most elusive thing because it's so much a combination of the involvement of Marg and Ron. But it is also the synergy of energies that people contribute to it," said the man who has helped mold its visual image.

"I have never been so impressed in my life by anything that compares with the quality of the people. I don't know whether they (Marg and Ron) hand pick the brightest people or if they are just naturally attracted to them. I have never had the privilege to be amongst so many bright people."

"It's pride," suggested Alan Golby, Maintenance Manager at Spruce Meadows. Strangers stop and pick up garbage. So do Marg and Ron.

"It all goes back to being nice to people, and that's the way the Southerns have always been. They talk to people and spend time with them, all of them. It's being part of the family and not wanting to disappoint anyone."

Former Canadian coach Tommy Gayford has had his differences with Spruce Meadows, but he still sees it as "one of the best, if not the best" in the world.

"I'm very proud of Spruce Meadows. You see the best in the sport breaking their necks to get there. They'll kill in Europe to get to Spruce Meadows. For Canadians it's the ultimate competition.

"Every Canadian kid's dream in show jumping is to ride out there in that big ring."

Swiss Chef d'Equipe Charles Barrelet argues it is unrealistic to even think of trying to duplicate the uniqueness of Spruce Meadows elsewhere in the show jumping world.

(photo by Cansport)

The numbers have changed, but Spruce Meadows continues to thrive on the enthusiasm, generosity and commitment of its staff and volunteers.

He believes with equal fervour, in fact, that it would also be foolish to try and clone any of the great venues.

"We've all heard the comparisons between Aachen and Spruce Meadows," he began. "Aachen is a fantastic show. It's versatile with its driving and dressage and the crowds are great. But the German character is stiffer and that is reflected in everything about the presentation, particularly in its organization."

> "I'm very proud of Spruce Meadows. You see the best in the sport breaking their necks to get there. They'll kill in Europe to get to Spruce Meadows. For Canadians it's the ultimate competition."
>
> (Tom Gayford)

"The thing that makes Dublin so wonderful," said Charles, "is the temperament of the Irish people." Similarly, in Calgary he sees the difference as the pioneer spirit that still seems to dominate and exude enthusiasm.

"So I'm not saying it would be wrong to try, but I do question if it could be done. It takes certain personalities and unless you have the same or similar personality, it won't succeed."

Fellow countryman Hans Britschgi has judged at competitions throughout the world and due to the depth of his understanding of all facets within the sport, he also is in great demand to conduct international seminars on protocol and regulations.

"At Spruce Meadows I feel at home. At Aachen . . . well it's very interesting but I never feel the human touch," said Hans. "They're (Aachen) friendly and very hospitable, but it's not the same. Here you are away from the city, so the whole group - riders, officials, trainers and fans - spend the day together. It becomes a friendly thing and it's not over-loaded."

In looking at the sport as it plays elsewhere in the world, Hans had some interesting observations:

". . . The whole of Eastern Asia can not create a show like the MASTERS simply because quarantine descriptions make it impossible to travel there with your horses."

". . .What the Japanese do to overcome this is invite very good riders from twelve different countries and give each of them two good horses to compete on. It creates a nice atmosphere, but it's still a club atmosphere."

". . . In Africa it is still very primitive but they are starting to do things. Australia has high standards, but its tournaments will never be international due to distances."

". . .The most developed show jumping nations can be found in North America and Europe. But in Europe we sometimes are too stuck to the old ways and traditions."

". . . You can learn something in Rome, but it's a special atmosphere built on high society. Beautiful fences, good people, but also very stiff. It probably wouldn't work outside of Rome.

"The Italians are happy when high society comes because when television must break for whatever reason - sometimes as long as an hour - nobody minds that the show is delayed. They just go out for a chat and a drink and come back as if nothing happened. Try that in Switzerland or Germany and the next time you would have no one in your stands."

George Morris, who has served as Chef d'Equipe for the United States team on several occasions, said Spruce Meadows "outperforms even the Germans" in its methodical, precise approach to management.

Riders view Spruce Meadows from many different perspectives, the most obvious being that it has made a few of them wealthy and provided many others with at least enough to comfortably prolong their careers.

"Spruce Meadows certainly provides opportunity," said Canadian team veteran Hugh Graham. "You don't go unless you have top horses.

(photo by Tish Quirk)

Canada's Hugh Graham enjoys another special moment at his favourite competitive venue.

"The Southerns run a tight ship, but they're great people."

Hugh, one of twenty prominent riders on the "all-time money won list"at Spruce Meadows, tells a delightful story about one of his grooms who was on his first trip to Spruce Meadows.

"We pulled the van in after a tough trip and I asked one of my grooms to find some grass and stretch the horses," began Hugh.

Ten minutes later, at a dead run and visibly upset, the groom returned mumbling something about a "crazy guy" who, while shouting and waving his arms, chased him and the horse off the grass.

"It was his first time to Spruce Meadows and I told him not to worry about it. It was a forgotten incident until the next day when he showed me where he had been grazing the horses. It was the International Ring."

And if that wasn't bad enough, a couple of minutes later he pointed out the "crazy guy" who chased him away. "You guessed it - Ron Southern. I told my groom not to leave the barn area for the rest of the show and made sure I was never seen with him."

Hugh speaks fondly of his trips to Spruce Meadows.

"It's become a ritual. You start in June for the NATIONAL and take in the nice country air. I always take the family and they enjoy the booths. There's not a better place for a family."

Hugh, who hasn't missed many of the tournaments in twenty years, enjoys the more relaxed atmosphere of the July NORTH AMERICAN, but stresses you can't beat the intensity of the MASTERS.

Former national team member John Simpson returned to Spruce Meadows as a major sponsor - presenting the Cana Cup to 1994 winner Ludger Beerbaum of Germany, together with his mother Mary and children, Christy and Luke.

Calgary's John Simpson was at the peak of his career when Spruce Meadows burst upon the international scene in the late seventies.

"I think back to when we first started international jumping at Spruce Meadows, and the way we were treated as riders was pretty amazing, and today it's still the same scenario," said John.

He finds it difficult to sit down with old friends who arrive at Spruce Meadows to compete, simply because they have no free time between all of the parties and dinners arranged on their behalf.

"Go anywhere else in the world to compete and you're sort of dumped out of the back door," said John whose company CANA Construction is a major sponsor at Spruce Meadows.

Facility for facility and dollar for dollar, he challenges anyone to find a facility that can compete.

"If you did an analysis of what you really liked about Spruce Meadows, and put the top twenty reasons on a check list, you could then go to any other facility in the world and I'll bet you couldn't check off more than five or six of those points at any of them.

"Aachen, for example, is great," said John, "but the barns are old, cold and damp stone. There's no real training area other than a field in back and a sand ring.

"At Spruce Meadows you have field after field to train in, and that's vital to riders.

"Hickstead," he continued, "may be beautiful, but again the barns are old, and many riders get stuck in temporary barns.

"The accommodation for grooms was so decrepit that my people preferred to stay with the horses in the stalls."

International grooms are given accommodation in ATCO bunkhouses at Spruce Meadows, the same structures that meet the highest of standards for drilling camps and other work-force housing needs around the world. The grooms are also invited to attend many of the special entertainment activities organized by Spruce Meadows staff, some of them specifically for them.

"I could go through every facility in the sport, and it doesn't get any different. And I haven't even mentioned prize money. One victory in the du Maurier is worth more than a dozen wins anywhere else."

Ian Millar said it's simply a case of continual "fine tuning" by the Spruce Meadows team.

"In the early going it was massive changes going on every year. That went into a fine tuning era, and now it looks like we're back to the big projects," said Ian.

"What separates the best from the rest is that the best keeps getting better. That of course is what Spruce Meadows is all about - people there keep finding ways to make it better."

A prime example, said Ian, is the International Ring. Initially the ring's footing was a nightmare after excessively hot, or wet, weather. It wouldn't drain properly in storms and water wouldn't soak in on the hot days. The result was a course either too soft or too hard, and while riders gave Spruce Meadows top marks overall, the International Ring failed miserably.

"Making a splash" at Spruce Meadows.

"We used to have a choice of hard, slippery or deep," recalled Ian. "A very sophisticated watering regime was established and that could take it from being too hard to just right. But at that point Mother Nature took control again and we didn't know if it would continue on to become both slippery and deep."

In the past few years they have done everything possible to improve that ring by aerating with sand, and it has made a "huge difference."

"I had a talk with Mrs. Southern and she described the process. Eventually the footing will get to the point where it will almost never be hard. Then it will get to the point where, no matter how much it rains, it really won't be that slippery. Then the point will be reached where it will take a serious flood before the sand will let you down.

"But the point is, give credit to the Spruce Meadows team. They already had an excellent venue in that International Ring, yet they weren't satisfied with just really good. They wanted it better," said Ian.

Pamela Carruthers has become an institution at Spruce Meadows, and even today as honourary technical consultant, she makes certain that the course design standards she introduced in 1976 are always maintained.

She feels deeply honoured to have been called upon by both Hickstead and Spruce Meadows to serve as resident course designer, and as a result she has had more influence on this sport than any other designer in history.

"If you have a job, and you're good at it, then you want to be amongst the best," said Pamela. "Spruce Meadows has offered all course designers the opportunity to be that."

She is constantly asked by her peers if there is any chance they could come to Spruce Meadows and just help out. Over the years they have all been there: Jon Doney, Richard Jeffrey, Olaf Peterson, Paul Duffy, Hauke Schmidt, Linda Allen and Leopoldo Palacios.

"They're not interested in getting paid. They just want the opportunity."

Marg and Ron Southern are openly embarrassed by the praise heaped upon them, but not by the accolades flowing to Spruce Meadows. They deflect credit directed at them to others, and thank them at every opportunity for contributing to the facility's successes.

It is a genuine humility that a casual outsider still might challenge if measured against society norms. But for those who have had the opportunity to share their dream, and maybe even help nudge it to reality, the sincerity of this family is beyond question.

"You wouldn't spend twenty years putting this kind of time and effort into it, if it was just for yourself," began Marg Southern. "We never did it for that. We truly wanted to put something back into the community and the people who helped us seemed to embrace this belief.

There is not a more magnificent sight than a majestic horse stretched to his limit above the gaping water jump at Spruce Meadows - Jill Henselwood and Canadian Colours.

"There are always some sceptics, and they don't believe it yet and probably never will," she said.

Spruce Meadows is open 365 days a year. Ron makes that point at least half a dozen times each tournament by inviting everyone to come out at any time. He doesn't issue that invitation to just friends and acquaintances, he delivers it to grandstands packed with as many as 40,000 strangers.

And on those rare occasions when he can't be at the microphone following an event, Marg, Nancy or Linda step in and inevitably they too will also stress the open door policy of Spruce Meadows.

"The coffee pot is always on. We'd love to see you."

Thousands accept the sincerity of that invitation and throughout the year there are

Resident course designer Pamela Carruthers of England helped create the Spruce Meadows masterpiece.

people wandering through the barns, stopping for coffee, and saying hello to the Southerns whenever they are around. That means just about every weekend of the year.

One groom recalls that on her first weekend she challenged a group of visitors as they walked through the barns.

"It's O.K.," she was told. "Ron invited us to come."

And of course they were right. He did invite them, and about eighty thousand others the weekend before at the NATIONAL.

American horse trainer and renowned hunter judge Victor Hugo-Vidal once asked a complete stranger to go back and pick up a cigarette butt he had seen him grind into a Spruce Meadows driveway.

"I told him: 'Don't leave that there sir. These people have gone to so much trouble to make this place look nice. Pick that up and throw it in the trash bin.'"

The somewhat startled visitor did as he was told.

Marg Southern speaks of the family's awareness of the fragile make-up of any success, particularly the one mistakenly taken for granted.

"I think everything you do is fragile, no matter which way the balance tips. You must never stop putting in the same effort that you did from Day One, because it doesn't take long for the tide to turn against you."

Marg gathers all staff together three or four times each year to impress upon them the importance of being friendly.

"If somebody comes by, say hello and be pleasant. Buildings don't mean anything if people are intimidated. They will only come if they are comfortable."

In searching for that moment when one can say with certainty that Spruce Meadows vaulted to international prominence, Ron Southern feels it came the second or third year into the du Maurier International (1982 or 1983).

(photo by Tish Quirk)

A powerful trio - together they changed the course of show jumping in the world - Ian Millar, Big Ben and the late Wilmat Tennyson.

"The great credit for that was due to Wilmat Tennyson (Chief Operating Officer of Imperial Tobacco, parent company of du Maurier). When the du Maurier prize money surpassed $250,000, people critical to this sport began asking if it would continue on. Wilmat assured them it would and that provided the stability that was needed to build some of the things you see here today," said Ron.

The Southerns were deeply saddened by the death of Mr. Tennyson in 1995. He had become a close family friend whose counsel and insights were profoundly valued. Later that year, on the day before the 1995 MASTERS, riders and friends of Wilmat and Helen Tennyson from around the world gathered at a small Riders' Chapel constructed within a horseshoe throw from the All Canada Ring. It was built in his memory by those who missed him the most.

The sport of show jumping has been marked by opportunism and a lack of ability by those with good intentions to stick it out. There have been sincere efforts in California and Virginia at matching Spruce Meadows, but

The Spruce Meadows Riders' Chapel reminds the world of the immense contribution made Spruce Meadows and the sport by Wilmat Tennyson.

neither had committed sponsorship or the presence of live television. After initial presentations, both projects faded away.

"Even though people have been kind enough to tell us they basically like Spruce Meadows, or thought it was great, it still takes them a long time to really believe it," said Ron.

"What happened here is that people kept coming back. They would see our family, volunteers and staff committed as much as ever and they would be convinced."

Ron chose his words carefully when talking about his early hopes for Spruce Meadows.

"In my mind always, and in my heart, was the belief that Spruce Meadows could be the best in the world," he said.

"I say that not because I want people to think we were geniuses with a plan. No, it was more along the line of occasionally thinking that is our challenge. We can't really define it, and we don't know how we're going to get there. But that's what we want to do."

Marg Southern suggested that for her the motivation was somewhat different, "but that again goes to our own personalities."

"We both grew up at a time in the world when expectations weren't very high. We worked very hard for what we attained, and we were fortunate in the sense that our commitment was always total - every hour, every day. A lot of people wouldn't want to live that way.

"It was easy for us, therefore, to fall into it again with Spruce Meadows. But I would never say Spruce Meadows is the best. I would say that we continue to make it better and better. But to be the best. I don't know what the best really is. 'The best' to one person isn't going to be 'the best' to another."

Financing the venture was costly from inception, and only in the nineties did Spruce Meadows finally manage to become self-sustaining.

There was a point in the mid-eighties when the Southerns were selling off personal assets just to keep Spruce Meadows running, and that in itself was a frightening realization that obviously couldn't continue very far into the future.

"When I think of commerce at Spruce Meadows," began Ron, "I look at it in two ways. First of all, the commerce of being able to sustain a sporting venue. We see that all around us in professional teams who do not have the ability to sustain themselves because of payrolls and other costs.

"Spruce Meadows is, in a sense, even more vulnerable because there isn't a large amount of money from the gate. That is the way we have always wanted it."

But any sporting venture still must have some form of internal economics to sustain it, or it will become a prohibitive drain on someone's resources.

"We are sensitive about this topic because people still believe that profit must be the reason we are involved, and that's not the truth at all. It's important that Spruce Meadows continues to develop and grow those areas of revenue that aren't done on the backs of the people that come here to enjoy it."

Marg's objective has not swayed from Day One.

"I just want to make sure that Spruce Meadows always stays for the horse and for the people to get enjoyment from it."

Ron said he is still amazed at the accomplishments of Spruce Meadows.

"I'm surprised at its basic underlying strength. I would have thought it would have been far more tenuous than it is. It is becoming both an institution and an influence."

The People of Spruce Meadows

People work arduously on behalf of Spruce Meadows, and among those working the hardest are the volunteers who have remained with the Southerns since Day One.

Most of them, like Marg and Ron themselves, waded in with a limited knowledge of the sport, but have gone on to become innovators and acknowledged leaders in their specific area of expertise.

It is said, quite honestly, that Spruce Meadows is the reflection of its people - widely varied in complexion and social structure - but very common in purpose.

It is through their efforts that, during the anxiety of competition, Spruce Meadows moves through the day at an orderly pace that shouts of confidence and purpose.

Collectively Spruce Meadows volunteers are known as members of the Pegasus Club and their numbers have grown from a handful in 1977 to several hundred. Many contribute their time, energy and expertise every day of every tournament, while others narrow their input to only one of the three annual competitions.

Although it is always dangerous to talk about specific individuals, simply because you must leave out so many who have contributed so much, there are a handful or so who must be given that special recognition.

Anne and Bas French certainly lead the list. Anne is a genius at organizing volunteers while making certain that proper protocol is never overlooked. Bas has shared the good times and the bad times with Ron, including a late-night session that found both of them ankle-deep in raw sewage.

The sewage escapade dates back to the late seventies when Spruce Meadows was still totally dependent upon a septic system. If the holding tanks weren't emptied regularly . . . well, you didn't want to be around for the consequences.

Bas and Ron were. It was late one Saturday tournament night when Bas and Ron ventured innocently into the basement of the Riding Hall to check on some equipment for the next day's competition.

"Not surprisingly, we smelled it first," said Bas, who has never shown any of the conservatism associated with his accounting background. "And then we saw it."

Raw sewage had backed up and was oozing across the floor to lap at their shoe tops. Desperately they looked around for some help, but there wasn't anyone within shouting distance. They did what they had to do. Shovels and boots were found and the two men started to shovel.

"It was," said Bas, "as gruesome as it gets." The two men spent most of the night gagging, as much from laughter as the choking stench.

"Ron kept telling me we were on the Poseidon and that we were going down," said Bas. "I couldn't believe I was there."

The two have travelled the world in search of good horseflesh. When more than one horse was purchased, they traditionally decided which horse went where by a flip of the coin. More than once they have missed planes because conversation locked away their minds from all other intrusions. They have taken riding lessons together, not a pretty sight according to their children, and they once spent an afternoon shooting in the general direction of pigeons destructively roosting in the Riding Hall roof. They killed far more roof tiles than birds.

As Competitions Manager, Bas has refined a scheduling procedure that is innovative and state-of-the-art. Tell him how many horses are in a class, include the specifics such as length, number of jumps, time allowed - and he will tell you to within seconds how long that class will take.

(photo by Cansport)

Dedicated volunteer, Casey Hansum, acts as Ring Master rain or shine, and yes, even snow - seen here during the 1992 MASTERS.

Anne French, affectionately known as Miss Anne for her gracious demeanor, matches volunteers to responsibilities with the uncanny insight of a clairvoyant. She also makes certain that no sponsor is ever left unattended at Spruce Meadows.

Dr. John and Chris Wood have done it all at Spruce Meadows. Chris, twin sister to Marg Southern, took on the duties that others would shun. She spent years hidden away in the kitchen making sandwiches for sponsors, volunteers and staff until ill health made it difficult. John Wood, with his gravel-voice and trademark cigar, was the tournament's first announcer and then moved on to any task that required the skills of a "real nice guy."

Wonneetta Hamilton gives new meaning to "presentation ceremonies" with her grace and soft nature. Judy Kley, wife of Riding Master Albert Kley, continues to keep track of award winners at every tournament.

There are hundreds of others; all have brought distinctive talents to the Spruce Meadows family. Most must take their holidays to work the tournaments, and their day is seldom less than twelve to fourteen hours long.

Only a few of the volunteer positions have an element of glamour attached. Most are tough assignments that bring neither glory nor outside recognition.

Standing for hours in freezing drizzle with a flag at the starting line is not a great deal of fun. Neither is opening and closing a gate in the warm-up ring, or hauling pop up and down stairs for a thirsty media corps.

Dave Williams, president of a Calgary-based oil company, would typically arrive at Spruce Meadows just after sunup to help daughter April groom her horse for competition.

He would then move on to his second job of the day, that of a volunteer gate man on the old Rocky Mountain Course. Usually it was raining. Like Superman, Dave would then dash into a washroom and emerge in seconds as a meticulously-groomed company president just in time to present ribbons in his company's class. If there was time, he would change once again before helping to cool down April's horse. Usually he did it in his suit. Dry cleaners love Spruce Meadows' volunteers. The only one who perhaps did it better was his wife Carol, also a volunteer.

A place for only the very brave -
Donna Marshall and Jack Hugill in Central Communications.

Checking a script - author Ken Hull, Marg Southern and Georgine Ulmer.

Donna Marshall spends most of her fifteen-hour day listening to as many as one hundred and ten people shouting at her on radios. Only the fact she is a nurse in the emergency ward of a Calgary hospital prepares her for such stress. Her partner and mentor in this madhouse is Jack Hugill, who used to be an air traffic controller. Spruce Meadows, he insists, is far more hectic.

"We once tried to find others who could help us out," recalled Donna. "No one lasted more than ten minutes, until Jack finally convinced his wife Jackie to join the team."

When Donna went back to nursing she was already a Spruce Meadows volunteer. She insisted that one condition had to be met before she could accept employment.

"I told them I would always have to take time off for the three Spruce Meadows tournaments."

For years, tournament announcer Bill Kehler shared facilities not only with the judges, but also with Central Communications.

"It wasn't the work that got you, it was the mental exhaustion created by the continuous humdrum of walkie-talkies, phones, questions, and then the bad weather. It would eventually get to everyone." There were lighter moments, however, and Bill's favourite story picks on Competitions Manager Bas French.

Bas called up from the International Ring and asked Jack Hugill to contact Riding Master Albert Kley and have him meet Bas on the course.

They began paging Albert when Jack noticed that he was already standing just a few feet from Bas.

"Thanks," said Bas. "I see him now."

A minute later, however, Bas was back on his radio to Central Communications.

"Jack, this is Bas. Do you know what it was I wanted to ask Albert?" Some days do that to a person.

Volunteers have found their way to Spruce Meadows under varied circumstances, but none quite so strange as those surrounding the recruitment of Ray Holt.

> When you become a volunteer at Spruce Meadows, you also become a friend of Marg and Ron Southern. You have been invited into their dream and that, you quickly learn, is a rare and honoured privilege.

Ray, who needed crutches to walk, was a big show jumping fan and travelled with his wife by car from British Columbia to attend one of the first MASTERS Tournaments. During an international class the magnificent Anglezarke, ridden by Malcom Pyrah of Great Britain, got loose and jumped over a series of fences and into a parking lot. The final leap ended on top of Ray's new car. The horse was fine, but Ray's car needed some serious surgery.

The Southerns had never met the Holts. But when they found out what happened they arranged to have their car fixed and also picked up hotel costs until it was ready. The Holts were so taken by the hospitality that Ray returned the next year as a volunteer and eventually became a permanent fixture directing the Rocky Mountain Hunter Ring.

When walking became even more difficult for him, maintenance staff constructed a special tower that was enclosed with a gentle ramp leading up to it. Ray used to tell everyone he not only had the best seat in the house, he also "had the best house."

From the time a sponsor sets foot on Spruce Meadows ground, a host or hostess will be at their side. These volunteers are well-versed on the sport, and more importantly, are themselves successful businessmen and women who appreciate the importance of good presentation.

"The attention to detail is unique," said Anne French. "Marg and Ron can easily relate to the sponsors and know exactly what they like to see and do. Of course, that adds an intensity to the tournament that most others wouldn't have to worry about."

On occasion you will have a special visitor with little or no interest in the sport, or even horses. It becomes the volunteer's challenge to keep these people very comfortable for up to six or seven hours. More often than not, they end up converting them into lifetime fans of show jumping.

The Southerns have an uncanny ability to remember names. Over the years at

Spruce Meadows Ron has never missed in introducing a string of sponsors and guests to the crowd. Not only will he refer to each by name, but he also relates detailed knowledge of their company. Be it before huge weekend crowds, or simply a handful of fans on a Wednesday morning, Ron will take as long as he feels comfortable to publicly extol the virtues of a company and its products. It is appreciated and remembered.

More importantly, the message is genuine. These people may be sponsors, but in his mind, and theirs, they have also become strong friends of Spruce Meadows.

Reflect once again on that comment, for it reveals what might be the most illuminating insight into the success of Spruce Meadows.

When you become a volunteer at Spruce Meadows, you also become a friend of Marg and Ron Southern. You have been invited into their dream and that, you quickly learn, is a rare and honoured privilege.

It doesn't matter who you have known in the past, or what project you may have been involved in. When you touch shoulders with this family, and when you listen to their excitement in relating the future for Spruce Meadows, you are hooked.

Marg and Ron both have the generous capacity to judge on merit, not reputation. Titles are not important when selecting volunteers. Those seeking personal gain by an association with one of this country's most influential families are quickly weeded out. It's not hard to do when the people at the top both lead by example.

Like the Southerns, Bas and Anne French feel their volunteer effort at Spruce Meadows is a way of giving something back to the community.

"I don't belong to service clubs and feel that my contribution to my community is through Spruce Meadows," said Bas.

"The contributions," he explained, "are the benefits derived by small business and tourism, as well as the enjoyment of the sport by thousands of fans.

"If it wasn't for the contribution to the horse industry and the community, and if I didn't see it helping small business, I wouldn't do it."

The 'Benefits Loop', for certain, does not stop at Spruce Meadows. Volunteers will tell you how their association with Spruce Meadows, not by design but by circumstance, greatly enhanced their lives and careers.

Pedro Cebulka may be the most vivid example. He certainly is the most colourful.

Pedro arrived in Calgary from his native Germany penniless and with a limited knowledge of English. He found his way to Spruce Meadows and was given a summer job on the maintenance crew in the late seventies.

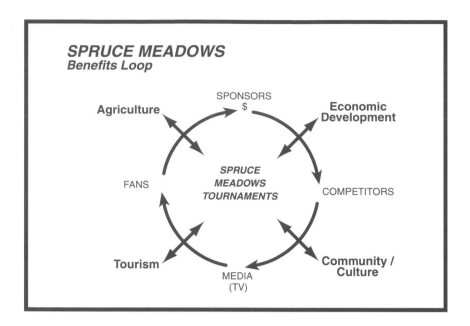

SPRUCE MEADOWS
Benefits Loop

Agriculture

SPONSORS
$

Economic
Development

FANS

*SPRUCE
MEADOWS
TOURNAMENTS*

COMPETITORS

Tourism

MEDIA
(TV)

Community /
Culture

His first task was to help paint lines in a parking lot and he was amazed to find that the guy working alongside him was Ron Southern.

Today Pedro will pick you up in his new BMW automobile and show you around one of his land developments in the British Columbia interior. But in between these two stages of Pedro's life, there was a lot of Spruce Meadows.

Devilment has always danced in Pedro's eyes, and this undoubtedly helped him rewrite the 'Good Book' on how to throw a horse tournament party. He didn't want the foreign grooms to feel left out, for example, so would entice someone to pick up the tab for beer and hamburgers and invite all of the grooms to his place.

From organizing pub crawls to leading the Southern family in a rousing rendition of "King of the Road," Pedro slapped more joy than paint onto Spruce Meadows.

If you happen to be on the grounds after midnight, when the only sound is the yelp of a coyote and the haunting, breathless sounds of Virgins of the Sun being played on a flute, you know Pedro has once again found his way into the Central Communications tower.

An accomplished musician, the solo is Pedro's siren to the equine gods, thanking them one more time for a pleasant day.

"A few times Marg came up and said the neighbours had complained because it was too loud, but she never asked me not to do it," said Pedro. "It was something I enjoyed for myself but it was also for the grooms in the barns that might be looking after sick horses."

More recently, Pedro attended a charity fund-raising auction and bought the right to direct the Calgary Philharmonic Orchestra for one number before a sold-out Saturday evening crowd. Resplendent in tails and proudly pinned with his Spruce Meadows Pegasus insignia, it came as a surprise to no one when Pedro selected the Spruce Meadows Victory March as the number he wished to direct. What did shake the somewhat staid audience, however, was the double row of boisterous friends in the back of the concert hall clapping in time with the music - a Spruce Meadows tradition

Pedro rose through the ranks quickly at Spruce Meadows and soon became manager of the burgeoning Equi-Fair, the continent's largest and most successful horse trade show. In between duties he would announce the German and Spanish results at the tournaments, and even learned Japanese when told of that country's upcoming appearance.

(photo by Al Savage)

Pedro Cebulka operates a hitching ring like no other person in the sport . . . and riders respect him for it. Damian Gardiner waits at the entrance to the International Ring with Pedro.

High blood pressure forced him to leave in the mid-eighties, but his commitment to the Southerns was a solemn oath - he would be back for every tournament.

Pedro now controls the International Hitching Ring where his good nature has earned him the respect of riders throughout the world.

"He's the best there is," said Ronnie Massarella. "I don't know of any other hitching ring where riders will co-operate as completely."

And why not? As often as not his call to order is either in rhyme or song. It's still a game to Pedro - a very important game perhaps - but the bottom line is let's do it right, but let's find a way of having some fun as well.

For years he helped Pamela Carruthers in the International Ring and she still describes him as "my absolute saviour." When she lost a ring given to her by her father, Pedro spent hours combing the ring until he found it for her.

When it comes time to give thanks for his good fortune, Pedro doesn't hesitate.

"I owe Marg and Ron immensely for what I learned from them. It was far better than going to university for ten years. They taught me about hard work and the value of honesty and effort."

Asked if that was the reason he felt an obligation to keep coming back, Pedro said:

"I owe them a lot, but I don't come back because I owe them. I come back mainly because I feel that I am part of the family. I was there from the beginning and if I missed a show now . . . it's impossible to even consider such a thing. I have to be there."

Day Three Continued:
Competition is Intense

Today's jumping attracts almost ten thousand spectators, a record for a Thursday. What this indicates is the presence of a growing number of hardcore fans who now come three or four days per tournament, sometimes all five.

More and more fans are beginning to look upon the five-day tournament as a competitive series, just like the World Series or Stanley Cup Final.

By the time Saturday and Sunday roll around, these fans are very aware of who is riding well, and who is not. This knowledge adds to the viewing intensity of events like the Bank of Montreal Nations' Cup and the du Maurier International.

Others like to follow the championship standings. The top Canadian rider, based on points accumulated in the five Open Division events, receives the use of a new Chrysler for a year. The top international rider, based on performance in the speed section of the International Division, receives a Rolex watch. The leading male and female riders in the International Division each receives a stunning diamond ring from the world-famous diamond studios of Fashion Diamonds of Holland.

American team member Leslie Lenehan wins today's first international class, the $15,000 Prudential Steel Cup. It is her first win at Spruce Meadows since 1985, the year after winning team gold at the Olympics.

She is excited about her chances aboard "Lenny" on the weekend, telling the press he can be "the best or the worst" depending on his mood.

"When he's on he can win any class. If not he'll do the opposite to everything you ask."

Ludger Beerbaum tells the media he will be having surgery on his knee as soon as he returns to Germany after the MASTERS. The $7,500 he had just won in the Cana Cup, he admits, helps ease some of the pain.

Rodrigo Pessoa of Brazil, the young man most believe will become this sport's next superstar, is second in the Cana event which saw thirteen horses advance to the jump-off. That's too many and you can be sure course designer Paul Duffy of Ireland will toughen things up tomorrow.

Most course designers traditionally look for ten per cent of their starting field to make it into the jump-off. Today that would have meant no more than five or six horses.

A jump-off in show jumping must remain intense. If you have too many horses, the crowd loses the sense of urgency to the rides, and it resembles any other round. But like overtime in hockey, or a playoff hole in golf, during a jump-off the big money is on the table and the rush of adrenalin hits rider, horse and fan.

After Wednesday's poor showing by the German riders, there is a lot of "I told you not to worry" comments after Beerbaum's victory today.

German Chef d'Equipe Herbert Meyer tells one local reporter that Saturday's Bank of Montreal Nations' Cup is second only to Aachen in importance.

"But please don't call them (the Germans) favoured," he pleads. "I feel everything but that. All of the teams are strong."

Tomorrow's events will be better barometers of just who is ready. The horses have had two days to adjust, and as seen by the huge jump-off field this afternoon, they love this course and are ready for more.

SPRUCE MEADOWS
Bank of Montreal
NATIONS' CUP

Meadowview

34

'MASTERS'

As horses jump outside, political and business leaders from around the world discuss global economic trends within the Spruce Meadows Congress Hall.

Day Four
A Different Day

Business suits dominate this morning's dress code, strongly suggesting that a somewhat different script is being played out somewhere today at the Spruce Meadows MASTERS.

The attire won't generate an inordinate amount of curiosity among the fans. They have come to expect the unexpected and a daily agenda that doesn't include something slightly off-beat or innovative is viewed as pretty pedestrian.

But for those not familiar with the pattern, it comes as a surprise to see that among this well-dressed entourage are former Alberta Premier Peter Lougheed, current Premier Ralph Klein and his deputy Ken Kowalski, as well as a bevy of high-ranking British officials, including Sir Nicholas Bayne, British High Commissioner to Canada.

Upon even closer scrutiny one discovers an imposing assembly of corporate and political leaders. The energy of this collective gathering begs to challenge just why such a group would meet at a show jumping tournament.

And then you remember this is Spruce Meadows, where inventive thoughts first become realities, and ultimately traditions. So, welcome to the MASTERS and the inaugural Britain-Alberta Economic Round Table.

Discussion at the one-day seminar, housed within the Spruce Meadows Congress Hall, is focusing on privatization and the "British Experience." Within the meeting are seventy-six people with enough political, corporate and economic clout to redirect the flow of international fiscal policy.

What would happen, one speculates, if this same austere body was given the mandate to work on national debt reduction? Think of the potential consequence if this collective cerebral fertility was unleashed with an accompanying promise of action without prejudice?

Interesting thought, and perhaps a corollary not that far removed from the impetus which introduced economic round table discussions to the Spruce Meadows tournament agenda.

From the very first competition it became apparent that those supporting this sport as sponsors, parents, riders and fans, were also the business leaders of their communities.

No one will ever know how many corporate agreements have been struck between men and women watching their respective children grind their way through a lengthy field of junior jumpers.

Such informal business liaisons became more frequent when specific days were designated by Spruce Meadows to celebrate relationships with participating nations: Holland Day, Mexico Day and British Day.

Prescribed business discussions, however, were not part of the celebrations. Business chatter may have crept into the pomp and ceremony of the day's agenda, but it was still spontaneous one-on-one dialogue.

One thing, however, became evident. The calm physical environment of Spruce Meadows certainly swept away the stressful trappings associated with the more conventional conference venues.

Day Four Continued:

The conference has broken for lunch and most delegates either head for the plaza, or adjourn to the solitude of the grassy banks of the Meadows on the Green show jumping ring.

Peter Green, president and chief executive officer of Cuddy International, talks about the uniqueness of the setting, particularly as it compares to the traditional convention centres.

"It's certainly the incentive in attracting the people who have come here," said the

London, Ontario executive. "This is a most significant gathering of industrialists and chairmen of large corporations. In fact the whole thing is a most unusual phenomenon, and to have it as part of an equestrian event adds the dimension that, frankly, is really quite different."

He also attended the first Spruce Meadows Economic Round Table held two months earlier in conjunction with the Spruce Meadows NORTH AMERICAN. It was billed as a Mexico-Alberta opportunity to discuss free trade.

"Look around. Delegates are being attracted that you normally would never get together in one room. Ron has got something going here, that's for sure."

Richard Gamble is group chief executive for Royal Insurance and was lured from London, England. Like most of the others in attendance, he turns down far more global invitations than he accepts.

"The venue is terrific because it has everything. There is a relaxed atmosphere which gets people prepared to talk and discuss the subjects, but at the same time it remains very professional and businesslike."

While the program content is both interesting and stimulating, he says it is "the aesthetics of Spruce Meadows" that makes it different from anywhere else.

A handful of key individuals helped the Southerns to create both a world-wide sport and economic summit venue unequalled anywhere on the North American continent. Among those people were (from left) - the late Wilmat Tennyson, Bank of Montreal's William Mulholland and the Honourable Peter Lougheed - all shown here receiving their Lifetime Honourary Memberships from Ron Southern.

As world-class jumping takes place just yards away, the Gallery on the Green Congress Hall reflects the diversity of its many faces - as an exhibition gallery, a banquet hall, reception centre and as a meeting hall.

The setting is indeed unique. The Pulsar Gallery On the Green/Congress Hall was opened at the 1993 MASTERS by Alfonso Romo Garza, chairman of Pulsar Internacional. He is a man who attracts many parallel comments to Ron Southern because of his innovative approaches to the sport of show jumping.

At this tournament the hall is home to a remarkable display entitled "Mexico Artesano", but at past tournaments has served as a window for the cultural works of other nations as well. An exhibition on tour, featuring paintings by the Great Masters of Europe attracted national attention, as did a startling display of journalistic photography.

In addition, Marg Southern will often purchase prints of famous art works from around the world and present them in the gallery.

The fifteen thousand square foot Congress Hall is equipped with many state-of-the-art audio/visual components and can comfortably accommodate up to five hundred people. The interior is tastefully decorated to enhance the tranquillity of its outdoor surroundings, which beckon enticingly through the banks of ceiling to floor windows.

A huge patio sweeps out to the eastern edge of the Meadows on the Green course, affording guests an exceptional view of competition.

Ron Southern is excited about the structure's potential and is confident it could become one of the world's great meeting venues.

"If you take a look at some of the great historical congregations of politicians, they have occurred in settings that are absolutely unique. The meeting in Quebec City during World War II between Roosevelt, Churchill and Mackenzie King was an example."

Although conferences of that stature are not being actively pursued just yet, Ron believes the two conferences held in the summer of '94 showed early potential in both a political and economic sense. That belief was substantiated the next year with two very successful conferences, and the concept now appears to be firmly entrenched.

The immediate and primary goal is to bring together key political and commercial interests within a relaxed atmosphere that promotes the best intentions of everyone.

Given the early successes and testimonials, there is a confidence that a high-profile summit is in the future for Spruce Meadows. Given the track record, most know better than to dismiss the prospect of one day seeing the signing of a significant world-order document to be known for ever as the "Spruce Meadows Pact."

None of this means Spruce Meadows is bent on becoming a major convention centre.

> Given the early successes and testimonials, there is a confidence that a high-profile summit is in the future for Spruce Meadows.

"No," both Southerns confirmed adamantly. "Spruce Meadows is no more than what it is . . . a unique venue that can have a group of people come together in a congress, with their families, and from that derive many benefits for many different people."

Ron sees the concept as a series of one-day economic round table discussions, and always before the key weekend of competition at the tournaments.

Special Events

The International Plaza reflects the mood of each of the three major tournaments. Even in its informal infancy, the plaza has always been a gathering point for fans, exhibitors and riders.

In the first half-dozen years, no serious attempt was made at the competition to try and create any form of commercial opportunity for exhibitors. The Spruce Meadows Tack Shop opened up a small outlet behind the main grandstand, and a few local artisans set up tables.

The plaza, as it is presented today, was still under grass although some benches and tables were there to offer a break in the walk between the International and Rocky Mountain courses.

Even then, however, it was apparent that a unification of kindred spirits was occurring at the plaza. Calgary has a strong ethnic make-up, and because of the sport's European heritage, there were strong bonds.

Walking through the area, then or now, is culturally unique even for Calgary. In addition to the richness of tone from their different languages, fans introduce a visual extravaganza by dressing in colourful attire native to their homelands.

Riders, particularly the British, Irish, German, Swiss, French and Dutch, began turning up on the plaza after events to meet with their countrymen. From out of nowhere accordions and other musical instruments would magically appear. Soon they would be joined by a crock of Schnapps, a jug of Guiness, a skin of wine, or some other delightfully enticing libation.

The impromptu parties became part of the inexplicable Spruce Meadows mystique, and reached a point where the celebrations could have stood alone as a festival of international prominence.

The International Plaza becomes a mosaic of many cultures where good sport, good fun and good friends become the order of the day.

The plaza began to assume a look of permanence in the mid-eighties as governments and major corporations became more and more aware of the exposure opportunities presented by the tens of thousands of plaza visitors.

But as exhibitions sprang up, a close watch was kept on content and exterior presentation. The Southerns went back to Europe in search of a booth design that would reflect the international flavour of the plaza for the MASTERS, the western hoopla of the NORTH AMERICAN Tournament, and a strong Canadian historical presence for the NATIONAL.

Through the creative use of snap-on trim, the plaza can today be dressed as a mountainous Bavarian village, or a raw and restless western town.

The Tournaments

Competition at all three Spruce Meadows tournaments is of the highest possible calibre. The visible difference amongst them is the uncommon way each is presented.

It is too soon to predict the success of indoor competition which will begin in the late fall of 1996 upon completion of the new Riding Hall. The indoor surface will be large enough to allow fence lines both up and down, as well as across the arena, and seating for up to 5,000 is planned.

Specific themes are assigned to each of the three major tournaments to reflect the origins of those competing. The NATIONAL, for example, was launched as a North American competition catering to riders from throughout Canada and the United States, but seldom anywhere else.

It also became the unsanctioned home of the Canadian Open Jumper and Canadian Open Hunter Championships, primarily because no other show in Canada had expressed interest in sponsoring the titles. Not even the Canadian Equestrian Federation (CEF) showed interest in promoting a National Championship.

Federation members, in fact, did their best to ignore this maverick title until its popularity demanded their recognition. Canadian riders were being introduced around North America and the world as Canadian Champions, yet the title had never been sanctioned by the sport's governing body.

Finally, in 1989, the CEF decided that a Canadian Championship was indeed a brilliant concept, but in its wisdom also decreed the venue must alternate between the west and the east. Since no other outdoor Canadian tournament attracted the calibre of

Audrey and Greg Greenough, past president of the Canadian Equestrian Federation,
present the Canadian Show Jumping Championship to Ian Millar

rider talent as the NATIONAL, it was a short-lived experiment and the Championships took on permanent residency at the Spruce Meadows NATIONAL.

Unofficially it became known as "Ian's Crown" as Mr. Millar managed to win the jumping title eight times between 1983 and 1994, four of them coming before the championship was officially sanctioned.

The NATIONAL Tournament is crucial to Canadian riders because competition traditionally serves as part of the Olympic, World Cup, PanAmerican and World Championship selection trials. American selection committees use it for the same purpose, although on an unofficial basis. Like Canadian officials, they know that if a rider/horse combination can tame the top events at the NATIONAL, the pair can handle pretty well anything that might come at them in Europe as well.

In a bold move from tradition the entire selection process for the 1996 Olympics in Atlanta will be held around the NATIONAL - two trial events during the tournament and two others the Wednesday following its conclusion.

In 1976 only two tournaments were offered, the INTERNATIONAL (which became known as the NATIONAL the next year) and the MASTERS, which featured provincial rather than international competition. A third Spruce Meadows tournament was added in 1977, and it is this competition that has undergone the most dramatic of changes.

It began as the Spruce Meadows JUNIOR, and as the name implies, it catered solely to junior riders in the Pony, Hunter and Jumper Divisions. In the eyes of the Southerns, Marg in particular, it was the JUNIOR that best reflected her dream: the creation of a world-class facility and tournament that would foster development of young western Canadian riders at a level equal to their European counterparts.

The tournament enjoyed great successes under the sponsorship of Texaco Canada, graduating many of the athletes who would represent Canada for decades to come.

What no one counted on, however, was Spruce Meadows' revolutionary impact on the Canadian and American riding scene. The number of riders attracted to the sport had increased dramatically since its inception, and since most were adults, a plea went out for more tournaments of the calibre of the Spruce Meadows NATIONAL and the Spruce Meadows MASTERS.

A fourth tournament would have been a logistical nightmare for Spruce Meadows, probably even destructive. The JUNIOR, however, could be modified to offer a limited number of adult classes, but still retain its youthful flavour.

The Spruce Meadows "Texaco" JUNIOR, to some degree, became a victim of its own success and in 1985 became known as the INVITATIONAL.

Not surprisingly, the introduction of open jumping into a predominantly junior event also changed the public perception of what this tournament was all about. The media and fan focus shifted so dramatically towards world-calibre open jumping, and away from the juniors, that a third name change was necessary to reflect the new continental tone of the tournament.

In 1991 the Spruce Meadows NORTH AMERICAN rose from the successes of the INVITATIONAL and almost instantly established itself as the continent's premier tournament. Although most eastern Canadian riders still chose to compete at home during the summer months, massive entries from the United States and Mexico more than made up for their absence. A Spruce Meadows North American Show Jumping Championship was introduced, and like the initial Canadian title, it had no official sanction. Now, however, it is recognized globally as one of the sport's most coveted honours.

In 1988, Calgary's Olympic year, the Jumping Calgary series (a series of smaller outdoor tournaments) was merged with the NORTH AMERICAN to provide ten consecutive days of competition, twice as long as any other tournament at Spruce Meadows.

Marg Southern, however, had not abandoned her commitment to the junior riders. There are now more jumper classes in the NORTH AMERICAN for juniors than ever existed in previous tournaments. At one point the decision was made to scrap pony events due to declining entries, but once the word got out, a lobbying campaign quickly convinced organizers to re-instate them after only a one-year absence.

The Spruce Meadows Queen Elizabeth II Cup was originally created as a competition that would stand on its own, separate from any tournament affiliation. The organizational difficulties created by that commitment were quickly realized, however, and two years later the event was merged with the NORTH AMERICAN to become one of that tournament's anchor competitions.

The inaugural presentation of the Queen Elizabeth II Cup on June 29, 1990 represented an astounding coup for Spruce Meadows since Her Royal Highness Queen Elizabeth II presided over all ceremonies.

Her Majesty Queen Elizabeth II with Marg Southern at the inaugural Queen Elizabeth II Cup in 1990.

*A moment that will live forever for North Salem's Alice Debany,
winner of the first Queen Elizabeth II Cup.*

A Royal Visit to Canada is a lofty event during which even a minute of the Queen's time is as precious as any crown jewel. For her to agree to attend a presentation that had neither political nor nationally induced overtones, was virtually unheard of.

She did, however, share a bond with the Southerns that centered on their families' common interest in the horse. Her husband, Prince Philip, served as President of the International Equestrian Federation (FEI) from 1964 to 1986, and of course their eldest daughter, Princess Anne, was an Olympic three day event rider who took over the helm of the FEI for almost ten years following Prince Philip's retirement. In addition, Her Majesty's personal passion for horses and horse sport is well documented.

"We had our interest in horses and that dominated most of our discussions," said Marg Southern, who was given the extraordinary honour of being asked by the Queen to be her Lady-In-Waiting during that entire Canadian tour.

It was perhaps the most singular highlight of Marg Southern's life, but the details of her seven days with the Queen are, out of a profound respect, never discussed by her.

Upon conclusion of that first Queen Elizabeth II Cup, the world looked on as twenty-two-year-old Alice Debany of North Salem, New York, swept into a perfect curtsy before Her Majesty to accept her $33,000 winner's cheque and a magnificent crystal and hardwood trophy.

It was the most gratifying moment of Alice's life, and flushed her with a glory that no other victory could ever equal.

The pomp and pageantry that went into the first Queen Elizabeth II Cup has become part and parcel of all other subsequent presentations. A representative of the Queen always oversees the precise military ceremony that has become distinctive to the show jumping world.

(photo by Cansport)

Special Features

This pageantry and respect for tradition also permeates the plaza where visitors traditionally enjoy at least one significant exhibition related to Great Britain and royalty, no matter what the tournament.

No one is certain just how large the plaza can become, but two decades of wild success probably dictates even more growth in the near future.

Randy Fedorak, Special Projects Manager at Spruce Meadows, suggests the plaza's future size and scope could be massive by comparison with today's presentation.

"I can see a huge exhibition tent for each participating nation of the MASTERS, as much as fifty thousand square feet of space for each. It will become like an annual international exposition unlike anything else in this world."

He accepts that there is not near enough space in the current plaza to accept such a vision, but points to a quarter-section of adjacent land and mentally transfers his image there.

Randy takes the proposal a step further, predicting the presence of international trade commissioners on permanent assignment at the respective exhibition centres. He also predicts the need for representation of the Horse Industry Branch of the Alberta Government and Agriculture Canada.

"And with all of this we suddenly will become the marketing centre for horses in North America. Just think! If you're a buyer in Japan looking for Quarter Horses, you can give us a ring a couple of weeks ahead of time and arrangements will be made to have the best two- and three-year-olds ready for scrutiny."

Some may challenge such a vision, but Ron and Marg Southern encourage all of their managers to send their minds out on frequent creative gallops.

One only has to think back to 1976 - examine the growth and development since that time - and then dare suggest that anything is impossible at Spruce Meadows.

A reminder of Canada's leading role as a peace-keeping nation within NATO - members of the Princess Patricia's Canadian Light Infantry perform the 'Feu de Joie' during opening ceremonies of the Queen Elizabeth II Cup.

Students from Monterrey, Mexico electrify a NORTH AMERICAN crowd with their enthusiasm and goodwill.

Day Four Continued:

At this year's MASTERS eleven nations are hosting pavilions with live entertainment reaching out to tempt you from seven stages. In total, more than two hundred exhibits exceeding thirty thousand square feet of space are located on five acres of prime real estate in the centre of the grounds.

It is difficult to imagine anyone not being enthralled by one or more of these entertainment opportunities. From a classical pianist to a thirty-strong corporate choir, from hard rock to classical music, it's all here.

Special occasions are not always reserved for competition. Nor is pure, raw excitement. One of the most inspiring afternoons at Spruce Meadows came during the 1994 NORTH AMERICAN when the enthusiasm of one hundred and forty young Mexican students from the Monterrey Institute of Technology spilled into a capacity crowd.

The young singers and dancers, guests of Spruce Meadows and Pulsar Internacional of Mexico, were on their way to the World Equestrian Games in Holland. Because of the close personal relationship between Pulsar boss Alfonso Romo and Spruce Meadows, the troop was allowed a dramatic detour and ended up at centre ring during the NORTH AMERICAN Tournament.

Delighted fans, most of them brandishing small Mexican flags and whistling windmills, were quick to pick up the beat. The students' zest settled into every corner of the sprawling complex, leaving fingerprints of joy on everything touched.

Like a titanic wave of energy, their bodies flowed as one across the course to wash away the few lingering frowns still among the thirty-eight thousand in attendance. Had a new tradition been born? Most would rightly argue that what happened that afternoon is not something that can be bottled or kept under cork until the next tournament. But that does not seem to be a deterrent at Spruce Meadows where a spontaneous creation finds a way to become tradition. The word "impossible" has always struggled in vain to gain any long-term support at Spruce Meadows.

There was a time when Ron Southern would get on the radio and close down plaza entertainment during key competitive events. It was seen by many as a challenge to the integrity of the sport to have a wave of heavy rock from the plaza wash across the course during a jump-off ride.

This sentiment was reversed as most correctly argued that not all visitors were at Spruce Meadows exclusively for the show jumping. If time and energy were spent to create a diverse package, then nothing should be done to stifle that diversity.

The Royal Canadian Mounted Police 'Musical Ride' is just one of several popular presentations.

If sipping on the golden lagers of Europe was the solitary objective of spending a day at Spruce Meadows, nobody will mess with that pleasure.

The heterogeneity of the plaza activities gave it a broad family appeal base, along with other Special Features such as Equi-Fair, the AGT Battle of the Breeds or Alberta Breeds for the World.

The plaza's charisma was built on universal participation, while the others targeted specific interest groups.

Ashford Prairie Dogs delight young and old.

It is tough, for example, to pass by an exhibition involving the Ashford Prairie Dogs. This wacky assortment of canines are locked in perpetual motion. When a more sophisticated group of dog owners from the Toronto area wouldn't appear because the money wasn't enough, a challenge went out to Calgary dog fanciers to come up with a better rendition.

They succeeded brilliantly without having to take themselves or their animals too seriously. The dogs, usually in teams, compete over courses of jumps, hoops and bars in a hilarious dash against each other and the clock.

Equi-Fair was undoubtedly the boldest experiment of the many supporting events attached to the MASTERS.

"The thought of complimentary enjoyment to the horse was always there," said Ron Southern, "but it was not an early priority."

He recalled an evening in Germany, watching a late night puissance class together with daughter Nancy and Spruce Meadows Riding Master Albert Kley.

"There were very few lights and the horses would appear from the darkness to jump the wall. I was seeing something far different from what is traditional show jumping. It was mystical and it had an impact on me." On that same occasion he also enjoyed the taste of the bratwurst and the companionship of "sharing a beer with friends," although his drink of choice was a Pepsi.

"So from the very beginning I understood it wasn't just simply a matter of sitting in your seat and watching sport," said Ron. "We always had family entertainment in our minds, but we were careful never to turn it into a carnival. I know that definition is difficult when you look around sometimes, but we always tried to introduce things that could be related to the horse."

The Prairie Dogs blended in perfectly. Dogs and horses are natural partners on the farm. Nor was it difficult to make a case for music, considering the dominant role of the horse in ceremonies of royal and military pageantry.

The quest for program diversity ultimately led the Southerns to Essen, Germany and Equitana, Europe's largest trade show for the horse industry. The Southerns struck a fifty-fifty partnership deal with Equitana owner Wolf Kroeber to bring a North American version of the exhibition to the 1983 Spruce Meadows MASTERS.

At the time success was predicated upon the number of quality European exhibitors that could be attracted to Spruce Meadows, and that would be Wolf's primary contribution to the partnership. Spruce Meadows would provide the infrastructure for the exhibition as well as staff. Operating expenses would be shared.

The partnership, however, just didn't work and was dissolved after two years. Wolf, said Ron, was unhappy because he wasn't able to affect the management decisions he wanted at Spruce Meadows. Ron found his German partner difficult to work with so the decision to split was mutual. Even though he didn't have to, Ron returned Wolf's share of the investment capital.

"He wanted to do it differently then we did," said Ron. "It was important to us that all people would find it interesting while walking through the exhibition. If exhibits were so technical they related only to avid horse people, most of our fans would not bother with it."

(photo by Al Savage)

Equi-Fair has become North America's largest and most successful annual exhibition for the horse and horse sport.

> Not only were riders
> encouraged to share social
> moments, but they also found
> themselves talked into playing silly
> little games and enjoying every
> second of it.

The first order of business was a name change and Equitana North America became known as Equi-Fair. The presence of European exhibitors remained critical to the success of Equi-Fair, but participants were now invited based on their uniqueness and character: master craftsmen of saddlery and tack, equine artists, etc.

By 1994 the re-direction of Equi-Fair away from its traditional trade show heritage and towards an exhibition of universal appeal was complete. It is now open all five days of the MASTERS as opposed to only the first two or three days. It has also been widely accepted by the public as an integral part of the entertainment structure of the MASTERS.

Equi-Fair is recognized as North America's commercial forum for the horse industry with virtually every segment of that commerce represented in exciting and entertaining ways. At Equi-Fair '94 more than twenty artists created on-site, including several sculptors working in everything from bronze to barbed wire.

In 1996 Equi-Fair was presented with a permanent home upon completion of the new Horse Industry Hall. Together with the original indoor arena, the two spacious structures will combine to give Equi-fair a greater sense of permanency.

Special events at Spruce Meadows are not organized exclusively for fans. Riders also have their moments.

The Nations Dinner has become a popular tradition at each MASTERS bringing team members, sponsors and sport officials together in a semi-formal setting. The atmosphere is light and dialogue traditionally focuses on that day's Nations' Cup competition, or speculation on the next day's du Maurier International.

More importantly, it is one of the few times in the sport when riders of different nationalities openly socialize. Traditionally, like members of opposing professional hockey or soccer teams, riders from different nations seldom mingle with their opponents.

It was a universal scenario Spruce Meadows deliberately set out to change. Not only were riders encouraged to share social moments, but they also found themselves talked into playing silly little games and enjoying every second of it.

The Spruce Meadows "Canada Cup" bears no resemblance to serious competition, and it would be impossible to mistake it for such. It disguises itself in a mini-Olympic format and then pits teams of riders, officials and the media against each other in such stalwart athletic challenges as hockey/golf; football/volleyball, grapefruit/croquet,

(photo by Cansport)

An all-star lineup - having a ball at the 'Canada Cup' are from left:
Antonio Maurer, Alfonso Romo, Nelson Pessoa, Jose Maurer, Fernando Fourcade and Rodrigo Pessoa

watermelon/basketball - and, well you get the picture. Put a hockey stick in the hands of someone like Harvey Smith and sit back and enjoy the show. Fellow riders brought him up just short of trying to take an oxer as he rode the stick like a toy horse.

When first asked to participate in the "Canada Cup", riders were hesitant and suggested they would prefer to return to their hotel rooms. Now it's among the first things they ask about. Most look forward to it and it definitely cracks the early stress associated with major competition.

Nobody, of course, plays by the rules and it is traditionally the most creative cheaters that emerge victorious. One year the media team was obviously too enterprising when it claimed a point total five times greater than any other. Team Captain Nancy Southern protested her team's elimination, but her pleas for mercy fell upon deaf ears.

The evening continues with a party during which each team presents a delightfully creative skit of song and dance - usually liberally laced with a lesson in morality, or lack of same. Members of one visiting militia unit brought the house down by grinding

A hit tune - they won't make the Top 40 charts but Thomas and Markus Fuchs Willi Melliger sing a song for Switzerland.

out a less than tantalizing strip tease in full dress uniform. It is also at this party that Marg and Ron, joined by Nancy and Linda with their families, blare out rousing renditions of "King of the Road" (Trailers for Sale or Rent) and "A Froggy Goes a Courtin'".

Harvey Smith of Great Britain started it all on his first visit to Spruce Meadows in 1982. The outrageous Yorkshireman approached a somewhat startled emcee, grabbed the microphone and proceeded to belt out a series of jokes, good cheer and song that lasted deep into the morning hours.

The upper lounge of the Meadowview Building has been set aside for riders and owners to watch competition. Initially riders would isolate themselves into team pockets, seldom breaking away to sit with others. Now, however, the atmosphere is far more relaxed and voluntary segregation is a thing of the past.

With the exception of the Nations' Cup, when riders merge to compete as a team, friendships are placed on suspension as soon as a rider enters the ring. It is very much an individual sport with everyone desperately searching for that one small aid to shave even a tenth of a second off a jump-off course.

Great Competitive Moments

During two decades of competition at Spruce Meadows there have been many extraordinary moments, among them several rides that would qualify as classics within the sport.

But greatness, at least in this sport, truly is in the interpretation of the beholder. What qualifies as exceptional depends very much upon the individual making the judgement.

For example, simply watching German legend Hans Gunter Winkler, four-time Olympic gold medallist on a horse was a vision of unforgettable wonderment for Ron Southern. The fact he did nothing sensational on his one and only riding venture to Spruce Meadows in 1979 was of no consequence. In Ron's mind, and for many others, it brought a presence of credibility to Spruce Meadows that no other rider of the time could.

Likewise, the competitive appearances of other great riders, also in the twilight of their careers, added a dimension of authority to the facility - people like: Australian Kevin Bacon, Austrian Hugo Simon, Canada's Jimmy Elder, George Morris of the

U.S., Liz Edgar, Harvey Smith and David Broome of Great Britain, Nelson Pessoa of Brazil, Hermann Schridde and Paul Schockemoehle of Germany and Eddie Macken of Ireland.

During its first two decades, every Olympic, World, European, World Cup, PanAmerican, Canadian and North American champion still active in show jumping competed at the MASTERS at least once, usually several times.

The same was true of virtually every medal team from an Olympics or World Championship. On several occasions the Bank of Montreal Nations' Cup at the MASTERS was the decisive event in determining that year's top show jumping team in the world.

There have been some classic showdowns in the Bank of Montreal event, including two instances when the Nations' Cup had to be resolved by a jump-off. In 1981 the Netherlands beat France in the overtime round after both had finished the mandatory two rounds with totals of twenty faults.

German riding legend Hans Gunter Winkler at the 1979 MASTERS.

The second occurrence was as energized as this sport can get. It happened in 1986 and even British coach Ronnie Massarella suggested the clash between his team and that of the United States was probably the finest he had ever seen.

Jumping by both sides was superb over the initial two rounds. Both teams finished with a total of four faults which meant they had to go to a jump-off, a rare occurrence in a Nations' Cup.

In the end, U.S. team members Robert Ridland, Hap Hansen, Jennifer Newell and Joan Scharffenberger triumphed over a British squad comprised of Malcolm Pyrah, Nick Skelton and John and Michael Whitaker.

Yet if you ask fans to recall their favourite competitive ride at Spruce Meadows, most become crippled with indecision. There have been "just too many" is the traditional response.

Instead there is a tendency among them to recall the sport in general, rather than specific terms. They don't cherish just one event, but link several together so that enjoyment comes every time a horse soars.

U. S. Judge Victor Hugo-Vidal said:

"It takes your breath away to see those horses on full burn, running across the field. You just sort of gasp and for those who haven't seen it before, they will swear the horse is out of control."

Surprisingly, riders remember their own achievements, but they too are usually at a loss when asked to recall the great rides of their competitors.

Other performances didn't command headlines simply because the special circumstances that made them different were never revealed: athletes who conquered the intrusion of blinding pain, or horses that jumped far beyond their scope even though they didn't qualify for a medal position.

There are some events where victory, no matter how it happened, commands attention. Certainly the Olympics and World Championships are examples, as is the du Maurier International. From a financial standpoint, for example, the du Maurier has no equal. Winners of the Chrysler and Shell Derbys celebrate their wins as major victories over exhaustion in show jumping's most demanding test of stamina.

Canada's Ian Millar, one of only four riders to win the du Maurier more than once (he won aboard Big Ben in 1987 and again in 1991) certainly regards those victories as benchmarks in his career.

Surprisingly, however, it is not a du Maurier victory that he remembers as his favourite Spruce Meadows memory. Instead he savours the particulars of the Royal Bank World Cup at the 1987 NATIONAL. The ride came aboard Warrior, a very good but not a great jumper who had limited speed.

They had just managed to squeeze into the jump-off and Ian remembers he watched from the warm-up ring as Canada's Lisa Carlsen directed Kahlua to a blistering round.

"As show jumpers we are percentage gamblers," said Ian. "We know the gamble and we know the risk/reward ratio. The risk obviously increases by going just a bit quicker.

"Well, Warrior was never a naturally fast horse. He was a little too lofty and his gallop across the ground was long and flowing, not a quick, active thing. For sure, it was tough for him to be as fast as most horses."

Ian, a student of the game at all times, watched the others and concluded there was no way Warrior could match or better the time of Lisa and Kahlua.

"But then I entered the ring, picked up the gallop, and said, 'Yes, but today's going to be different. Today Warrior will go faster.'"

By the time three or four strides had been covered, Ian was convinced he would win the competition. He had gone from a normally rational thinking individual to an athlete completely detached from reality.

"I pushed Warrior as fast as he could go. When I had finished I knew of course that I was clear, but I wasn't sure of the time. The crowd was cheering and I looked around at the scoreboard and it said 'No. 1.'"

His reaction was spontaneous. For the first time in a lengthy and distinguished career, a refined Ian Millar stripped off his hard hat and tossed it high into the air.

"I was excited because it was a very special win for that horse. Warrior went past what he should have been able to do that day. He was bigger than life." Ian enjoyed nineteen major victories at Spruce Meadows aboard Big Ben, but it was their du Maurier International win in 1991 that will be remembered by Ian as his partner's finest hour.

The course was set that year by Hauke Schmidt of Metzengen, Germany, a designer of straightforward, but killer-big courses.

"Those jumps were seriously big and the footing was medium at best and getting deeper with every ride," said Ian. "That second round came down to a bit of a brawl. It was tough and would take some serious efforts just to get into.

"Ben, however, stepped up to the plate that time. He just fought like hell to do it, and that really stays in your mind.

"I remember turning the corner to the last two jumps . . . it's like it was two minutes ago. The effort it took from Ben was unbelievable. That was a special one."

It is said within the sport that domination at the international level is virtually impossible. There are simply too many good rider/horse combinations to expect that one pairing could consistently beat all others.

It will happen in tennis, occasionally in golf, quite often in boxing, but never in show jumping. To suggest that one rider/horse combination could come into a tournament like the MASTERS and sweep the International Division would be ludicrous.

But that does not mean that at any given time, one particular horse couldn't justifiably be called the best in the world. It simply means that by the next major tournament, that may no longer be true.

Looking through the records of the eighties and nineties, several horses stood hands above most of their competitive adversaries.

Big Ben reached such a lofty scale in the mid-eighties, as did John Whitaker's Next Milton. Everest Forever with Britain's Liz Edgar certainly dominated in the late seventies and it was tough to beat France's Pierre Durand aboard the scrappy little Jappeloup. Others that earned super-status included the likes of Norman Dello Joio of the U.S. on I Love You, David Broome of Great Britain on Philco and Sportsman, Germany's Paul Schockemoehle aboard Deister, Malcolm Pyrah of Great Britain on Towerlands Anglezarke, Canada's Michel Vaillancourt and Branch County, Jos Lansink of Holland on Egano and Libero, Ludger Beerbaum of Germany on Classic Touch, Greg Best of the U.S. on Gem Twist, Michael Whitaker of Great Britain on Mon Santa and teammate Nick Skelton on Apollo and Dollar Girl.

All of the above horses could devastate the competition, and when conditions were perfect, each was unbeatable. All of them, of course, also lost far more events then they ever won.

> To expect such athletic euphoria day after day is unrealistic. It is said, therefore, that only an exceptional horse can finish in a medal position even thirty per cent of the time.

But there is a tickler in this equation. Show jumping takes two athletes and each must be firing perfectly for the team to attain perfection. If a rider is feeling flat, he or she can talk about it in search of an antidote. A horse, obviously, doesn't have that luxury.

There are those magical occasions when a rider finds that the fire in his heart is also ablaze in the heart of their horse. It is as if the same high-octane adrenalin is pounding through the arteries of each. So when it happens, look out! No man-made obstacle is high enough or wide enough to stop them. Reality gives way to fantasy and the team takes flight.

To expect such athletic euphoria day after day is unrealistic. It is said, therefore, that only an exceptional horse can finish in a medal position even thirty per cent of the time.

In September of 1979, Ireland's Eddie Macken and an aging Carroll's Boomerang made a mockery of all such statistics. Among world-class competition that included Great Britain's Malcolm Pyrah and Caroline Bradley, 1982 World Champion Norbert Koof of Germany, Canada's Johnny Simpson and New Zealand's Graeme Thomas, Eddie and Boomerang put on a riding exhibition that will never be equalled.

The International Division of the MASTERS is divided into two sections. Section I is designed to test the speed and agility of world-class horses over courses that focus more on the animal's dexterity than brute strength. At one point, Grand Prix horses on the down-side of their careers could find extended life in the "speed division". Today the demand for precision and speed is so intense that riders must find and develop horses specifically for these events.

Section II classes are traditionally the featured events of the competition where courses are as large and wide as the rule book allows. By the closing weekend of the MASTERS, Section II tracks are equal in difficulty to any Olympic or World Championship final.

At the 1979 MASTERS, Ireland's Eddie Macken and Carroll's Boomerang put on an exhibition of riding mastery that has never been equalled.

Boomerang, deep into the twilight of his brilliant career, had no trouble winning the opening event. The rider he beat was John Simpson of Calgary aboard Texas, and ironically the class was sponsored by Cana Construction, a company founded by John's father and now run by the former show jumper.

The next day the good fortunes of Ireland continued to radiate upon its favourite son, and Eddie joined Boomerang in the winner's circle of the Canada Cement Lafarge Mixer. Teammate Lt. John Roche was a distant second.

People had noticed the back-to-back victories, but Eddie really had them talking when he made it three straight on Friday. Once again it was Lt. Roche forced into the best man position as Eddie and Boomerang sailed effortlessly over a tough field of big jumps in the Imperial Oil Esso Extra.

Considering the exceptional calibre of riders chasing him, Eddie told reporters it was very unlikely he would make it four in a row.

The next day saw the talented field gathered for the final event of the 1979 MASTERS, the Rothman's Grand Prix. A hush of deafening disappointment fell upon the crowd when Boomerang pulled his first rail of the tournament in the second round. Although he had gone clean in the initial run, it now appeared the shamrock had wilted and Eddie would not accomplish the impossible after all.

Two Canadian aces, Mark Laskin and Bo Mearns, could snap Eddie's miracle streak by riding clear in the second round. Both, however, sent lumber flying.

As only the luck of the Irish would have it, Eddie and Boomerang joined a field of three others - all with four faults each - for the jump-off. They were Bo Mearns, Johnny Simpson and Germany's Julius Schulze-Hesselmann.

Eddie was again flawless aboard Boomerang, a marvellous flying machine. John Simpson came closest and actually beat Eddie's time by almost four full seconds. Unfortunately for John and the partisan crowd, Texas also clipped a rail.

Eddie Macken and Boomerang would not be denied. Together they had defied all odds by sweeping every event in the division, something that no one else has even threatened to do since. Nor can anyone, including Macken, believe it will ever be done again.

Eddie continues to thrill crowds at Spruce Meadows, however, and took great pleasure in directing the Irish team to a convincing win in the 1995 Bank of Montreal Nations' Cup.

His performance at the '79 MASTERS was an extraordinary display of power. To this day, John Simpson insists that even though he didn't win an event, his battle with Eddie in all four events remains the highlight of his career.

"He beat me every time out," said John, "but they were great rides. In the Grand Prix I thought I had him because my time was so much quicker. I didn't know until I had left the ring that I even had a fence down."

One of the sport's most popular wins, yet one that was somewhat unexpected, was registered in the 1986 Texaco Derby with Calgarian Jonathan Asselin at the controls of a very inexperienced horse called Brigadoon.

Jonathan, since married to Nancy Southern, is a talented rider who still has never quite managed to find the big ticket horse that all riders seek. Certainly Brigadoon was not such a candidate as his owners of the time were struggling with very little expectations to find a home for him, even as a moderately-priced junior jumper.

On that day, however, the magic wand appeared to touch this pair. Brigadoon was spectacular under the careful urging of Jonathan and cleared the monster course. No other entry came close.

For Jonathan Asselin of Calgary and his mount, Brigadoon - magic happened in the 1986 Texaco Derby.

Most of the credit must go to the exceptional riding abilities of Jonathan. But the conquest also vividly demonstrated what has been said many times throughout the sport: when the mix is perfect, look out because the impossible will probably happen.

Not surprisingly, Brigadoon was sold soon after at a far higher price than that being asked for the day before the Derby. Although he never again found a spotlight quite so brilliant to bask in, the victory did give Brigadoon a new confidence that greatly extended his competitive life.

There is no doubt that each and every tournament produced a career highlight for one or more riders. To finish ahead of Ian Millar on Big Ben or John Whitaker aboard Milton in any competition was a dream come true for riders of limited talent and mounting.

Or imagine the thrill for a fifteen-year-old junior rider who had been allowed to move into the Open Division and ride on the International Ring for one event - the Double Slalom - and ride against the world's best?

You can bet there was some big time pride on display when these youngsters talked about running head-to-head against a World or Olympic Champion. And on occasion these teens would soundly trounce their worldly opponents.

As one veteran rider once confessed, looking to his left at the starting line to face a wild-eyed youngster primed to win at any cost was one of the most frightening things he had ever encountered. His stated objective at that point was simply survival because he knew the younger rider would be full out. If he couldn't be well ahead, he wanted to be well behind and out of the way.

It is unlikely that anyone enjoys the sport more than Ron and Marg Southern. With the exception of a couple of missed days due to family or personal illnesses, both have been there for all of the rides in the International Ring.

Ron respects the commitment of a good rider and marvels at the power and abilities of the horse. He has difficulty remembering any bad rides, simply because he sees a degree of wonderment in every performance.

"I will never forget Eddie Macken (Ireland) winning the four classes, or the fact the Grand Prix total paid only $15,000 for such an extraordinary performance." (Winning the same four events in 1995 would have been worth $261,500 to Eddie versus a total of $5,700 in 1979.)

"Norman Dello Joio (U.S.) with I Love You was absolutely spectacular, but equally amazing in my mind was Paul Schockemoehle (Germany) not winning with Deister at Spruce Meadows, and in fact sharing the horror and disappointment when they actually stopped out twice in the du Maurier."

Now this is fun . . . isn't it? Canada's Ian Millar and Linda Heathcott go neck-and-neck in the ATCO Structures Double Slalom.

Among the best young riders in the sport - Frank Selinger and Judi Gorsline - were stifled by conditions beyond their control.

He also expressed concern for the missed opportunities of some juniors.

"Frankie Selinger (Calgary) and Judi Gorsline (Edmonton) were the two best junior talents ever at Spruce Meadows and could have been the best in the world. I feel they were denied that opportunity due to economics beyond their control.

"I remember a ride by Britain's Nick Skelton (the 1985 Alcatel Canada Wire Parcours de Chasse) on a horse called Apollo that was the most dramatic speed ride I have seen anywhere. He did not take that horse back one inch. It was a blazing round and it was the most spectacular piece of riding I have ever seen in my life."

The Rider

When asked to name his top three riders, Ron didn't hesitate: Canada's Ian Millar, Alwin Schockemoehle of Germany and Great Britain's David Broome.

"Alwin is certainly the best judge of horses I have had the pleasure of knowing. His two clear rounds on Warwick Rex to win the Montreal Olympics also put him in a class of his own." Alwin was only seventeen when he became the star pupil of Germany's revered Hans Gunter Winkler.

"But if you're looking for tough, they don't make them tougher than Ian Millar," he continued. He endorsed Ian's 1991 win in the du Maurier as perhaps the best single effort he had seen at Spruce Meadows.

"David Broome is the complete horseman. He had so many great horses, but it was his skill that made the difference," said Ron. Yet when the depth of emotion secreted by memorable victories at Spruce Meadows is finally measured, the outpour of pride that erupted after the 1990 Spruce Meadows NATIONAL and the Shell Cup Derby will certainly add volumes. Mark Laskin, always a favourite before a Spruce Meadows crowd, wanted so badly to re-establish his presence as a world-class rider.

But as fate would have it, his only international horse Voila didn't have the experience or the scope to deal with the monster length of a Derby course.

"But she got it together that Sunday," said Mark. "She got brave and won the class and I don't think I have ever felt better."

Mark's goal as a rider at Spruce Meadows is to just once make it into every Victory Ride, a formidable task since he traditionally rides two horses in every class.

"I don't need to win. That's great of course, but if I can get into the money, I'm very happy. The closest I have ever been is seventeen out of eighteen," said Mark, one of the best catch riders in the business, and also one of its most superstitious.

He still has his superstitions, "but I'm getting better as I get older," said the young man who once took a year off to teach blind children to ride in Israel. "I used to have just one favourite bathroom. Now I have several to make it easier." But he would fight to the death if someone tried to abscond with the tattered hard hat that has been with him since Day One.

Michel Vaillancourt will forever treasure the memory of his Olympic medal ride, but he also loves to talk about the day in 1982 when he edged Calgary's Alan Brand for the Canadian Championship at the NATIONAL.

They were tied for the title going into the final event, and both had their hearts set on the new Chrysler vehicle that was to go to the winner. As fate would have it, they were also the only two to make it into the jump-off. Alan went first and dropped one rail. Michel was slower, but he was also squeaky clean.

"I walked out of that ring and said 'Alan, you're a good sport. For that I'll take you out for dinner and I'll even pick you up in my new car.' Funny thing though. He didn't laugh too hard."

International judge Tom Michiel put a different twist on his recollections of greatness at Spruce Meadows. His qualifications are impeccable having judged at every tournament since 1976.

Officials team: Judges Francois Ferland of Quebec, Tom Michiel and Ray Antonuk of Calgary and Chief Steward Dr. Eric Ratledge of Calgary.

"There is no doubt about the greatness of Big Ben, Jappeloup, Boomerang and others that have appeared here," said Tommy. "But you tend to think only of these world-class champions, and not those who come year after year . . . sometimes upsetting the stars, but always legitimate contenders."

He spoke highly of Bo Mearns and The Flying Nun, a valiant mare that tugged at the hearts of show jumping fans across North America. The Victoria, B.C. rider directed the floppy-eared Nun to many superb rounds in Calgary, including those that climaxed in a Canadian Championship in 1979 and two Leading Canadian Rider Awards in 1979 and 1980.

Theirs was a storybook relationship. Bo bought the unhappy young Thoroughbred off the race track for $400 and would consign her care to no one else. Bo trusted no one but herself to take the wheel of the half-ton and small trailer that negotiated the mountain trek to Calgary three times every year. She never really had much interest in going any further.

Eventually their talents could no longer be ignored and Bo and The Flying Nun were named to the Canadian Team.

Bo retired her "best friend" in a moving ceremony held at centre ring during the 1981 NATIONAL. She had spoken earlier of how difficult it would be to enter that ring one last time on a horse that was so trustful she had never, in almost a dozen competitive years, tossed Bo from the saddle.

Perhaps the big mare was listening. As Marg Southern approached with a blanket of flowers, The Flying Nun, in her first defiant act reared like a wild young pony, and Bo slid unceremoniously to the ground.

Without Spruce Meadows it is unlikely that Bo and The Flying Nun would have ever crossed the mountains in search of competition. Spruce Meadows brought fame to that pairing, but both gave all of it back in goodwill and honest effort. It is just unfortunate that Spruce Meadows didn't come a decade earlier for Bo and The Flying Nun. No one will ever know just how exceptional they really were.

Upon losing The Flying Nun, Bo returned unannounced to Spruce Meadows the next year and walked directly into the show office to volunteer her services. Minutes later she was on course with a flag in her hand.

There were other riders who, for a variety of reasons, appeared only once.

People like Bum-Yong Son, a thirty-five-year old fishing company president from South Korea. He had been riding for fifteen years in pursuit of a dream: to ride for Korea in an Olympic Games.

(photo by Rick Maynard)

Bo Mearns of Victoria, B.C. and her courageous mare, The Flying Nun.

To gain confidence and experience he dipped deeply into his savings account and financed excursions into the United States in 1983 and 1984 to compete in smaller regional shows. Although these tests were no match for the international courses he hoped to face as an Olympian, they still provided far tougher competition than the small army shows he dominated back home.

Bum-Yong wanted desperately to ride for Korea as an individual in the 1984 Los Angeles Olympics, but his country's Olympic Selection Committee decided he must first prove himself worthy of such an honour.

They told him he could ride in L.A. if he could finish the Canadian selection trial course at the Spruce Meadows NATIONAL with twenty or fewer faults.

The Royal Bank World Cup course was posted on his arrival and, through an interpreter, he confessed it was the most terrifying thing he had ever seen. But he would use the open events of the first two days to prepare for the Saturday showdown in the Royal Bank World Cup.

His first venture into the Spruce Meadows International Ring was not encouraging. He finished the course, but with thirty-four and one quarter faults. The next day, however, there was cause for celebration: only two down for eight faults.

Course designer Pamela Carruthers announced she would be setting a tough test for the selection trial. Anything less would be unfair to those aspiring to ride for Canada at the Olympics.

Bum-Yong cleared the first four fences and appeared to be on his way. But he came out swinging on the next two obstacles and his horse froze at the seventh. With fifteen faults he decided it was enough and retired voluntarily, he was concerned for his horse who had injured itself on an earlier knockdown, and he would take no further chances. His horse's safety was far more important than even a lifelong dream.

But before he left Spruce Meadows he asked for a video-tape of his earlier eight fault performance in hopes it would still persuade the committee to reconsider and allow him to compete in Los Angeles. Unfortunately, permission was never given.

Details of the most unusual ride at Spruce Meadows were never reported by the media. American riding legend George Morris was at the reins and saw no reason to mention it during the press conference which followed his victory in the 1988 du Maurier International.

George, a man with an extraordinary reputation for excellence, was on the comeback trail at an age resting just above the half century mark. He was aboard a talented but devil-bred horse called Rio. Never one to ride the easy horses, he preferred instead to hand the soft ones over to his riders while he tackled the mavericks.

> "I walked into the ring to accept my cheque (the largest of his career) and Ron ordered me to get off. That was the scariest moment of my career. Ron didn't know what was happening, but all I could think of was this is exactly how I broke my leg on Rio before."
>
> (George Morris)

Rio was impossible to mount in a normal fashion. He had already broken George's leg once, and the only sure way to get aboard was to shank him tightly back at the barn, blindfold him, and then get on fast.

Once astride this horse you didn't get off until the day was finished. Chances of ever remounting were very unlikely.

"The easiest way for me to get Rio ready for the du Maurier was to get on him for the noon parade," said the man whose many triumphs include a team silver at the 1960 Olympics. "But then I would have to stay on him for the day, which was a better choice than getting off and having to get back on."

If anyone noticed a grim-faced George Morris wandering with his horse among the trees behind the hunter ring they didn't say anything. He couldn't even capture a moment of rest by taking his feet out of the stirrups because he knew if he did that Rio would bolt. He couldn't lengthen or shorten the irons for the same reason.

"Well I went clear in that first round and now things were getting uncomfortable. I didn't have enough time to get back to the barns and get off him between rounds, so back I went into the trees to await the start of the next round."

George and Rio won the du Maurier that day. And despite the euphoria of that win, George had now been on Rio for four and a half hours and he was looking forward to ending the day, no matter how monumental it might become among future treasured memories.

"I walked into the ring to accept my cheque (the largest of his career) and Ron ordered me to get off. That was the scariest moment of my career. Ron didn't know what was happening, but all I could think of was this is exactly how I broke my leg on Rio before.

"I thought for sure he would bolt, but I was told to get off and I did. I gave the horse to a groom and he was fine. I couldn't believe my luck."

That night, between "terrible cramps", George enjoyed dreams of his new-found riches and incredible good fortune.

There have been very few controversial on-course incidents at Spruce Meadows, but the worst occurred during the 1986 du Maurier. Great Britain's Malcolm Pyrah, a pre-tournament favourite, was approaching the first fence of the second round when one of the jump crew suddenly walked behind the fence.

British coach Ronnie Massarella watched in disbelief as the distracted horse fell into the fence and suffered injuries that proved serious enough that he had to withdraw.

"I went berserk. I'll always remember it. Nancy (Southern) was doing the television and stuck a microphone in front of me. I told her that if they (Spruce Meadows) wanted to call it the biggest and best Grand Prix in the world, they ought to run it like that."

He saw Ron Southern that night and wanted to discuss the incident, although he was also prepared to tone down his remarks. Before he could, however, course designer Pamela Carruthers came up "and played hell with me for what I had said to Nancy on the television". Others, however, said the comment was justified because they had seen what happened and there was no excuse for it.

The next morning the two Rons met and the British Chef d'Equipe unloaded his concerns about the incident the day before. He also took advantage of the moment to add a few new ones.

"I told him: 'You had better make certain everybody in that ring knows what is going on. And besides that, you overload the ring because of television time and I understand the need for that. But if you're going to let them in early you had better have people in there telling them where to go. Those are the best horses and riders in the world and they're only looking at the next fence.'

"He wasn't pleased with me at the time," said Ronnie who has been forced into making some tough decisions in his life. As a soccer coach he once had to permanently bench his veteran star and team owner because he could no longer keep up. That person was himself.

When he met Ron Southern the next year, Ronnie told his host he sincerely hoped the du Maurier event would indeed be the biggest and best Grand Prix in the world.

"He laughed and told me that everyone had learned a lot from the previous year, and they had. You couldn't believe the efficiency after that."

For every bad experience there have been hundreds of good ones.

Jim Elder, a member of Canadian Olympic teams that mined gold in 1968 and again in 1980, remembers a humorous exchange with British riding legend Sir Harry Llewellyn.

"It was in the big ring and Sir Harry was in the playpen serving as a technical delegate. I believe he was also President of the British Equestrian Federation at the time.

"I had gone clear and was coming in for the jump-off when Harry shouts over: 'Gee Jimmy, aren't you getting a little too old for this sport?'

"I told him that he, if I remembered correctly, was older than I when he quit riding and he laughed saying that he didn't think so. Anyway I won the class and on my way out I looked over to him and shouted: 'See Harry, I guess I'm not too old after all.'"

The Athlete

It comes as no great surprise to anyone to learn that all great riders are also gifted athletes.

Dig deeply enough into their pasts and you will find they excelled at other sports as youngsters. Mark Laskin can still burn up a hockey rink, and if called upon, Hugh Graham could still rope a runaway steer. Many of the European riders were exceptional soccer players, nor should we forget the wrestling prowess of one Harvey Smith.

Canadian veteran Jim Elder ran track and also showed some promise as a hockey player, but his size kept him from getting too serious. Rising Canadian star Eric Lamaze is a whiz on the tennis court.

"Ian (Millar) would have probably made one heck of a basketball player with his natural abilities, and he probably would have made more money," said Jim. "But what you have to remember in this sport is that you not only have to be very athletic, you must also have incredibly quick reflexes."

After winning team gold in 1968, Jim Elder became a prized catch on the banquet circuit, right up there with hockey legends Gordie Howe and Bobby Hull and Canadian football greats like Russ Jackson of Ottawa.

The problem, he said, was uncertainty on his part over what to say.

"These other guys were talking about how good their sport had been to them, and how fortunate they were to be part of it. So I sat down one day and prepared a list of what show jumping gave me. I came out a way ahead of all of them."

What, he challenged, can a retired hockey player do other than put on some skates and take a slow turn around the rink. They aren't competitive any more . . . at least not against the best in the sport.

Jim Elder, however, can still win a major Grand Prix with young legs beneath him. And he can always be better since he still learns something about the sport every time he enters a ring.

"I don't have to get on a slow horse and have him take me for a walk around the ring," said Jim. "I can jump them, I can ride them, I can take them here or I can take them there . . . and maybe if I had played hockey I might have got over to Russia, but with my horses I have been all over the world."

And if injuries had ever cut short his riding career, Jim Elder still could have spent his life with horses - breeding, driving or training them.

"And look at my age. I'm 60 and I can still do it all. And I love it."

Unfortunately for show jumping, the visual image projected in the ring doesn't embody the true depth of intensity needed to participate in this sport.

> "The first thing I'd do is get rid of the pretty pink coats and ties. What other sport asks its athletes to put on ties and wear little peaked caps. It's ridiculous."
>
> (Jim Elder)

(photo by Peter Llewellyn)

Hervé Godignon of France favours his country's distinctive blue jacket with a red collar rather than the traditional red.

Comdt. Gerry Mullins of Ireland wants an image change for the sport.

"The first thing I'd do," said Jim, "is get rid of the pretty pink coats and ties. What other sport asks its athletes to put on ties and wear little peaked caps? It's ridiculous."

The sport of show jumping is one of speed and danger, he said, and the uniform of the rider should reflect that. Riders don't put on snow white breeches and starched shirts while training their horses in the dust and mud.

"This is a tough sport. People see the finished product, not the days, months and years of training that evolves into a good rider or a good horse."

He suggested the donning of racing silks similar to those worn by jockeys "bright, exciting and flashy."

Or, he added, a nice windbreaker with a turtleneck sweater. But never a shirt and tie because "that's to wear downtown to Bay Street to sell stocks and bonds."

And once that concern was settled, Jim would like to find a way of dumping the conventional peaked hard hat.

"If you go down and catch the peak on a pole, it will either break your nose or give your neck one heck of a jolt." He believes what he preaches and that is why Jim Elder has always managed, with a defiant toss of his head, to lose his hat by the second fence of any round.

He gets some support on the dress code. Ireland's Comdt. Gerry Mullins agrees that an image change is essential.

"It's time to move away from having all riders dressed the same. If you look at racing, each stable has its own distinctive colour combination," said Gerry. "But in our sport you can have riders from ten different countries and they're all dressed alike. Identification from the public point of view becomes very difficult."

What riders wear, however, doesn't really interest many coaches. They are more concerned what is beneath the clothes, or even the skin.

In their hunt for a potentially great rider, they start their search for somebody who is a gifted athlete. If that rider is also brave, totally committed and very intelligent, they might have a chance.

"Number one, you have to find out if they have the guts," said British coach Ronnie Massarella. "They must have the will to be good, and while it is fine to be frightened, they must have the spirit that will take them beyond the fear of pain."

Ronnie looks for a young rider who "has the will to want to be a star" and one who is determined in many different ways.

"Are they interested in working the horse, or do they just want to ride? Are they a good horse-master, and do they really know how to look after them? Are they interested in going to all types of competitions and earn their credentials, or are they just hoping to find a good horse and go right to the top?"

Most coaches add a word of caution. Although a natural rider's ability becomes evident at an early age, don't arbitrarily ignore older athletes entering the game. Paul Schockemoehle never rode a horse until he was twenty-six, and Harvey Smith didn't climb aboard until he was sixteen.

Not surprisingly, Ronnie identifies David Broome as the "greatest show jumper that ever walked this earth." The two men remain the best of friends and their mutual respect never wavered through some difficult athlete/coach confrontations.

"He has a natural flair about him, but like all great riders he educated himself with every ride," said the British coach.

"Spruce Meadows only saw David in his latter years. In his heyday he was magic. He would go to Hickstead on a Sunday and the next day would be riding at a small country show. And he was just as tough riding in a class for fifty pounds as the one worth ten thousand."

> "If they are totally and absolutely determined, they will win their share of competitions. But if you can get someone who is married to that determination and will to win, as well as someone who has the feel and touch, well then you get, well you get an Eddie Macken."
>
> (Ned Campion)

David was at his best in a jump-off, yet he never walked a jump-off course. Nor would he watch those riders who went before him.

"It used to hold you in awe looking at him. Before a jump-off he would simply look at the board. He knew what he was going to do with his horse and he knew the maximum he could get out of it. He seldom had time faults because he had a clock built in his head," said Ronnie Massarella.

Harvey Smith was self-taught and reached world-prominence by absorbing the lessons of other riders. He also brought laughter to the somewhat staid atmosphere of British show jumping.

Ronnie likes the man a great deal and takes delight in recounting just how Harvey was introduced to the sport.

"Harvey was watching a competition from the side of a ring one day, and although he had never been on a horse, boasted to all around him that he could ride better than all of them."

Sure enough, Ronnie said, he returned the next week and guess who was dashing around the ring - bareback. Ronnie had a feeling he would be seeing more of this brash youngster in the future.

"I don't think there's a man in the world who has won more Grand Prix than Harvey. A brilliant rider, he had something more. He had charisma. When he rode for Britain he was a handful, but he sure could ride."

Ronnie believes it is possible to determine a youngster's ultimate potential by the age of fourteen or fifteen.

"You can't say if they will be brilliant because that also takes a great horse. There are a lot of very good riders, but most are never lucky enough to find a great horse."

Talented horses don't seem to change hands and that globally may be a problem plaguing the sport of show jumping.

"I saw a lovely horse last winter and I offered a fair price of 6,000 pounds. But the owner was shocked and told me she wouldn't sell for a million because the horse was part of the family.

"Many people who are riding today have good horses, but they never develop because the kids are never good enough and the horses become family pets."

Ronnie also bemoans the disappearance of the traditionalist, both at the rider and trainer levels, and said it has become particularly difficult to find young riders who can stand pressure.

"We have some good riders in England, but they won't work. They're used to having a good time, the playboys. When I first went around with the likes of Harvey Smith, Caroline Bradley, David Broome, Malcolm Pyrah, and Ted and Liz Edgar . . . now they were workers. We would have breakfast at 7:30 a.m., be at the training grounds by 8 a.m., and work the horses for at least two hours.

"Now you have to kick them out of bed in the morning; the new breed. They think that all they have to do is buy the horse and it's going to go."

Swiss coach Charles Barrelet measures great champions by their successes aboard many horses, not just one.

"Firstly, every rider who makes it to the international level is a very good rider," said Charles. "But if you go back in history and look at major championship winners, you will find many who excelled on one horse but then weren't heard from again."

These riders, he added, were still competitive on other horses, but they never again reached that ultimate championship level.

"The great champion is the one who can adapt his or her own riding style and character to the character and temperament of whatever horse they may be riding. Then through hard work and diligent training these riders are able to build champions.

"Among those blessed with such abilities," said Charles, "are Nick Skelton of Great Britain, Ludger Beerbaum of Germany and both Thomas and Marcus Fuchs of Switzerland."

His counterpart in Ireland, Chef d'Equipe Ned Campion, suggests the most dominant factor in any great rider's makeup is their "will to win and the will to just do it."

"Like everything else in life," said Ned, "if a rider wants it badly enough they will achieve success.

"But I can't teach that."

> "That's my biggest fear today. All we're seeing is shallow horsemen with limited abilities. When everything is going right, or they're on a certain horse that can do a brilliant job, they are fine. But if something goes wrong, they can't recover."
>
> (George Morris)

Linda is always in the hunt and has earned recognition as one of the sport's strongest woman riders.

He also spoke of something he called "the feel."

"If they are totally and absolutely determined, they will win their share of competitions. But if you can get someone who is married to that determination and will to win, as well as someone who has the feel and touch, well then you get, well you get an Eddie Macken.

"Macken," he said, "can be so strong and determined in his quest for victory that pressure doesn't even become a serious factor.

"The greater the pressure, in fact, the more likely he is to win. But he does it with such style as well. It's marvellous to be there."

The supply of quality horses around the world is severely limited, and that adds to the frustration of those riders of irrefutable quality.

"If you are a top jockey in horse racing you are

In the top five on the Spruce Meadows all-time money won list - Canada's Laura Balisky always seems to save it for the big event.

practically assured that you will get quality mounts," said Ned. "But here that's not the case at all. In fact it is quite often the amateur who has the best horses and they aren't about to give them up to a better rider.

"That," he added, "may not be as bad as it sounds since it does give others a chance and brings new blood into the sport.

"If show jumping was restricted to the top riders, others would soon lose heart and before long no one else would be even trying to get there."

Canadian coach Tommy Gayford searches for intelligence as the prime attribute in his riders.

"There are a lot of athletes, in all fields, that are good athletes. But they're not always smart," said Tommy. The truly great riders, however, are also very intelligent which means that in addition to their natural ability ". . . they can also think and they can reason.

"The next crucial ingredient," he said, "is dedication."

"We have a lot of people around who can ride horses," said the former Olympian who at age nineteen competed for Canada on a team that included his father Maj. Gordon Gayford. "What you look for is the athlete who gets up early every morning and gets out there and works their horses all day, every day. There is nothing else important to them. They're dedicated and that dedication makes them tough."

It's not always outwardly evident, but the great riders also have computers for minds and nothing ever rattles them, according to coach Gayford.

With most riders, he said, you invite disaster by using a negative approach. Tell a rider to watch a certain fence and nine times out of ten they'll knock it down.

"With the great ones, like Ian (Millar), you can talk about the difficult areas and he will work out a way to beat it."

Tommy shows no hesitation in identifying Ian as the greatest competitor he has ever seen. "The stronger the competition, the stronger he becomes."

Ian is flattered by the accolade and admits he does thrive on tough competition. But he also believes that one of the fortunate aspects of show jumping is the training process.

If there never was a competition to go to, said Ian, he would work just as hard training and riding the horses because he enjoys that phase as a rewarding end in itself.

"I think of a swimmer who gets in that cold, clammy vat of chemicals at 6 a.m. and rages up and down the pool, Lord knows how many times, just to have themselves fit and strong for the race.

"In fact, I've heard athletes say that much of the reason why they retired is they just couldn't get their minds around the grind of the conditioning and preparation any more. It was just becoming too tough mentally and physically."

For Ian, time spent in training and preparation is the most intriguing and rewarding.

"My idea of a great Christmas Day is to come out and ride the horses. The phone's not going to ring and I'll climb on Big Ben while the kids get on their horses. Lynn (Ian's wife) will come and watch and we all just sort of hang out with the horses. That's a wonderful thing."

George Morris is not sure that great riders can be made. To become one of the best, he said, one must be fortunate enough to be "born into it."

"A lot of people would like to become horsemen and some spend a lot of time trying to become one. But it has to be in your blood."

His secret ingredient to success is "passion". If a rider just goes through the motions in quest of the big prize money they will never last. There are, he said, too many ups and downs in show jumping for anyone who is not 100% committed.

"Many long hours go into making a good rider or a good horse. Years, in fact, into a horse like a Deister or Big Ben. The instances of glamour are so short and quick compared with those spent in training and searching for the right horse."

George suggested that today's "new breed of rider" is far different then the one prominent in the forties and fifties.

"We all grew up running down and mucking out a stall or two or three, filling the water buckets, feeding the horse, grooming the horse and then after all that was done, assuming it was done properly, we would be allowed to ride."

Now, said George, everybody else does the job for the rider.

"That's my biggest fear today. All we're seeing is shallow horsemen with limited abilities. When everything is going right, or they're on a certain horse that can do a brilliant job, they are fine. But if something goes wrong, they can't recover.

"This is not a mechanical computer game. It's a contact sport with an animal and the more you can be with that animal, in or out of the barn, the better chance you will have of making it as a rider," said George.

As a man who makes his living from horses, George Morris has an interesting theory on why great riders are lousy coaches.

"They may be wonderful riders, but they got there because of a natural talent. They don't know what the average rider does wrong simply because they never did it wrong themselves."

oking it over - Linda can only wonder about the grass on the other side of this wall. Fellow Calgarian John Anderson has no problem . . . it is greener.

There are exceptions; among them are Americans Anne Kursinski or Katie Monaghan-Prudent because they wanted to learn how to teach, said George.

"But around the world there are few great riders who are also great teachers."

Germany's Paul Schockemoehle, he suggested, is the most notable exception.

"As an instructor he has a track record a mile long. He is not a stylish rider, but he is a great rider and an even greater winner. He can impart his knowledge because he is intellectual . . . a student and therefore a teacher."

Paul, he added, is also one of the best at dealing and selling horses making him one of the few in the sport that "has it all."

Something that is often over-looked in show jumping is the fact that women compete against men on equal terms. That does not happen in any other sport.

Depending upon the horse, a woman rider could hold a distinct advantage over her male counterpart. The same, of course, could be said about male riders.

British journalist Peter Churchill has analyzed the differences many times.

"A woman rider, and we are talking about Grand Prix show jumping, doesn't usually have the depth of leg or the depth of seat to get deep into the horse's back. They can't, therefore, pull up that power by wrapping their legs around and squeezing the horse up to the next fence.

"To make up for it," he added, "women riders become exceptional technical riders." A strong example is Linda Southern-Heathcott who is short in stature but whose knowledge of the horse reaches considerable heights.

"There are also some horses that will go better for women," said Peter. "The horse feels that it is looking after them, and women knowing that will take advantage of the situation.

"Some of the great horses," he said, "have shown over the years they don't like to be dominated and feel a woman won't try it. They'll go sweet enough for a woman rider, yet I've seen a male rider get on their back and they're on the floor in seconds."

Course designer, and former U.S. Team member Linda Allen finds that a cool set of nerves remains crucial to any success.

"There is a tremendous amount of pressure on the rider, particularly if you are riding a top horse," said Linda. "You know the horse is as good as it can be, therefore if a mistake is made, it's your fault."

She also projects an interesting theory on why it is that over the years the United States has consistently produced good technical show jumpers. Most horsemen will argue that dependency upon the race track for potential jumpers is bad. She, however, believes it has made American riders stronger.

"Why? Because we must search for our horses among race track rejects, and that means we are buying horses with a lot of bad habits and very few good ones. There is a lot of work that must go into the development of these horses, and as a result, riders have to compensate for weak points in their horses."

The bottom line, said Linda, is that a lot of riders with natural talent became very good at getting the very best out of every horse they ride.

"What seems to be a little out of kilter now, however, is we're still developing riders using that same system. But many of them don't have that rough and ready, do-it-all ability to handle the horse. They don't have the foundation to apply the polish and they never will unless they are prepared to ride all kinds of horses . . . not just those that have been trained by somebody else."

Even rarer is the trainer or rider with the natural gift of recognizing potential champions among horses.

The very best, according to Linda, is Canada's Terrance "Torchy" Millar. "He is an absolute genius at recognizing talent in a young horse."

> "If you go home and train the horses, and you have a really good day at it . . . that's really wonderful. That's really what it's about. You should ride because you like the animal."
>
> (Albert Kley)

Spruce Meadows Riding Master Albert Kley agrees that the best instructors do not necessarily come from being great competitors.

The finest he studied under was Otto Meyer, Riding Master at Germany's prestigious riding academy, Landes Reitschule Hoya. "Otto," said Albert, "was equally proficient in both show jumping and dressage, something you seldom see in today's riders.

"The harder you worked for him," said Albert, "the better the horse he would allow you to ride.

"Riding is so much feeling and experience that it is hard for anyone who has not trained a horse to understand what you mean," he said. "How can you hope to explain this to someone if they have never had that special feeling?"

Shortly after being hired by the Southerns, Albert shocked a young Nancy Southern - who was already riding at the top Grand Prix level - by making her ride almost a year on the flat without stirrups to develop a better seat.

The difference between riding a well-trained horse and one that isn't, said Albert, is as obvious as the difference between driving a car without power steering and power brakes.

"Once you have driven the car with power you won't ever go back to one without it. Why? Because it's so much more comfortable and you enjoy the feeling. The same thing happens in riding. When you talk about how a horse gets light in the reins, you have experienced the feeling."

Albert suggested that if a rider did nothing but compete, life would quickly become pretty boring.

"But if you go home and train the horses, and you have a really good day at it . . . that's really wonderful. That's really what it's about. You should ride because you like the animal. Then you learn to like to ride and when you get good enough you can enter a competition.

"The animal," he stressed, "must always come first."

And, at least according to Ireland's Comdt. Gerry Mullins, they usually do.

"I don't know of anyone that takes better care of their animals than show jumpers," said Gerry. "We check them every morning and we make certain they are fit to start any season. Their diet is looked after and in return we expect them to jump for perhaps two minutes a day."

There are some riders, he said, who might try and win at all costs, but they are the exceptions and they don't stay around very long.

"In the main the horses are extremely well looked after. Even when they retire, instead of selling them or putting them down, most riders will mind that horse until the day it dies. That's quite a thing to see," said the Irish army officer.

Riding Master Kley concurred, and added his definition of a "class" rider:

"For me it's not those who are always winning. I watch how riders behave around the tournaments to the people, to the spectators, to the sponsors, and most important of all, to the horse. Those who do it right are my kind of people."

Nancy Southern is quick to add patience and discipline to the attributes of a great rider.

"Even if you are bitterly disappointed, or even very angry, riders more than any other athlete must control themselves," said Nancy.

"If you have a temper, learn how to control it. You can't express temper with a

Resident course designer Pamela Carruthers in a photo taken early in her legendary show jumping career.

horse, because just like people, the horse will lose complete respect."

It doesn't happen often, but anyone who has attended show jumping has seen at least one incident when, after being abusive to their horse, the rider is unceremoniously dumped to the ground. Ususally the crowd cheers the horse when it happens.

British course designer Pamela Carruthers loves horses and everything about the sport. When away at school as a youngster she convinced her parents to send money for a fur coat. She used it to buy her first horse.

A "natural eye", said Pamela, is a must if any rider is to gain prominence.

"There's too much catering to those who won't ever get to the top, and don't deserve to get there," said the world's most prominent course designer. "In North America there's too much trainer involvement. It bothers me, for example, that most trainers feel it is essential to count exactly how many strides the horse must take between fences for every student on every ride."

There is no way that all horses are going to take the same number of strides in the big rings of Spruce Meadows and Hickstead, she explained. The rider, not the trainer, should be determining the precise take-off point when he or she is on course.

"Unless you have a good eye, you'll never make it. It's a question of having the horse between your leg and your hand and you being able to adjust if the stride needs to be lengthened or shortened."

Eventually, however, riders must face the dilemma which haunts most careers: the financial bottom line. Usually it is not very attractive.

"On the scale of professional athletes we're pretty well at the base of the pay scale," said Edmonton's Mark Laskin, "particularly when you figure how much it costs to play the game.

"The highs are high," said Mark, "but the lows are rock bottom.

"The hardest thing is figuring out how to deal with the mental aspect of it all. We fail far more often than we succeed. If a horse wins one Grand Prix a year that's pretty good. If they win two, it's a darn good year. If they win three it's fantastic, but that's still only three out of twenty starts and it might be worth $6,000 - unless it's the du Maurier.

"So how many riders can make a living without teaching or trading? Maybe one or two, but that's all. You have to do the other stuff."

So why do it?

"Maybe we're crazy. But when you get good at something, and you enjoy it, why not?"

In England, top sponsored riders like the Whitakers and Nick Skelton receive roughly $100,000 per year from their sponsor. They also keep all prize money, and when the sponsor buys them a new horse, the rider pays the tax but also retains a one-fifth ownership interest in that horse.

That is a deal that only the best of the best can negotiate. Others will receive anywhere from twenty-five to seventy-five per cent of purses and a limited amount of appearance money, although appearance money has never been paid at Spruce Meadows.

Two of the best - brothers John (left) and Michael Whitaker (right) of Great Britain have shared the most generous of rewards at Spruce Meadows.

It is a sport in which you need breaks, said John Whitaker, but sometimes "you have to make your own breaks."

"Show jumping," he continued, "is an expensive sport and it is probably impossible to get to the top without some big money behind you.

"But that is not the main reason we (brothers Michael and John) do it. It's because we enjoy it. We never worried about getting up at five in the morning to get our horses ready to show."

(photo by Katey Barrett)

Great Britain's Nick Skelton, together with the Whitaker brothers, have been a dominant, steadfast team since the mid-80's.

Ian Millar held no illusions about what it takes to win.

"You have to be sitting on the best, and the best costs a lot of money to acquire, maintain and develop."

When Ian first hit the Grand Prix trail he remembers that Jimmy Elder on a medium horse was a real threat.

"Today, if I may be so bold, Ian Millar on a medium horse is not really so much of a threat. I must be sitting on as good a horse as anyone else in that class, and I have to be right on my game, if I expect to win.

"There are," he added, "so many quality riders that the error ratio is generally so low that the only thing that will decide it on that day is the quality of the horse."

Day Four Continued:
Friday's Competition

Germany's Franke Sloothaak holds the hot hand this evening pocketing $16,500 for his win aboard San Patrignano Weihaiwej in the Canadian Airlines Challenge. The World Champion collects another $9,250 for directing his speed horse San Patrignano Dorina to a first place tie in the Alberta Power Circuit six-bar competition.

Once again, conditions are perfect although shadows are creeping into the International Ring by the time Franke leads the top twelve back for a jump-off round in the Friday evening feature competition.

It leads one to speculate on how long it will be before one of the courses is fully lit for night competition, but it's not a subject that gets a great deal of attention. Certainly, in the near future the Southerns are hoping to introduce winter jumping as part of a Christmas fantasy setting, and that probably will also bring about stadium lighting.

Artificial lighting is not a necessity for the NATIONAL and NORTH AMERICAN. Because of Spruce Meadows' northern latitude, daylight during the summer months will linger until almost 11 p.m. By September and the MASTERS, however, the sun has bid its adieu by 8:30 p.m. and in December Old Man Sol is snoring by 5 p.m.

Of the twelve riders returning for the jump-off in the Canadian Airlines event, only three managed to repeat the effort. Switzerland's Beat Grandjean takes the cautious route around the course but it is costly in terms of time and he finishes clean in 49.97 seconds.

Nick Skelton of Great Britain punches the pedal hard but his 44.27 running time is still almost a full second slower than the rapid Sloothaak.

Franke shares honours in the Alberta Power event with Ireland's Peter Charles. It is a popular event with the fans, with six vertical jumps set in a straight line at centre course. At the discretion of the judges, heights increase with each round until only one horse remains. If only two horses remain and both have knockdowns, as was the case tonight, the winner's purse is shared.

Tonight is also pay-back time at the MASTERS as fans, riders and organizers pay tribute to the horse. It is so fitting that the primary entertainer in the "Evening of the Horse" celebrations is . . . the horse.

In addition to superb competition, the record crowd of 24,687 for a Friday evening is delighted by a traditional Parade of Athletes, J. Michael Wigen and his aerobatic plane "Cyclone", five daring skydivers, the usual collection of marching bands, and an explosive fireworks display.

By 10 p.m., long after the formal festivities have ended, thousands linger throughout the plaza area.

British coach Ronnie Massarella isn't nearly as relaxed. In his nineteen years at the MASTERS, this tournament marks the first time a British rider hasn't won an event through the first three days of competition.

"It's the worst year we've ever had," he says in reflecting over the year's results.

But he is hopeful that history will repeat itself. After a disappointing sixth at the Barcelona Olympics in 1992, the Brits gained revenge by beating all of the medal teams at the MASTERS just one month later.

Tomorrow they bring another disappointing sixth place finish from the 1994 World Championships in Holland into the MASTERS.

Don't count them out yet.

Show jumping is a sport that has no age restrictions among its diversified followers . . . as reflected by the three generations of this family.

Day Five

A Sport Worth Watching

Of all the professional sport audiences in Calgary, none approach the diversity of a Spruce Meadows crowd.

Hockey crowds are comprised primarily of middle-aged to older patrons and traditionally reflect the upper middle class. Seats are expensive, and an evening game is treated by many as an outing of considerable social significance.

Football attracts a somewhat younger, working-man throng. Moderate pricing makes it reachable for more families, although it is predominantly a male following. Baseball plays host to the youngest fans of all, particularly teens, and more family groupings than either hockey or football.

None of these sports have a significant ethnic mix among their fan base. Several attempts to introduce professional soccer to Calgary, the one sport associated with multi-cultural followings, failed miserably in the late seventies and eighties. It was good soccer by North American standards, but it wasn't of the high calibre most Europeans were used to. They wouldn't be fooled.

A Spruce Meadows crowd suffuses the age, social, ethnic, economic and gender spectrum. There is no slice of society not vividly represented at a tournament, nor does one specific group dominate the mix.

(photo by Cansport)

There's always a comfortable piece of grass for a break and a picnic.

Today's crowd is once again typical. There is no discernible dress code, but overall it is far less formal than the attire of show jumping audiences in Europe. Today will be favoured with sunshine and warmth, so the closest thing to a standard uniform is shorts and a wild assortment of light shirts and other tops.

For many families packing a picnic basket is an essential part of the show jumping experience. It is something not seen as often at the major European tournaments, although packing along a lunch is very popular at their smaller presentations.

The family presence today is exceptionally strong, and that is a bit of a rarity for Canadian sports crowds. You don't often see two, or even three generations attending a sporting event in this country. Most sports are too specific in nature to satisfy the eclectic demands of Canadian society.

Show jumping's base of appeal is far broader since there aren't many who can't relate, in some way, to the horse. Those who defy such a contention however, can easily fill a day with assorted delights at Spruce Meadows without stopping even once at a competitive ring.

There are those who will tell you about the somewhat inexplicable, yet very fervent pride that engulfs all who become fans of Spruce Meadows. They protectively regard it as their own, and treat it accordingly. They will stop to pick up trash and admonish those who toss it around indiscriminately.

There is also a politeness to the crowd, never boisterous to the point of insulting, but appreciative of good sport and good entertainment. Fans collectively feed on a joy that mystically shields them from the explainable discomforts of rain, sleet, snow and hail - all frequent intruders of Spruce Meadows' domain. Nor will you suffer through the antics of

> It truly is a great place to be on an exquisite Alberta Saturday.

drunks or other narrow-minded boors who delight in making it uncomfortable for others.

It truly is a great place to be on an exquisite Alberta Saturday.

There isn't, however, much sparkle in the eyes of the Mexican riders. A power failure at one of the host hotels forced them, together with several hundred tournament guests and officials, into the streets at 2:30 this morning. It took four hours to get the lights back on, and only a lucky few rediscovered the comforts of sleep.

Pamela Arthur, one of those booted unceremoniously into the snappy morning air, has her hands full this morning. She is the steward responsible for behaviour in the main practice ring. Somebody has managed to sneak a couple of square rails into the ring and they are being used with enthusiasm by those who recognize the edge it provides. Pamela quickly has the rails removed.

Another concern is raised because one of the French riders has set up a series of three small verticals with ground lines in front so that he can bounce the combination. Pam explains that if the line isn't part of today's course, it is illegal to practice it. She gets a polite argument from the rider, but confirms her assessment of the rule with Dr. Eric Ratledge, Chief Steward. The rider unravels his creation without a lot of concern.

"Once in a while they'll test you," Pam said of the international riders, "but usually they are very good."

The Horse

Not surprisingly, there is a universal respect for the horse among show jumpers that borders on adulation. Unfortunately there are still a few who will abuse them in the quest for money, power and fame. But riders are now policing themselves in a determined effort to keep the sport's image squeaky clean.

They know the public will not tolerate even a hint of animal abuse, particularly since their future very much depends upon public support and respect. Too many reported incidents of brutal training procedures, together with the horrors of alleged horse killings for insurance money, have already seriously tainted that image.

Fortunately, the vast majority of riders and owners protect their horses with parental passion. Like millions of others through the ages, they have been captivated by its nobility, power and creative diversity.

But is this animal nearly as complex as its distinctive talents would indicate? And where did it really come from?

Amazingly enough, the horse as we know it today probably emerged from a prehistoric region within a two-day ride of Spruce Meadows. Over a period of millions of years primitive breeds migrated from North America to the Old World across the Bering land-bridge which used to connect Alaska and Siberia.

Scientists believe the last single-toed representative of the genus Equus also followed this route and evolved into our present-day assortment of zebras, donkeys and wild horses. Mysteriously their relatives in North America died out 10,000 years ago, were re-introduced in the early 1500's by conquering land forces into the Antilles, and then spread into Mexico and up through the Americas.

When they returned to the Western Hemisphere four centuries ago it was in the humiliating role of ship ballast. Those that survived provided transportation in both labour and war. By the time the horse found its way back to the Americas, its spirit was wonderfully wild once again. It didn't take long, however, for the Plains Indians to bridle this zeal as they faced the imposition of western Canada's first white settlers.

(photo by Cansport)

As shown by this team of Clydesdales, the majesty of the horse can come in many different dimensions.

Today there are more than three hundred breeds of domestic horses and it is now accepted they descended from several, rather than just one specific breed.

Neatly logged, the equine world breaks into purebred, warm-blood, cold-blood or pony breeds.

Cold-blooded breeds are typically of calm temperament and huge bulk: Percheron, Belgians, Clydesdale, Bretons, etc. Warm-blooded horses are those whose ancestry, usually the sire, includes one purebred (English Thoroughbred or Arab). They include the Hanoverian, Holstein, Trakehner, etc. - breeds that have collectively dominated all disciplines of modern equestrian sport.

Anatomically, the body of a horse is a perfectly crafted running machine. Its parts have been set in flawless balance with massive muscles to propel it effortlessly, and with boundless energy.

Nature, it has been said, delivered great honesty in the evolution of the horse because every detail of its form has been dictated by its function.

Unlike humans, who must traverse the earth in only one exhausting gait, the horse has four and utilizes each with efficiency and grace. It is also both intelligent or "limited" depending upon your partner in conversation.

British humorist W.C. Sellar wrote:

"To confess that you are totally ignorant of the horse is social suicide. You will be despised by everybody, especially the horse."

Once man discovered its agility, and then found he could stay upon its back, the horse has served with humility in countless tasks of toil and pleasure. It has been a partner in war and in peace, law and universal order, commerce and sport, as well as being a life-giving friend. It was Sir Winston Chuchill who said "There is something about the outside of a horse that is good for the inside of a man."

The horse evokes all emotion - joy through anger - and tests the limits of both love and patience. Poets and bards have exhausted the depth of man's language skills in search of words to honour its conquests.

German Riding Master Manfred Lopp said that only a dog challenges the horse in terms of servitude towards mankind.

> Unlike humans, who must traverse the earth in only one exhausting gait, the horse has four and utilizes each with efficiency and grace. It is also both intelligent or "limited" depending upon your partner in conversation.

"But man looks down to the dog and up to the horse," said Manfred. "But you must also remember that while you may look up to the stallion, you must never be under the stallion. You are the boss."

Many heart-warming tales of the horse have withstood the strains of time, yet new equine legends are being created because of the animal's prolific potential.

It is fair to say that the magnificence of Spruce Meadows sprang from the profound obsession one little girl held for the horse. Nancy Southern's life-long infatuation with the animal continues to intensify, and it is one she now eagerly shares with her own children.

The future of Spruce Meadows definitely rests within the hands of Nancy and sister Linda.

Linda will preserve the dream and direct its future with careful and loving attention. Yet as its designated president, Linda also knows she must operate Spruce Meadows as a business in a most efficient and professional manner. If not, future generations will be robbed of the cherished resource and legacy she and others hold so precious. Linda understands the horse better than anyone else in the family, and is firm she will not be emotionally distracted from making difficult decisions because of its captivating properties.

As detailed in earlier chapters, Linda awaits this challenge with an eagerness and confidence that far exceeds the tenderness of her years.

She is bolstered in this challenge by many people, but none more welcomed than the commitment and support dedicated to her by sister Nancy.

Nancy is a leader with an intuitive business sense that will earn her international accolades as she moves toward, and ultimately occupies, the chairmanship of the ATCO Group of Companies.

Her future role at Spruce Meadows will not be as much a "hands-on" experience as it will be for Linda, but it will be both distinctive and vital.

She will become the keeper of the dream. Not just as it seems today, but as an ever-changing vision cultivated with creative commitment and belief.

In preparation for this role, Nancy has been blessed with all of the right tools: compassion for the horse, love for the sport, a confidence in the future, and the remarkable ability to perceive, and then pursue, exactly what is right.

On top of this she has the human qualities to pull it all off - believability, sincerity and just enough naiveness to allow her to chase the fantasies of her dreams.

Most close friends of the family suggest Nancy is a reflection of her father, and

Linda her mother. Although flattered by the comparisons, both Nancy and Linda disagree and say just the opposite is probably closer to the truth. Reality is probably somewhere in between. Both are exceptional young people who are equally distinctive.

Nancy's position within the global business community will ensure continued progress of Economic Round Table discussions at Spruce Meadows, as well as maintain a crucial peer presence among sponsors of the sport.

Between the two daughters, in fact, the strengths and attributes of their parents are nicely covered and the future of Spruce Meadows is on very solid ground.

"Those are two very smart women," close family friend Wilmat Tennyson said in an interview conducted just months before his untimely death in early 1995. "Depending on timing, but with some interim understandings, I think the future of the corporations and Spruce Meadows is in good hands."

In the same fashion that both Marg and Ron created trust from colleagues and board members, so will Nancy and Linda require loyal friends they can count on, added the late du Maurier executive.

If you close your eyes and listen only to the message, not the voice delivering it, Nancy sounds very much like her father.

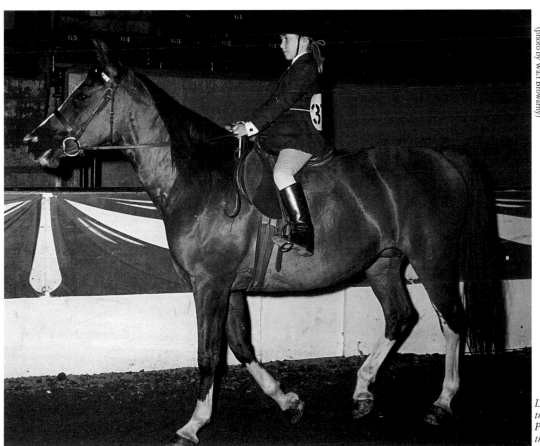

(photo by Walt Browarny)

Linda, perched proudly on the back of her pony Prissy, already showing the poise of a champion.

Nancy and Benny - a partnership that provided inspiration and belief.

On those few occasions when neither he nor Marg can publicly thank a sponsor of an event, Nancy steps in. Her presentation skills are akin to those of her father - relaxed, sincere and very smooth.

And like her father, Nancy ventures into the future with that same thrust of unbridled energy. No mental or physical barrier is big enough to slow a good dream.

If Nancy has a visible flaw it might be her vulnerability to the horse. Others, however, would see it as a compassionate strength. She still weeps when reading Black Beauty to son Kyle and abuse of any degree or description enrages her.

When, as a toddler, she set out across that vacant field in hopes of finding a horse, nobody realized she also had the future of a family in tow.

On her tenth birthday Nancy was given "the best present of my whole life" - membership to a week-long riding camp at St. George's Stables. At the end of the camp most of the girls were allowed to buy their horses, but her parents weren't yet convinced.

"My Grandpa Visser (Marg Southern's father Charles Visser who was affectionately known in the Calgary Oil Patch as "The Big Dutchman") took me out to an old cutting horse man who was a great horseman. His name was Bill Renaud and he had a horse named Connie Kil O'Bar, a world champion for about five years running," said Nancy.

He wanted $5,000 for the horse and Nancy's Dad made it clear there was no way he would spend that kind of money for a horse.

"So we ended up with a 14.3 hand Arabian-Welsh horse nicknamed Prissy. I thought she was wonderful but she definitely lacked talent. All I wanted to do was jump, and she wanted no part of it."

This all led to the purchase of a horse, through Mr. Joe Selinger, called Benny - a big lovable Hanoverian that forever changed the Southern family, and ultimately the face of show jumping in Calgary, Canada and the world.

"Benny really started it all," said Nancy. "He taught us everything that is precious about the horse and for almost thirty years was the silent inspiration that guided us."

Benny was born in Germany on April 14, 1963 and carried the name Sentgraf until his arrival in Calgary four years later. That was when he met his new owner, a spirited twelve-year-old who felt he "just looked like a Benny, so that's what I called him."

"He was a good keeper and ate himself sick on the boat," recalled Nancy. "He was so fat when he arrived . . . anyway there was no way I could sit on him and he was so big I really couldn't control him."

It didn't take long for Benny to shed the weight and show the spirit of a jumper capable of transporting a little girl and her dreams over the most distant of moons.

Nancy was not allowed to ride Benny for almost a year. She could walk him, feed him and groom him all day long, but she was not allowed on Benny's back.

Finally Nancy grew into the horse, and although Benny's gusto may have been under control, he was a long way from being docile.

"At first I didn't really ride him," Nancy now confessed. "He sort of carried me around the courses."

But that would change in a very dramatic fashion. It wasn't long before Nancy was confidently calling the shots, and together they notched significant wins at every junior jumping competition in the country. Their sights were firmly set on the open jumper ring.

"Riding was everything to me. Thinking back on it now, both my Mom and Dad were very good athletes and although I liked other sports, I wasn't that good at them. I didn't have the same co-ordination as they must have had, or as Linda has now. But riding was something I could do very well."

She tried every sport through junior high, but eventually concluded she was "a bit of a klutz."

"I was always a bit self-conscious of that, yet with riding and Benny I thought I could conquer the world."

Her world, however, took a nose-dive on an early June morning in 1970. While schooling Benny at St. George's Stables, she heard an ugly crack and felt Benny pull up. Although initial diagnosis revealed nothing serious, Benny stayed lame and it was decided to call in Dr. Barry Grant, a world-renowned large animal vet from Pullman, Washington.

A new set of x-rays was ordered and he discovered that there was a sagittal fracture of the long pastern bone. His verdict was the cruellest of all:

"The horse has to be destroyed."

Dr. Grant was with the Southerns when Nancy arrived home to hear of the grim decision. Bursting into tears she told them he would not be put down.

"He's mine and I'm not going to let him die."

Nancy would not listen to reason. At best, she was told, they could put the leg in a cast, but the horse would surely kick it until it shattered. A second possibility was traction, but Benny was so big that the resulting pressure sores would be cruel and unbearable.

And besides, operations on a break this severe were only experimental and carried no guarantees.

But Nancy had finally heard what she needed: there was an alternative that included a chance at life.

"I can say this now," Nancy confessed several years later. "At the time nobody in our family really knew that much about horses. If we had, we probably wouldn't have given the approval to go ahead."

They looked after each other, but together Nancy and Benny enjoyed some magnificent victories.

> "And then one day he (Benny) simply had enough and jumped out of his corral. It was his way of telling us to stop the nonsense and get on with the show."
>
> (Nancy Southern)

Benny endured an eight-hour operation. The bone had been broken in three different places and two galvanized compression screws bolted the splintered bone together again.

Benny stayed at the University of Washington for almost a year and Nancy fought to be there whenever possible. During his recovery he never walked for more than ten minutes a day, and doctors warned that even if he survived, he probably could never be ridden again, and most certainly would never compete.

Healing was slow, but steady, and finally Benny came home where he was restricted to a simple exercise program for another year.

"And then one day he simply had enough and jumped out of his corral. It was his way of telling us to stop the nonsense and get on with the show."

Benny and Nancy enjoyed almost another decade of competition before this courageous horse was retired. She had other horses in her climb to becoming one of the country's finest show jumpers, and on paper some of them were probably better than Benny, but she never had a better friend.

"They say every rider might be lucky enough to get one special horse. Benny was mine."

He passed away in 1993, leaving behind a legend of memories and a new definition for the word courage.

The two foundation stallions of Spruce Meadows, the Hanoverian Young Wolfsburg and the Thoroughbred Anforan, are the only other horses that came close to touching the heart of Spruce Meadows in such a profound manner.

Young Wolfsburg's gait was imperial as he strutted into a competitive ring. The sun would reflect radiantly off his burnished chestnut coat. Every rider, young and old, took note of his grandeur in hopes that someday they too would have a horse that delivered such perfection.

Brilliant in the ring, his jump was of such immense power that no fence seemed a chore. But he was also in great demand as a stallion, and with his mind focused on natural instincts, he often got into trouble within the ring.

Spruce Meadows Riding Master Albert Kley was the only one strong enough to control both the mind and the body of this superb Hanoverian, but even that was only on occasion.

Albert Kley and Spruce Meadows foundation stallion - Young Wolfsburg.

He was retired from the show ring after a career-ending injury in 1984, but he continued to stand at stud until his death almost a decade later.

The Thoroughbred Anforan beat the impossible odds on cancer after grooms discovered a huge lump on his jaw in 1982. A five-man surgical team was assembled, but no one held out a great deal of hope since the surgery being attempted was experimental and had only been previously tried on humans and canines.

Following a tracheotomy to allow breathing, his right jaw was removed except for anterior and posterior positions which were left to anchor the front and back teeth.

Although this courageous stallion survived the trauma of surgery, at one point it appeared he would starve to death because he couldn't swallow.

(photo by Rick Maynard)

Young Wolfsburg's power was awesome, but Riding Master Albert Kley was one of the few with the strength to handle him.

Oats dropped to the ground and hay clogged in his throat as his weight dropped more than three hundred pounds, to leave the stallion unable to walk.

Anforan was not the friendliest horse in the stable, but he was probably the most intelligent. His disposition towards handlers changed abruptly during the crisis, however, as he calmly and gratefully accepted their life-giving assistance.

A food mixture was finally found he could consume, and although recovery was slow, within the year he was back breeding.

From that day only one stallion is allowed to lead the Parade of Mares and Foals at a Spruce Meadows competition. Anforan had earned that honour.

After listening to many of the world's best riders describe the powerful attributes of a great jumping horse, one might be left to ponder just who - man or horse - is really in control.

Edmonton rider Mark Laskin is probably the most honest when he confessed his objective is simply to "co-exist with my horses." Never, he warned, try to dominate them.

"In the long run, when you really need something from your horse in a competitive situation, they must try as hard as you are. If you try to dominate them they say, 'no way' and just don't give the effort."

In developing a young horse, said Mark, every step must be a progression where advances are taken in small increments. That way if there is a regression, the horse only goes back one move instead of destroying the entire foundation of its training program.

Basically the rider/horse relationship comes down to "friendship," stressed retired Canadian team coach Tommy Gayford.

"I don't really know of any rider that doesn't consider the horse as their friend. But just like some kids, you still have to swat them on the bum once in awhile. Letting him bump into a fence now so he won't do it again, could save that horse from falling into a fence and really hurting himself in competition."

Canadian Show Jumping Team member Jay Hayes instigates every new alliance with a horse believing one thing: he will make that horse the very best it can be. "You can't make a normal horse exceptional, but you can certainly, through mistakes, make an exceptional horse normal. The key is to identify them, not ruin them," said Jay.

Spruce Meadows Riding Master Albert Kley believes training must start the day the foal is born. It does not need to be a formal program, only a simple case of touching the foal and sharing time with it to develop a lasting friendship.

"There must be no fear between the rider and horse, but that trust comes slowly."

A young horse shows strong promise during a free-jumping exercise in the Riding Hall.

Serious training at Spruce Meadows, said Albert, begins when the horse turns three.

There is no great rush at Spruce Meadows to get the horse into a competitive position. That is the general rule throughout North America, but does not hold true in Europe where horses generally are brought up through the jumper divisions at an earlier age.

As three-year-olds at Spruce Meadows, horses spend the first 12 months in a confidence-building program that also stresses muscle toning and general conditioning.

"At four years we start jumping and at five years they will start attending smaller tournaments. Keep to that schedule," said Albert, "and your horse will mature with a lot of confidence.

"If you don't, then you shouldn't be surprised when they stop. When that happens with a young horse it is almost always because of a rider mistake.

"A horse will always try to please its rider, but if you have made him scared, or if you have taught him poorly along the way, then a horse will stop. He won't if he is trained properly."

It is, Albert added, not unlike raising a child. If the trust between parent and child is ruined, it will take a great deal of time and patience to regain that confidence.

Look after your horse like he is your best friend, is the wisest piece of advice course designer Pamela Carruthers can give.

"The more you can be with him, the more you're going to get out of him in competition. They remember. Also be patient," added Pamela.

> **"When I was a kid the old horse dealers used to say that a show jumper should make a shape over a fence like cream being poured from a jug."**
>
> (Peter Churchill)

"You mustn't try to win all the time at any cost. If you gallop your horse off his feet in every preliminary class just to win money, it will eventually lose form. Only those people who have shown patience with their horses make the grade."

British author and sports journalist Peter Churchill spent the first half of his life riding horses. Now all of his time is spent writing about them, or broadcasting their accomplishments.

"Unlike in flat racing, where you ask a horse to run to a line as quickly as possible," said Peter, "show jumping asks the horse to behave in an unnatural manner.

"By asking a horse to jump man-made fences," said Peter, "we are also urging them to go against their natural instincts, as an animal is most comfortable within the protected confines of its herd. The horse, therefore, will only jump under the urging of man and this requires immense trust if any reliable degree of accuracy is to be achieved.

"There are," he added, "some horses that take that accuracy to an art form.

"I love to see the power of the horse coming up, the way he buckles those front legs as he goes into the air, gets on top of his fence, kicks the back end to the sky, and then softly comes down and lands.

"What," he challenged, "could be more beautiful?

"When I was a kid the old horse dealers used to say that a show jumper should make a shape over a fence like cream being poured from a jug.

"To learn," said Peter, "just watch the truly great riders - individuals like Franke Sloothak of Germany.

"He's a tall, big man, but he rides like he was six stone eight (ninety-two pounds). He's got a lovely light touch as a dancer would, as any artist would. He makes it all so simple. He's not pulling at the horses, he just presents them and then sits still as if to say 'You do the jumping, not me' and they do it."

Ron Southern is an intense student of the sport and acknowledges that the skilled rider - the man or woman who makes a living from show jumping - must have a horse of exceptional talent.

"But that isn't necessary for a junior or beginner. I don't think it wise, and I say this after having made the mistake myself several times. I too have bought some expensive horses, and without exception, all of them were bad horses," said Ron.

"I wish that I could say that I hadn't done that because I knew better at the time and I sure knew better after.

"Begin by finding a good trainer," he urged. "There is so much for the young rider to absorb, but the vast majority of it can be learned on very modestly priced horses.

"The problem today," he said, "is that everyone, and that includes riders and parents, wants to be competitive right from the start. They put up a lot of money, buy a proven horse, and are in the winner's circle the next day.

"My advice would be to bite your lip and don't follow that procedure . . . even if you can afford it," said Ron. "I believe that in the end you judge an athlete in this sport not by their wins, but if they are better people for the experience.

"If you tried as hard as you could, but still didn't win, you shouldn't be afraid of being beat. You're building character and you're building people.

"By buying the best, no matter what the cost," explained Ron, "parents are only teaching that child that success has a price tag, and that is a flaw that nobody should place on their children.

"The sport," he continued, "can be marvellous in the hands of a good trainer, but unfortunately many of them are only anxious to sell newcomers very expensive horses. Be very reluctant to such pressures," he cautioned.

Mark Laskin will get more out of a horse then most, but he also knows that people can buy their way to the top. That makes it difficult for him and others to stay competitive.

"You can manufacture winning riders. There's a system that allows you to plug in an average rider by mounting him on a great horse. As long as the rider

Through study and observation, Ron will always enrich his wealth of horse knowledge and on occasion will test his theories himself.

is even half-smart, he or she can win a Grand Prix.

"Because that individual is on a much better horse than the professional, who has vastly superior skills, the professional will still lose more often than not. If, however, you have a naturally gifted rider and put them on a great horse, then the programmed rider won't stand a chance."

The one thing Mark is most proud of is that his Grand Prix victories have been earned aboard several different horses.

"You can't," he said, "go looking for shortcuts in the development of a competitive horse. There simply aren't any.

"You always have to keep the big picture in mind with horses, and some people forget that and try to do it too fast. If you press too hard or too early, that horse will never turn out as well as it could."

Mark has been fortunate in dealing with owners who have shared this philosophy, and has never faced huge pressures to win every class or put ribbons in the tack room.

"You learn it's more important to win the big ones, but you can only accomplish this by allowing your horses to reach their potential."

And even if a superb horse is found, sometimes it's difficult to keep it around since few riders can afford such a financial luxury.

"Tomorrow I could walk out to the stall and have the vet tell me my best horse has developed arthritis in the coffin joint and it will never be the same again. In just a matter of seconds, the horse has gone from an Olympic prospect to a horse that is no longer saleable."

Selling was never a decision that had to be faced by Ian Millar about Big Ben. It wasn't even a distant thought. Officials, said Ian, must be aware of the fact jumping is all about show business and business in general. But it is also imperative they remember it is primarily about the sport.

"Let's remember who the king is. The king is our horse and the sport he provides. Everything else at a competition is only there to enhance it," said Ian.

"I never get the impression at Spruce Meadows that the horse and the sport are playing second fiddle to anything else. I always get the feeling that they are the focal point. To me that is very correct."

As he spoke Ian was watching his wife Lynn work with a young Thoroughbred on the lunge-line. He responded with remarkable insight when asked to describe what he felt as he watched.

"I'm seeing the horse's balance, his attitude, his learning abilities and how he understands Lynn's lessons. I'm looking to see how much co-operation there is in him, how tough and determined he is and yet whether that can be controlled so it becomes a liability."

Placing an evaluation on any horse - its mind or body - is both an intriguing and fascinating exercise for Ian Millar.

It helps him to understand, among many things, the element of danger attached to show jumping. Fortunately very few riders have suffered serious injury at Spruce Meadows, but Ian Millar's terrifying spill at the 1990 INVITATIONAL (NORTH AMERICAN) was probably the worst.

Riding a young speed horse called Domingo, the pair crashed with sickening speed into the Spruce Meadows wall. Ian was tossed like a rag doll into the solid wooden bricks, but Domingo amazingly avoided stepping on his unconscious rider.

Taken by ambulance to hospital, Ian was diagnosed with a severe concussion and, against a doctor's recommendation, flew home that night. Further testing at home revealed a far more serious brain hemorrhage that thankfully cleared with treatment. The injury, however, prevented Ian from competing in the 1990 World Championships in Stockholm where he had been among those favoured to win, since both he and Big Ben were performing as well as any other partnership in the show jumping world.

A terrifying moment for Ian Millar and Domingo.

(photo by Cansport)

Despite this near disaster, Ian Millar continues his flirtation with danger by placing his life in the hands of a horse several times every day. Even though he is as skillful a rider as there is in the sport, Ian knows that in any given year he will fall from a horse five or six times. Half of the tumbles will come when the horse inexplicably falls and the others will occur when he is caught off balance or something goes wrong during a ride.

As long as he can get up, it's never a bad fall.

"Why do we do it? That's an interesting question. We have this great big strong animal, who, it is said by some, has the intelligence of a four-year-old child. They operate most of the time on their own agenda . . . yet we do in fact trust our lives to them."

> "We have this great big strong animal, who, it is said by some, has the intelligence of a four-year-old child. They operate most of the time on their own agenda . . . yet we do in fact trust our lives to them."
>
> (Ian Millar)

Ian believes that in the final analysis the horse is a very gentle animal blessed with speed and the sharpest of eyesight to solve and avoid problems.

"They are," he added, "generally non-adversarial which explains why during training, horses would rather avoid testing their strength and determination against the rider's training techniques.

"That is why we're able to train them. They yield because they are easy-going animals that prefer to avoid conflict.

"The trick," said Ian, "is not to ever take advantage of the horse's good nature, but build upon it instead.

"I can't tell you the number of times in my career when I have fallen and the horses have turned themselves inside out to avoid stepping on me. Or if we fell together, those horses did everything in their power not to land on, or step on me.

"Horses also like to take care of themselves. If something goes wrong on course they will do whatever necessary to avoid danger . . . once again protecting the rider."

Ian is amazed by the forgiving nature of the horse.

It is tradition that a trainer gives novice riders a sequence of things to do correctly to evoke a certain response from the horse.

"That rider may get it wrong nine times in a row," said Ian, "and therefore gets either no reaction or the wrong reaction. But then on the tenth try the rider gets it right, and like magic, the horse reacts perfectly.

"I always marvel at that point. I think you are such a wonderful, generous and forgiving animal. You have gone through this exercise nine times and you patiently wait. Finally when they get it anywhere in the ball park you give them a 100 per cent good reaction.

"And please," implored Ian, "don't fight with your horse.

"To begin with you're probably wrong. It doesn't matter what the horse did, because even if you think you have won the fight, by that time the horse has forgotten all about why it started and hasn't learned a thing.

"Just suppose," he continued, "you could talk to a horse that had just endured a battle with its rider:

"Well, how was your ride? you ask.

"Terrible, responds the horse. I had this horrible fight with my rider.

"What was it about?

(photo by Tish Quirk)

By their expressions, neither John Pearce of Stouffville, Ontario nor Vagabond appear anxious to tackle the next fence.

The elegance of the Hanoverian stallion - Goodwill.

"I don't know, I forget.

"So did you learn anything from this fight?

"Yeah. I learned that my rider is a bad-tempered son-of-a-gun. Frankly it was all pretty negative and I'm not looking forward to tomorrow at all.

"But if you went to the rider and asked how it went, the response would probably be: It wasn't a good session because my horse wouldn't do what I had taught him. But I fixed him good and you can bet that tomorrow he'll be listening to everything I ask of him.

"There ain't," said the usually articulate Ian, "no art of training there.

"Quite often," explained Ian, "it is the horses with the worst reputations that turn out to be the best competitors.

"They're tough to train but when they walk into the competition venue they are all business. The footing can be deep or it can be slippery or hard. It can be far too hot or far too cold. But these horses always manage to find a way to fight for you and fight to be the winner. They are the special horses, the ones that come on strong. As the saying goes," concluded Ian, "it's not the size of the dog in the fight, it's the size of the fight in the dog."

Canadian national team coach Michel Vaillancourt will tell you that horses are his job. But great horses, he stressed, are his hobby.

"When I am given the opportunity of working with a great horse, that isn't work anymore, that becomes pleasure."

"It is amazing," said Michel, "to stop and think of what man can get a horse to do.

"Yet it is not the power of being able to control them that keeps you interested. It's a matter of really sharing with them, working with them, and appreciating what they can do for you."

He said it is interesting to note that while some horses perform better at Spruce Meadows than anywhere else, there are also some who will never perform well there.

"Rarely is a horse successful at Spruce Meadows the first time out. Like a young rider, they're not used to the large crowds. They sense the pressure as they walk into that ring."

Others thrive on the expectations that are generated by a boisterous crowd. Big Ben is probably his best example.

"Ben used to gain six inches just by walking through the Clock Tower."

"The best horses pick up signs of urgency from their riders," explained British coach Ronnie Massarella. "They can feel the adrenaline rush in their rider and prepare accordingly.

"Typically," he said, "a rider can compete at Spruce Meadows Wednesday through Friday without doing anything special, and then on Saturday and Sunday things explode.

"The whole thing changes, for horse and rider. Even I change. Instead of being quiet and placid I am agitated by the time Saturday arrives. If anyone says or does anything slightly off colour, I'm on their back. That's what big competition does to you and your horse."

He tells the story of British jumper Malcolm Pyrah who had come to the Spruce Meadows MASTERS just weeks after finishing second to Germany's Norbert Koof in the 1982 World Championships in Dublin.

Malcolm desperately wanted revenge for himself and Anglezarke, and the perfect opportunity beckoned in the du Maurier International. He advanced to the jump-off. Among the three German riders who also made it to the jump-off round was the outstanding Koof and his world-champion mount Fire II.

"I could see Malcolm there waiting

The very best of two decades have passed beneath the Clock Tower on the International Ring.

*Great Britain's
Malcolm Pyrah
and his moment of
revenge at the
1982 MASTERS.*

to go in and he was feeling mean", said Ronnie. "I told him this was his day, and that even though he had been beaten before, he now had the chance to show the world that he was still a winner."

"I could see Malcolm and I could see the horse. There was a tremble in the horse's legs and I knew Anglezarke was ready for the job that day. That's what is magnificent about these animals. They sense it. They sense everything about the big occasion. Some fall by the wayside because they can't live up to it. But great horses, they come on a great day."

Malcolm and Anglezarke went first and set a quick, clean pace. Norbert, the last rider out, blistered the track and was an unbelievable two seconds ahead of Malcolm coming up to the last fence. The tricky liverpool gobbled him up, however, and this time it was Norbert offering congratulations.

It is interesting to look at other finishers in that competition, one of the best du Maurier Internationals on record. The legendary Fritz Ligges of Germany was third, Canada's Mark Laskin on Damuraz was fifth and David Broome of Great Britain was sixth. It reflected a very elite and powerful international lineup for a tournament only six years old at the time.

"I knew that day Malcolm would win it," said Ronnie. "I can usually tell ahead of time how the horse is going to do.

"Stand at the gate," he said, "and watch the horses as they wait for the big class.

"The ones that go in and have a decent round, but have an unlucky four, they're the ones that have stood there placid and relaxed. But the good horse, he's on edge. You can see his legs moving. You can see his muscles rippling and you can feel his heart pumping. And as soon as he hits the public eye he knows he has a job to do."

How do you find them?

"You've got to be lucky to get a good horse. It's not money that finds them. I mean Milton cost nothing and I bought Mr. Softee for 360 pounds in Ireland as a four-year-old . . . and those are two of the best four jumping horses I have seen in the last quarter century."

The other two? Gem Twist (Greg Best of the U.S.) and Jappeloup (Pierre Durand, 1988 Olympic Gold Medallist from France).

Course designer Pamela Carruthers observes that horses are not unlike humans in that ". . . some are absolute fools and others are not."

"But you must have an intelligent horse that realizes his rider is going to give him the best opportunity. Many simply don't have the powers to cope with big fences in the same way some athletes can jump six feet and others can jump seven feet.

"But you can," she said, "communicate with a horse, and those that say they can't will never achieve anything but a minor role.

"And the horse will answer back. How? By not knocking down fences."

British broadcaster and author Peter Churchill also has trouble buying into the dumb animal theory.

"They do have a language, but we must be prepared to read it. If you're not perceptive enough to work out the dialogue flowing between you, you'll never get to the top.

"But it is there," he insists, "and it's a body language as well as a sign language.

"The horse," said Peter, "has lived with man for so long that we are now the substitute for his herd. Man is now his head stallion and everything in his life.

"I have seen remarkable intelligence in horses, to the point of what you could honestly and intelligently analyze as the power of reason."

But the great thing about the horse, he concluded, is that it is naturally people friendly.

"It's in their blood. They are no longer wild animals. They've been so domesticated it is part of their life that people are around. A horse won't fall back to the wild ways as your dog would.

"Professional horsemen cannot afford to wear their emotions on the sleeve of their riding coats. Yet many will tell you it's amazing what they feel while waiting to enter the ring on a 'big occasion' horse.

"You feel the horse come up from under you. They get those springs ready as if they're winding them like a watch coil. It's a fantastic feeling to ride down to a big fence and actually see what we call a stride, but in reality is the rhythm of a distance.

Doug Henry of Aurora, Ontario on Big Bird - the horse nobody but Doug could ride.

"And then the split second when you feel the power on the hind end come underneath you and the horse is in the air. The great horses for some reason seem to hang on top of the fence, It feels like ten minutes, but again it's only a split second," said Peter.

"For the professional," he added, "it isn't about love and devotion between horse and rider. It's about performance and loyalty.

"In the end Ron Southern was absolutely right when he introduced the word 'excellence' to describe what our sport can and should be all about. There isn't a better word."

Doug Henry of Canada is one of the truly delightful characters of show jumping, combining a bouncy sense of humour with a skill that kept him close to the top of the national circuit for almost three decades.

In 1985, at the tender age of 45, he arrived at the Spruce Meadows NATIONAL perched atop a 17.2 hand maverick named Big Bird.

Nobody knew much about this gangly horse, and that remained the case throughout the five-day competition because he didn't do much to draw attention. On the closing Sunday, however, Big Bird became very popular. He won the first ever $50,000 Chrysler Classic.

One reporter asked: "What can you tell us about this horse?"

The response, laced with humour and gilded in drama, was enough to make a Disney script writer writhe in envy.

"Big Bird," began his rider, "was initially owned by a trick rider whose only success was making the big animal buck . . . on or off command."

Between lessons, however, it was noticed Big Bird entertained himself by jumping between paddocks. The owner figured he should capitalize on this talent and began to show him at smaller jumping tournaments.

"The amazing thing," said Doug, "is that he would tie Big Bird to a fence post while he went about his business and the horse just stood there dozing like an old cow pony."

But he could jump and Doug was only one of several riders drawn to this strange creature who had been bred and raised in the wild. He half-thought about buying him, but before he could make up his mind a deal had been made with another rider.

The new owner, a young woman, couldn't stay on him. In fact, nobody else could either. But that didn't deter Doug Henry. He had liked what he saw earlier and bought the horse.

Big Bird was trucked to Doug's Aurora, Ontario farm and turned over to his top groom. "Ten minutes later she was on her way to the hospital, so I asked a second groom to climb aboard. She went to the same hospital as the first."

Doug knew at that point it had to be him. "I was running out of grooms and good help is hard to find."

He decided to train Big Bird in what would be his natural environment: a bucking chute. Slowly Big Bird accepted the weight of Doug on his back, and once he was aboard, the horse no longer had any desire to dump him.

"But I still have to mount him from a special box that I bring with me to every show. If I don't come down on him as light as a feather, you can kiss old Doug Henry goodbye."

> "I believe that Secretariat could have been a great jumping horse because horses with heart are horses that want to win."
>
> (John Simpson)

That delightful tale certainly substantiates the one contention of Irish coach Ned Campion that horses, like people, have vastly different personalities.

"They respond to different stimuli, or at least respond to the same stimuli in different ways," said Ned. "It becomes a measure of every rider's sensitivity as to how well they can gauge this in their horses and then utilize it to the maximum."

From the viewpoint of coaching, it's important that the coach can suit the rider's personality to that of the horse in an effort to bring them that much closer together.

"It's all a matter of experience and observing," said Ned, "and then measuring just how the animal interacts with the human."

He concurs with others who argue that the most common mistake, and unfortunately also the most crippling, is over-facing the young horse during its formative years.

"If a horse has a bad experience it will become defensive and will never be disposed of giving its best."

As a side note, the Irish Chef d'Equipe had an interesting theory on why it is best that riders own their horses, rather than ride on behalf of another.

"I think it might become a little bit like cars for rent . . . and I'm not sure just how well they would look after them."

Calgarian John Simpson rode Texas at the top of the sport for almost a decade and believes that great horses could probably have been outstanding athletes in any equine sport.

"I believe that Secretariat could have been a great jumping horse because horses with heart are horses that want to win."

John rode a half-brother to Texas called Dallas, a horse with a bigger jump then Texas, but one that could also go through a jump as easily as over it.

"Dallas had more power. When you sat on him it felt like you were sitting on steel. Unfortunately, sometimes, his brains were also steel."

Many of the world's most heroic show jumping horses have been huge, and from a Canadian perspective, certainly Texas and Big Ben fell into that category.

Swiss coach Charles Barrelet, however, is among those who don't see size as a major plus.

Nothing like a good scratch after a tough day on the job . . . access to horses is a bonus for Spruce Meadows fans.

"It's athletic ability," he stressed. "Size doesn't come into it. We have all seen small horses just barely over fifteen hands jump houses, while horses two hands higher couldn't get it together on even the smallest of jumps."

Charles said he preferred an average-sized horse for the same reasons human athletes of average stature usually dominate most playing fields.

"If you are too tall in any sport, human or animal, you must also be exceptionally co-ordinated to make it work."

Everyone has known natural athletes who didn't have the common sense or desire to capitalize on their athletic gifts. There are horses with the same problem. The horse with the biggest jump isn't always going to win.

"Horses and women," philosophized former Canadian coach Tommy Gayford, "make fools of the smartest businessmen. And the ladies can say that men and horses also fool the smartest of ladies."

"But there's something about a horse," he said. "I mean I love them and I'm an idiot. I'd never be in the sport if I ever sat down to figure the dollar return on my time, effort and everything else."

When he was only eighteen his father's secretary told him she was trying to determine precisely what the horses were costing and what his Dad was getting in return.

"I told her to stop it before my Dad fired her and killed me."

Canadian riding dean Jim Elder said it depends on what you are measuring the horse against when trying to determine its degree of intelligence.

"If a horse could live with you in the house like a dog, I am sure he would pick up on things: horse come here, horse do that. But mainly he learns by repetition.

> "I have never known a horse with a bad character simply because, if left alone, that would not be possible. When you say a horse has a bad character you are really saying that it has a temper created by a bad rider or owner."
>
> (Hans Britschgi)

"But they are all so different," said Jim. "Some you give just a light touch to move, and others you have to put spurs into for the same response."

You can suggest that Ian Millar's Big Ben is a very intelligent horse because he answers the challenge.

"But," stressed Jim, "you also must realize that Ian Millar prepared him for that challenge. Some horses will rise to the challenge naturally, others must be pressured into it."

And what about a horse's character?

There's no such thing according to Hans Britschgi, a Swiss-born international judge who has seen the best and the worst perform on every continent.

"But let me clarify that," said Hans. "I have never known a horse with a bad character simply because, if left alone, that would not be possible. When you say a horse has a bad character you are really saying that it has a temper created by a bad rider or owner.

"There are," he said, "three essential ingredients to a great show jumping horse: physical abilities, temperament and training.

"If the first two factors are good, then it is up to the human to finish it by showing patience and understanding."

Linda Southern is quick to agree.

"Horses are very much like children," said Linda. "You can mold them however you would like, within reason. Some are more timid, others very aggressive. You can work around some of those things, but I think their basic makeup is probably how they are.

"The secret," she added, "is not to try and dramatically change it, but have those differences work for you as a rider."

George Morris is a very pragmatic man. His directness is refreshing and because of his outwardly stern disposition, it is unusual to hear him suggest horses have a "magical affection."

"First of all they are so beautiful an animal, and they're unique in what they can do for people. I always tell riders that if they can use their own brain and the horse's body they will become one and then can accomplish anything."

Nancy Southern will concede that a horse is missing the pure qualities of devotion and commitment demonstrated by the family dog, but she will also argue that the bond with the horse is more powerful.

"It's almost stronger than a person bond, even a love relationship," said Nancy.

"A horse is something that you can't control. You can't even manipulate a horse. But you can have a horse work with you. It's the implicit trust that the horse has to have in you to do the things you ask."

It's also the joy of seeing your child's eyes light up when they see their first pony. And it's seeing the horse become the legs of a child otherwise confined to a wheelchair.

"It's so many things," said Nancy. "It's everything."

Ron Southern said he feels totally inadequate when in the company of competent horsemen. Through intense research and observation, however, he has learned far more about the horse than most men.

"I like the research and I suppose that is one of the reasons that I was attracted to the Hanoverian. The breed had a history where people had tried to develop the form and the function of the animal. That appeals to me."

He doesn't believe the horse is that intelligent, but like Jim Elder, he said it depends on how you define intelligence.

"The horse can do some reasoning, and is certainly a creature of habit. He really is a placid animal and I think he probably responds more to gentleness then he does to determined discipline.

"It is important," Ron continued, "that when the horse is young he is not abused, as success very much depends upon working with man as his partner.

"But as you might expect, the best performances of these two athletes only comes after numbing hours and numbing years of repetitive practice.

"The relationship between rider and horse," he said, "is not so much mystical as it is one of great respect and joy.

"I remember very vividly, a long time ago, sitting in a Calgary restaurant between Liz Edgar and Caroline Bradley, both representing the British team at the 1978 MASTERS.

"Certainly the two best women riders in the world at the time," said Ron, "they were talking about young horses and the pleasure they derived from them before being overtaken by the pressures and demands of competition.

"Those two riders talked of the joy and the frivolity of the younger animals and the fun they were having training them. And they moaned about losing this fun to the repetition necessary to prepare for competition. They felt sorry for the animals.

"That kind of feeling for the horse is remarkable, but it is one present in all the top riders. Some develop shells and affectations that won't allow you to get that out of them, but I believe it's still there with most of them," said Ron.

Saturday's Competiton

Herve Godignon of France wins the $60,000 Amoco Cup, and is brilliant in the process. Anytime you can win a competition of this calibre by almost two full seconds, you know you have presented the audience with a daring ride.

Michael Whitaker of Great Britain finishes second while Switzerland's Markus Fuchs holds on to edge Canada's Mario Deslauriers for third.

More amazing than the victory, however, is the size of the crowd. It's 12:45 p.m. and almost one hour before the Parade of Nations for the Bank of Montreal Nations' Cup event. But you can't get near the International Ring and nobody seems anxious to leave.

This has never happened before and polite ushers must inform fans there is no more room. Some head toward the parking lots, but the vast majority simply shrug and head over to the Amoco Festival of Nations or Equi-Fair. Perhaps the time has come for one of two things: more seating in the International Ring beyond the thirty-eight thousand now possible, or one hundred per cent reserved seating for major events of the tournament.

More grandstand seating is only possible by going up. At one point that would have been tragic since it would have distracted from the softness of the sweeping prairie landscape to the north and east. Now it doesn't matter as the only loss is a view of encroaching and monotonous subdivisions.

Those struggling to find space in the International Ring are fearful they will miss the

(photo by Rick Maynard)

Hollywood legends like Cary Grant usually ask for a low-profile visit and they always receive their wish.

farewell appearance of Ian Millar on Big Ben, scheduled to happen between the first and second round of the Bank of Montreal Nations' Cup.

Others just want to watch the parade and then they will back off to allow others in. The parade is a wonderful tradition that riders now tolerate far better than they did at first. They have accepted it as a rare opportunity to forge a visual link with the show jumping public, and their future is dependent upon that bond.

The parade is a marvellous event on its own with as many as four hundred and twenty horses often highlighted in a forty-five minute procession. Included in the parade are marching bands from around the world, ethnic dance groups and special guests ranging from royalty to national and international sport and political luminaries.

It's surprising how many movie idols have attended a Spruce Meadows presentation, but usually they beg for anonymity and watch from behind tinted windows. They include Cary Grant, Kirk Douglas, Olivia Hussey, Diahann Carroll, Christopher Reeve, Wilfred Brimley, Jennifer O'Neill, Jill Ireland, Charles Bronson and Kate Jackson. Mikhail Gorbachev and every Canadian Prime Minister since the mid-

seventies have been among the political luminaries in attendance. Even the Stanley Cup, flaunted by Edmonton Oiler forward Glen Anderson, visited Spruce Meadows as did figure skating stars from the past and present: Barbara Ann Scott, Kurt Browning and Elvis Stoijko.

Just moments before the 2 p.m. start of the Nations' Cup there are almost as many people outside the International Ring as in it.

Results of the first round are devastating for the pre-tournament favourites and the scene is building for a major upset.

Less than one fault separates the top four nations - Switzerland and France are tied with twelve each, the United States is in third with twelve and a half and Canada is in fourth with twelve and three quarters. Young Eric Lamaze has Canada's only clear aboard Cagney.

Ireland has an outside chance struggling in fifth with twenty-two and a half and the Brits are languishing in sixth with twenty-four faults.

Young musicians of the Calgary Round-Up Band pace a lively competitors' parade.

The final emotional appearance of Ian on Big Ben at his retirement ceremony in the International Ring.

But no one can believe the collapse of the powerful German entry. Together with the Mexican team, the Germans have been eliminated from the second round. Franke Sloothaak had his team's foremost effort, a very routine eight faults.

It will demand a close look at the entry list for tomorrow's du Maurier International. Did the Brits and Germans leave their best horses in the barns today to pursue a larger share of the huge $680,000 du Maurier purse tomorrow?

Actually not. The next day's entries will show that with the exception of Franke, who you will remember had the best round for Germany in the Nations' Cup, all others on the British and German teams returned Sunday astride the same horses.

There is a stir among fans closest to the entrance tower. They sense the arrival of Ian Millar and Big Ben and when the big Belgian-bred gelding breaks through the entrance way he seems slightly confused. His ears pierce the sky in a familiar hunt for the starting point of today's course.

But there will be no jumping today. And when Ben realizes it, you would swear he looks disappointed. You know that Ian Millar is.

Big Ben's spirit visibly lifts when applause rolls like thunder around the ring. The intensity is soon deafening and the loudspeakers must struggle with the music of the song, "Wind Beneath My Wings."

International rules state that at nineteen this magnificent horse is now too old to compete, but surely the calendar must be wrong. Today Ben has a child's bounce to his gait and Ian flows with him as lightly as a feather resting on a soft wind.

They stride with joy along the edge of the big ring, staring into the misted eyes of their legions of fans. Ben, so unsettled in his early years that he couldn't be ridden during victory parades, dips his head into the crowd like a spoiled dog in search of one more scratch.

Soon they find themselves at the top of the Spruce Meadows bank where they are joined for a brief ceremony by Marg and Ron Southern and Ben's long-time care-giver, groom Sandi Patterson.

Choking back tears, Ian quietly thanks those in attendance.

"For eleven years the mighty Ben has been coming to Spruce Meadows and he's being doing it for one reason . . . to jump for you Calgary, because you're the best show jumping fans in the world.

"He's been the wind beneath my wings for a long time and I know when I say that 'he's my hero' he's really a hero to all of us."

Moments later it appears that the ceremony is over, but Ian and Ben aren't about to close that final gate quite yet. They want one more tour around the ring that has been their playing field for more than a decade.

Ian kicks Ben into high gear and they explode at jump-off speed. As they enter the backstretch before the main grandstand, Ian's hands fall to Ben's neck. His smile is born of sheer gratitude as he gives Ben loose reins to enjoy those last seconds in a magical dash of unbridled freedom.

There truly is wind beneath his wings.

The second round of the Bank of Montreal Nations' Cup is about to begin when half a dozen members of the Spruce Meadows jump crew vault mysteriously over the east wall.

They run out about twenty feet into the course and, holding a rope, form a barrier in the shape of a half-moon. Several hundred fans rush onto the course and the open grass is quickly jammed. The Southerns have found a way to accommodate more fans.

As an experiment, the F.E.I. has decided today's Bank of Montreal event will be operated under a new "crowd-pleasing" format. Traditionally each nation will take a turn during each round of this competition, until just one rider from each country remains to go. Today all four riders from each nation are riding in succession.

It eliminates all of the doubt for the also-rans, but does heighten the intensity and drama towards the end of the competition for the contending nations. The teams return for the second round in the reverse order of finish from the first round.

The unlikely twist generated in the first round takes on even stranger dimensions in the second. The two teams tied for first, Switzerland and France, collapse and it is the two North American entries - the United States and Canada - that finish first and second. For the first time in nineteen years nobody in the media pool predicts the order of medallists in the Bank of Montreal Nations' Cup.

Ron Southern congratulates U.S. Chef d'Equipe George Morris. It is the fifth Nations' Cup win at Spruce Meadows for the Americans, but their first since 1988.

"I hope the Chefs will allow me to pay a special tribute to Canada," Ron Southern tells the crowd. "I can't go through all the nations assembled, but I think you will understand me when I congratulate Michel Vaillancourt and the Canadian team for an absolutely terrific performance in what I consider to be the toughest field that ever rode here."

The second place finish equals Canada's best ever showing in the Bank of Montreal Nations' Cup.

"Also, it's very rare to get a double clear round and I think we should all show Eric Lamaze of Canada, the only one to do that, a very special tribute."

At the press conference George Morris flashes only as much excitement as his reserved personality and lazy drawl will allow.

"I was hoping to do well. Our country has had so many problems over the last four years, it needed this shot in the arm. To win the Nations' Cup here is one of the blue ribbons of our sport."

Transplanted Englishman Tim Grubb turns in the strongest performance for the Americans aboard Elan Denizen. Tim, who emigrated to the United States in 1980 and took out citizenship in 1994, had only one down in the first round and then ices it for the Americans with a clean run in the second.

Tim says he made the decision to take out American citizenship when it became apparent he could no longer afford to take eight or nine weeks out of his life to return to England and participate in British selection trials.

"I didn't want to retire from top class international riding, but if I didn't return to England I was going to sacrifice any chance I might have of going to any championship in the future. That made up my mind for me."

Leslie Lenehan, anchor of the U.S. squad aboard Charisma, doesn't even have a chance to walk the course before the Bank of Montreal event. She is back at the barns nursing her second horse Lenny through a slight case of colic. Teammates fill her in quickly, however, and she records a pair of four fault performances, adding a quarter time fault in the second round.

While Eric's twin cleans were brilliant, strong performances are also recorded by Beth Underhill and Monopoly for the Canadians. She opens the class with four and three-quarters faults and repeats the effort in the second round. Ian Millar on Future Vision has a pair of knockdowns in Round One and three down for twelve faults in the second.

The final crowd estimate is just under fifty thousand. That is arguably low because so many people left when the main ring was stuffed to capacity. A crowd of closer to sixty-five thousand is probably more reflective of what is the largest crowd to ever attend a day of competition at Spruce Meadows.

Tomorrow, if the sun will again lead the way, should attract that many again to closing day action.

(photo by Cansport)

Canadian team member Beth Underhill enjoys the rewards of the 1994 Canadian Show Jumping Championship, including the use of a beautiful Chrysler convertible.

*Mother Nature has lost all battles to dampen
the enthusiasm of a Spruce Meadows crowd.
(photo by Garth Pritchard)*

Day Six
A Tournament of Milestones

They slosh across the parking lot like a family of happy ducks.

Rain drops, like tiny little brushes, slap at their faces in an unsuccessful attempt to scrub away infectious smiles. Their bodies are encased in plastic and they haven't bothered with umbrellas which would only slow their progress.

One carries a large sheet of heavy plastic to spread on the soggy grass bank of the International Ring, the family's favourite spot to watch a Spruce Meadows MASTERS.

"Why," they are asked, "would you come here on a day like today?"

The parents, appearing somewhat insulted by the query, turn to their teenage daughter to allow her the pleasure of an answer.

"Because our heroes are here," she replied in a matter-of-fact tone.

They left their southeastern British Columbia home before daybreak to attend today's final competition. They would have been here earlier in the week but business commitments made that impossible this year. Maybe next year.

"My daughter is fourteen and the horse is the common interest we share," stresses the father. "We're outdoors people. We don't have problems with bad weather."

A September rain in Calgary is unlike rain anywhere else in the world. It is not a warm, gentle mist that slips quietly over the mountains to caress the parched landscape below.

It is a mean-spirited leak that should be fixed. It is always just a degree away from turning to sleet, and it can never come on its own but must always be chaperoned by an equally nasty wind.

West Meadows wrapped in a rainbow.

And the rain loves show jumping. It hasn't missed a MASTERS in twenty years.

Bad weather has become a standing joke in Calgary. If this is rain, goes the refrain, then they must be jumping horses at Spruce Meadows.

The rain, of course, doesn't simply fall at the MASTERS. That would be too easy to deal with. It attacks in endless waves of assault, and when those troops are exhausted, Mother Nature sends in the heavy artillery: sleet and hail.

During the first few years fans did the sensible thing when bad weather struck. They went home. But as the sport's popularity took hold, the number of faithful bloomed and no weather system was tough enough to beat them.

The Southerns would constantly apologize for the poor weather and once were so concerned about the discomfort of fans that they handed out hundreds of free Spruce Meadows rain coats.

Only twice in the first two decades has an entire tournament played under a sunny blue sky. Both were NORTH AMERICAN presentations that happen to fall in that illusive time period known as summer, a span on the calendar that in Calgary can extend for either months or hours, depending upon the year in question.

Maintenance staff had to shovel snow off the International Course on Sunday, September 13 at the 1992 MASTERS. Hail had stripped flowers of their blooms in just seconds and jumps had to be secured with stakes to allow competition to continue.

But the weather has never succeeded in forcing Spruce Meadows to unravel the white flag. A major event has never been cancelled due to inclement weather.

Competition was once moved from the International Ring to the All Canada, where footing was only just slightly better. Another time an event was put on hold for more than an hour when the sky collapsed into a foreboding black hole. It eventually emerged, but only after a spectacular lightning show serenaded by thunderous rolls of drumming hail.

Ron Southern, like a sea captain in a hurricane, will always ride out the worst of any storm at the helm of the good ship "Playpen" in the middle of the International Ring. Usually he has convinced at least one sponsor to stay with him to accept the abrupt salutes of riders.

During a horrendous storm at the 1993 MASTERS, Jeffrey Chisholm, Vice-Chairman of Corporate Services for the Bank of Montreal, escaped between rounds of the Nations' Cup to the warmth of the media room. His shoes were so drenched he had to wring out his socks and paddled through the room naked from the ankles down. The colour of his face and hands blended perfectly with the chilled-blue of his business suit, but he asked for no favours. Just when it appeared circulation might return, he peered out at the course and couldn't believe his eyes.

"Rub-a-dub-dub" - 3 officials in a tub - Competitions Manager Bas French, Announcer Bill Kehler and Spruce Meadows Television V.P. Ian Allison.

"My gawd, he's going back. Don't bother with my socks, just give me my shoes."

Seconds later the sockless executive caught Ron at centre ring and within seconds was once again returning the salutes of unbelieving riders.

But they weren't alone. Like a giant box of mail, the fans of Spruce Meadows were always delivered. Neither sleet, nor hail, nor snow, nor fog stopped them from reaching their stated destination - a good day of show jumping at Spruce Meadows.

They are the most committed fans in the sporting world. Rain has emptied football stadiums in just seconds, yet you can drench, freeze or blow-dry a Spruce Meadows audience and it just hangs in for more.

And when Mother Nature finally gives up, sending Old Man Sol in to mop up, they cheer his arrival and unfurl their bodies like college students on Spring Break.

A rain squall that would at any other tournament chase riders to warmer and drier confines, has no clout at Spruce Meadows. In fact its intrusion seldom justifies even the limited comfort and protection of rain gear for the athletes. You don't see football players pounding it out in raincoats, and you won't often see riders jumping at Spruce Meadows with them on either.

At first they grumbled at the edict. But now, unless they're starting to dissolve, they know it's no use even asking if they can wear any rain apparel into the ring. The sport's stalwart image would definitely suffer if riders appeared on course looking like balloons tethered to their horses.

Ian Millar has endured the toughest of all elements at Spruce Meadows, but the strangest came one Saturday in a NATIONAL Tournament.

"The day had started off all right, a little cool perhaps but still reasonably sunny. I was second to go, and I wasn't liking the order because the sky was quickly becoming overcast."

The first rider, Laura Balisky of British Columbia, was quickly eliminated, pushing Ian into the ring even sooner than expected.

"It was starting to rain when I entered the ring and by the time I picked up my gallop into the first jump it was really snowing. I'm freezing to death. My hands are numb on the reins but somehow I go clean and in fact win the class."

The victory, however, is not why Ian relives the ride.

"When it came time for presentations the sun was beating down and it was as warm and as beautiful a Calgary afternoon as you can imagine," said Ian.

"I just thought at the time how the weather that day really was symbolic of the roller coaster which show jumping is on. It went from perfectly normal beginnings into the depths of despair and then finished on this sunny up-beat."

Comfort is the only order of attire at a Spruce Meadows tournament.

The Fans

Hopefully Ian's sun will find its way back to today's MASTERS. It's now 11 a.m. and the rain is coming down even harder, yet fans appear oblivious to it as they continue to pour through the gates. The question begs to be asked time and time again:

"Why are you here on this miserable day?"

The next to respond is a young Calgary couple who look like a rock concert would be more to their liking than show jumping.

"Last year we bought this blanket, this sweater and what else did we buy . . . anyway all in all about $100 worth of stuff to keep warm at the MASTERS. We didn't want it to go to waste, and besides my wife is a Big Ben nut."

Other responses?

"I wouldn't go to a football game in this weather, but for a Grand Prix I would sit all day in a snow storm. In fact we often do."

"Why would a little rain scare me away? I have a big heavy sweater and I have my umbrella. And besides, horse people are fanatics anyway."

"For the price you can't find anything to compare in Calgary. The service and the sideshows are unbelievable and we were lucky enough to get a sponsor's pass, so it has cost us nothing."

Finally, some people are seen heading back to the parking lot.

"Had enough of the rain, have you?" they are smugly asked.

"No, not at all," comes the cheerful reply. "We're just taking some of the souvenirs we bought back to the car."

The most delightful message erupting from these brief encounters is the realization of just how serious Calgary fans take this sport. If they were in search of only a pleasant day in the country, they would have bypassed Spruce Meadows today.

The day, however, still presents them with an opportunity to watch the very best riders and horses in the world. Apparently Mother Nature has nothing in her arsenal strong enough to stop them . . . or at least not today.

Bad weather at Spruce Meadows, it seems, is no more than a measuring device to test levels of fan sincerity. Today's readings have shot right off the scale.

The other thing you learn at Spruce Meadows is that bad weather is fickle. Just when it threatens to bring organizers to their knees in frustration, it abandons the area in its rapacious search for new targets.

More often than not, Spruce Meadows days that are traditionally spawned in the depths of despair usually manage to clamber up a ladder of sunshine, and hopefully today will be one.

Sponsors

One could never overstate the significance of the Spruce Meadows family of business, corporate and individual sponsors.

With one hundred and ten companies and businesses proudly associated with at least one tournament, and often all three, the allegiance has created the healthiest and most unique sponsorship program in sport.

When the Southerns realized operating costs in the first decade left them to absorb a $1.6 million shortfall, they also knew something had to be done about it or the facility itself could collapse.

It hadn't drained them of their last dollar, but it had virtually eliminated their life savings.

At this point in time (1985 and 1986) sponsorship was strong and had nothing to do with the incurred debt. There were, even then, long lineups of potential sponsors waiting in the wings. The problem was the opposite. There was no opportunity for growth since every competitive event was under full sponsorship.

These commitments helped defray expenses, but the vast majority of sponsorship funds was returned to riders in prize money. The Southerns were left to pick up all other expenses.

Although profit was never a motivation for construction of Spruce Meadows, breaking even at least was part of the plan. New revenue was imperative, and the Southern family think tank submerged for some serious deliberations.

The result was creation of new sponsorship opportunities that were not linked directly to competition, but to associated activities that still reflected the distinctive Spruce Meadows mystique.

Corporate sponsors, for example, were happy to attach their names to the plaza celebrations at all three tournaments. It proved to be a stroke of promotional genius for these companies since association with such a positive and fun-filled venue was like displaying your corporate logo at Disneyland.

It was found, in fact, that every special event had a strong, valued attraction to the family. Companies discovered there were huge benefits to be derived under any association with Spruce Meadows. It didn't come only as a sponsor of a major competition.

AGT quickly picked up the sponsorship package for the Battle of the Breeds, while Petford Resources enjoyed the fun of sponsoring the Spruce Meadows Prairie Dogs. The real Canadian Superstore, a major grocery chain, made a lot of friends sponsoring the best Stampede breakfast in the city during the NORTH AMERICAN, and Häagen-Dazs became the tournaments' official ice cream.

All riders and officials fly to Spruce Meadows on Canadian Airlines International and, as the official film supplier, all photos are taken on AGFA film.

NOVA literally jumped on the bandwagon picking up sponsorship of all marching bands appearing at Spruce Meadows, while Canadian Pacific gathered attention as patron of the Lord Strathcona's Horse, official honour guards at Spruce Meadows. And the list went on.

By 1987 Spruce Meadows was spending roughly $160,000 annually on newspaper advertising, yet event sponsors had never been approached to develop a cost-sharing program. Spruce Meadows' management organized a seminar to introduce the benefits of co-op advertising. It was so successful that it now costs Spruce Meadows only a fraction of what it once spent on newspaper advertising. The tournaments, however, are getting more promotional exposure through the medium then ever before.

"I've always felt that unless you have something that's economically viable, it's not sustainable," explained Ron. "It would be such a pity to have Spruce Meadows end when Marg and I aren't around."

The man who had generated financing strategies for international mega-projects on behalf of his own companies and those where he was a director, faced a new challenge. He had to find a financial security for Spruce Meadows that would extend through generations. "In the end," he stressed, "the best legacy Marg and I can leave for Spruce Meadows is a pool of young professional people, together with an economical, viable base. You need both."

When they first discussed plans for Spruce Meadows, the Southerns went to Revenue Canada and told them of their goals.

"They too are fans of Spruce Meadows, but the law is clear. You have to have a reasonable expectation of making a profit, otherwise you can't deduct all of these expenses. When I pay $1.6 million, I'm taking an $800,000 tax write-off, and they don't want that."

When time ran out, it created a crisis in their lives, but it was a crisis whose solutions led to a positive experience.

"I've always felt that in the end you can't do anything about dying," said Ron. "But problems are a different thing, and most can be solved if you reveal them and then go after them using people of good intent and great enthusiasm."

Concerns, not then and not now, are never hidden from Spruce Meadows' managers and staff. The Southerns met with key personnel and told them specifically what had to be done while also encouraging them to pass the word on to those who worked for them.

The solution, perhaps obvious now, surfaced only after countless hours of debate and close scrutiny. Spruce Meadows had to generate more revenues and the best opportunities rested with television and new sponsorship concepts.

With few exceptions, Spruce Meadows did not have to actively solicit new sponsors. Instead, interest was generated by creating opportunities for those companies who were already waiting in line, or had made earlier inquiries.

"We weren't aggressive in our pursuit of new sponsors because most of them came on their own volition," said Ron. "Once here, then we would pursue them. But we didn't go and search them out. They came to us and said they must be involved at Spruce Meadows because there was a good fit with their corporate image."

The campaign did succeed and everyone - Spruce Meadows, the sport, the riders and the sponsors - continue to benefit.

The money crisis had cooled by 1994 and the financial security of the facility was solid, and will remain so for generations to come.

During its first two decades, Spruce Meadows lost only a handful of sponsors and they withdrew due to internal economic adversity. No one has ever left in anger or after expressing disappointment with the treatment and benefits their company received.

Describing the Spruce Meadows corporate lineup as "family" is not excessive. It is, in fact, a term favoured by the sponsors themselves once they've been exposed to the Spruce Meadows experience.

There is a sense of belonging that runs far deeper than a cheque book, and it probably will never be fully understood except by those who have been participants.

No one expressed it with more sincerity and grace than the late Wilmat Tennyson, President and COO of Imperial Tobacco. What began as a business strategy in the early eighties, blossomed into a friendship of intense mutual respect.

The Southerns came to appreciate Wilmat Tennyson for his extraordinary vision and marketing brilliance. They cherished him and his wife Helen as the closest of friends because of their remarkable gifts of commitment and belief in Spruce Meadows.

"The du Maurier contracts Wilmat provided to Spruce Meadows granted us the stability needed to convince others to participate and invest. With that kind of an anchor in place, it really pushed others through the threshold of believing," said Ron.

Money definitely talks. When the du Maurier International offered prize money of $506,000 in 1988 to become the richest show jumping event in the world, it gave Spruce Meadows and the MASTERS a credibility that most believed would never grace the sport of show jumping.

In that one day, it joined golf, tennis and motor car racing as a big ticket sport. The full impact of that move is still being felt, and will for years to come.

Wilmat Tennyson refused, right to that untimely moment of death, to claim even a hint of the credit.

"I always remind myself that I was only the messenger with other people's money," he insisted. "I don't claim any personal credit for that at all. I just thought it was an extremely fortunate convolution of circumstance among like-minded people."

His reward, and also for his wife, went far deeper than commercial riches or recognition.

"We took to the Southerns, and to their children," he said. "We found a kind of haven of enjoyment and achievement in this relationship.

"It was through the funds that were made available to us that we could achieve something we felt was truly wonderful. I don't want to sound like an Amish preacher," said Wilmat, "but I never thought of our sponsorship at Spruce Meadows in commercial terms."

Instead he reflected on the inferiority complex Canadians have about themselves and saw Spruce Meadows as an opportunity to show the rest of the world "we can do something really good."

His first meeting with Ron Southern came just moments before dusk gave one final summer brushing to the Spruce Meadows landscape. He had spoken to Marg a year before to settle on a "modest sponsorship" and recalled the difficulty justifying the sponsorship to those in the company who believed show jumping was a Toronto-based elitist sport.

"As we walked through part of the undeveloped acreage, Ron talked about his dream. He said it would become the most respected show jumping venue in the world, and beamed when describing what it would mean to the people of Calgary and Alberta."

> "It was just another way of demonstrating that once you get involved with the Southerns and the prevailing sentiments at Spruce Meadows . . . you get caught up in a wave."
>
> (Wilmat Tennyson)

Ron can, said Wilmat, become "very dramatic if he wants to."

In a whisper he leaned toward Wilmat: "Can you hear the crowds cheering? Can you see the flags? Can you see the cars in the parking lots?"

"And of course by that time I could . . . Ron Southern is one hell of a salesman.

"Sure he put the arm on a lot of people. So what? You can't admire people that don't do that. I mean he makes Lee Iaccoca (former Chrysler CEO) look like an amateur."

"Much of what Ron achieved at the sponsorship level," added Wilmat, "was done through creative, corporate power politics.

"But there were no false promises. The only promise he made to me was: 'If you and I are going to do this together, I'll do my part, you do your part, and together we'll make this the best in the world.'"

And when they got there, Ron never re-visited the proposition.

"He never came back to me to say: 'By Gawd, we've done it'. But that's him. That's history. What about tomorrow?"

For Wilmat it was all reinforced the first time he arrived to officially represent du Maurier at a Spruce Meadows MASTERS. Although he retired in 1992, it was a trip he would continue to make until his death in 1995.

"Ron was talking to the crowd and telling people if they liked to ride and didn't have a horse to come on out and he'd put them on one. Bring your mother and father, brothers and sisters and enjoy a picnic at Spruce Meadows.

"To me," said Wilmat, "it was unbelievable that a man of his stature would be so magnanimous toward people, and I was genuinely impressed with his unadulterated love for them."

Wilmat recognized in both Marg and Ron their need to give back some of what life had allowed them to achieve.

"That really set Helen and I on a roll as far as Spruce Meadows was concerned. After that, things happened so rapidly."

Wilmat recalled the MASTERS' Press Conference of 1987, the year after Gail Greenough of Edmonton won the World Championship.

"In an unguarded moment I told the reporters what an honour that achievement was, and because of Gail Greenough du Maurier would increase its prize money in the du Maurier International by $250,000.

"It was," he explained, "just another way of demonstrating that once you get involved with the Southerns and the prevailing sentiments at Spruce Meadows, you get caught up in a wave.

"To be part of Spruce Meadows," Wilmat continued, "makes one feel good about yourself. That's about the best way I can explain it."

1986 World Champion Gail Greenough of Edmonton, Alberta - the only Canadian and the first woman to win a World Championship.

Over the years it was remarkable that no one went searching for issues that might bring controversy to Spruce Meadows, or to those associated with it.

That is not to suggest there are any skeletons hidden in a Spruce Meadows closet. But the presence of a tobacco firm as a major sponsor had certainly launched missiles of discontent among other sports.

Tobacco companies have struggled world-wide with a poor image, yet it never became an issue at Spruce Meadows. That is probably due to one-of-a-kind ground rules established between Wilmat and the Southerns at the outset of their sponsorship agreement.

"If you go back through the archives you will find that we never showed a package of cigarettes in any Spruce Meadows events," said Wilmat. "We never asked any athlete to smoke or show tobacco products or even packaging. I tried to stay as far away as possible from the product itself and to weave an image, a dream around Spruce Meadows itself.

"It would not have worked, or been accepted by the Southerns, if du Maurier had insisted on the traditional approach to sponsorship," said Wilmat.

"I was overly concerned and I think that made the sponsorship acceptable to both Marg and Ron," he said.

From a corporate standpoint it worked wonderfully.

"By inference it helped place the product of sponsor, despite what that product was, on a pedestal."

It is customary at every presentation ceremony for the Southerns to present sponsors with a bouquet of flowers. Helen Tennyson has received far more than any other. What she did with her flowers, however, was noticed by only a few.

Nobody told Helen to do this, but by instinct she always surveyed the scene of people standing behind her at the barrier around the ring. She would then make a mental note of where one elderly lady was standing, and when the ceremony was over - and when no one noticed her doing it - she would walk up to that lady and give her the flowers. Usually the result was instant tears.

When Wilmat questioned his wife about it, she told him that was her symbol of Spruce Meadows.

"You take and you give. Those ladies will remember those flowers for the rest of their lives. That's what the Southerns do to you."

The relationship with Spruce Meadows and its people had an immense impact on Wilmat and Helen Tennyson.

The Horses are Coming

FINAL OLYMPIC TRIAL
CANADIAN CHAMPIONSHIPS
SPRUCE MEADOWS 'NATIONAL'
JUNE 3-7

HIGHLIGHTS OF THE TOURNAMENT

Wednesday, June 3, 1992
5:00 pm LUSCAR "Welcome"
7.00 pm INVESTOR'S GROUP "Welcome"

Thursday, June 4, 1992
5:00 pm NORTHWESTERN UTILITIES &
CANADIAN WESTERN NATURAL GAS
COMPANY LIMITED "Blue Flame"
7:30 pm CBR CEMENT "Challenge"

Friday, June 5, 1992
5:15 pm WIRE ROPE INDUSTRIES
Intermediate "Strength"
7:00 pm NESBITT THOMSON "Canadian Cup"

Saturday, June 6, 1992
11:30 am SMIRNOFF "Cup" – Parcours de Chasse
2:00 pm ROYAL BANK "World Cup"
Olympic Trial

Sunday, June 7, 1992
12:15 pm ATCO ENTERPRISES Double Slalom
2:30 pm $100,000 SHELL CUP – Derby

South on Macleod Trail, west on Hwy. 22X • General Admission $5.00, Seniors and Children Free
• Tickets available at the gate

Canadian ◆ 🐚

WIN! A TRIP FOR TWO,
ENTER AT
SPRUCE MEADOWS
CANADIAN AIRLINES
COFFEE HOUSE

$1500.00 FORMULA SHELL GASOLINE
ENTER ON SPRUCE MEADOWS DAY SHEET

du Maurier Arts Ltd.

🎵 FESTIVAL OF MUSIC 🎵

BAND CONCERTS, PETFORD PRAIRIE DOGS,
MUSIC, PARADES, ENTERTAINMENT & MORE!

FREE SHUTTLE BUS
Friday: 5:00 pm – 9:30 pm
Sat & Sun: 10:00 am – 6:30 pm
From Anderson LRT, courtesy of
Pacific Western Transportation.

A co-operative advertising program has greatly increased pre-tournament exposure.

SPRUCE MEADOWS

The Horses are Here

SPRUCE MEADOWS
July 6th - 10th

NORTH AMERICAN CHAMPIONSHIPS
Tournament Highlights

WEDNESDAY, JULY 6
4:30 pm	Zeidler Forest Industries "Cup"
7:15 pm	LaFarge "Cup"

THURSDAY, JULY 7
4:30 pm	Home Oil "Stake"
7:30 pm	Interprovincial Pipeline "Cup"

FRIDAY, JULY 8
11:30 am	Trimac Jumper
2:30 pm	Canadian Western Natural Gas "Blue Flame"
5:00 pm	Alberta Treasury Branches "Albertan"
7:15 pm	Western Gas Marketing "Cup"

SATURDAY, JULY 9
9:30 am	Frontec Jumper
11:30 am	Northern Telecom "Direct"
2:00 pm	Queen Elizabeth II "Cup"

SUNDAY, JULY 10
9:15 am	Sunlife Jumper
10:45 am	Canadian Pacific "Cup"
12:45 pm	Pulsar International "Challenge"
2:00 pm	Mexico Day Ceremonies
3:15 pm	Chrysler Classic "Derby"

Red Arrow Shuttle Bus from Anderson LRT Friday evening, Saturday, Sunday 10-6.
Tickets available at the gate.
General Admission $5.00. Seniors and Children Admission Free.

8015T990

Tournament advertising always tries for balance among key sponsors.

"It's probably one of the two great satisfactions in my life . . . my wife and Spruce Meadows," said Wilmat. "I grew up in South Africa and have no family or relatives here. It was only when I became sixty-five years old that I realized I had no village. I had no family farm to go to and I had no roots. That's the price you pay for the fast track life."

Spruce Meadows became his family village.

As a final wish, Wilmat did return to Spruce Meadows one last time. His ashes will forever be part of the facility and sport he so dearly loved. The Riders' Chapel dedicated in his name beckons as the focal point of the village this extraordinary man called home.

In 1985 Xerox Canada Inc. went on the hunt for perspective board members. As with many companies before and since, Ron Southern's name was at the top of the list.

Dave McCamus, President & Chief Executive Officer of Xerox Canada Inc., had gone to great lengths in searching for individuals he felt would bring the appropriate Canadian representation to the Xerox Canada board.

But, explained Kevin Francis, Vice-President and General Manager of Xerox Canada, as his boss recruited Ron Southern, Ron was also recruiting Dave McCamus. Both came away happy.

"Once on board, Ron promptly invited Dave out to Spruce Meadows," said Kevin. "He was just blown away. He had never seen anything like it."

The impact of the meeting came as no surprise to anyone. Ron Southern, said Kevin, is probably one of the best marketers in the world, and so is Dave McCamus.

"The two of them were dangerous together. They came up with every wild idea imaginable," said Kevin.

Xerox was looking for ways to position itself regionally, but in such a way that some national value would also be realized. The company's initial commitment to Spruce Meadows began modestly with a junior riding scholarship. It quickly expanded into something called the "Xerox Fax," a highlights package featured on all "Spruce Meadows Today" programs.

Before long the company had added a horse, Spirit of Xerox, ridden at international levels by Linda Southern-Heathcott. All of Linda's competitive horses are now sponsored, an enviable position for Linda and one that more and more riders are moving towards. From a Xerox perspective, the rider/horse relationship provided some significant wins.

"Spruce Meadows has a national forum, yet it also has enormously high regional content," said Kevin. "To Calgary firms, the facility is a fantastic and highly sought after event to participate in. Residents of the city are passionate about the place and take an enormous amount of pride in what's being accomplished.

"Spruce Meadows," he added, "may be owned and run by Marg and Ron Southern. But make no mistake about it, Calgarians call it their own."

Tournaments provide Xerox with high profile venues in which to showcase technology, whether it's facsimile equipment, work stations, laser printers or colour technology.

> "Ron got up in the middle of the field and without hesitation told fans to 'fly Canadian.' He told them Canadian Airlines was supporting the sport they loved, and deserved their patronage in return."
>
> (Charles Barrelet)

"That's wonderful exposure for us - an international media centre where people can experience what Xerox can do in document intensive application."

It also enables a sponsor like Xerox to get its major customers out of the office and into a setting they enjoy. It's far better than a downtown lunch, primarily because it allows all family members to participate.

Despite these many successes, however, Kevin doubts if Xerox would become involved with any other show jumping venture.

"For us I don't think it's about horses and I don't even think it's about show jumping per se," he explained. "It's about what Ron and Marg have uniquely done in Calgary. That's what we want to be part of.

"There is no such thing," he suggested, "as being a little bit involved with the Southerns.

"I mean you just jump into the deep end of the pool and learn real quick," said Kevin. "There's no wading, no putting your toe in to test the water. As a result, everybody becomes an ambassador for Spruce Meadows.

"By comparison," Kevin said, "although Xerox is also involved with sponsorship at the B.C. Open, it's just not the same.

"We sign up, give them a cheque, enjoy a couple of photo opportunities . . . but it's a golf game. There's no passion about it, it's strictly a business.

"Spruce Meadows is definitely different," said Kevin.

"You're proud to be part of it and you talk to people about it. You know, when Dave McCamus told me ten years ago we were going to do this I thought he was nuts. And now listen to me. I can't believe I'm saying these things."

And make no mistake about it, tournament organizers around the globe look on at such testimonials with varying degrees of envy. They often won't admit it publicly because that would be admitting to failure on their part. Yet in their desperate search for clues as to why it hasn't happened at their venues, they overlook the obvious.

The lessons to sponsorship success are as naked as the blank cheques in their wallets. They are plainly dealt out three times a year at the Spruce Meadows tournaments, and all people must do is open their eyes to the sights around them.

In the final analysis there are no secrets to sponsorship success at Spruce Meadows. The Southerns and staff simply treat all sponsors with the respect and attention they deserve. Sponsors are, after all, the economic life-blood of any tournament, and ultimately of the sport itself. Why would anyone want to do it differently?

An example?

Swiss coach Charles Barrelet will never forget the words Ron delivered spontaneously at an early nineties MASTERS competition.

It was a Friday night and most of the 20,000 who had just watched a Canadian Airlines competition were still on hand for the presentation. Primarily this was because an opportunity to win air tickets for two loomed in their future. But over the years more and more fans had come to appreciate these ceremonies and stick around for them.

Charles remembered that Canadian at the time, like so many other airlines around the world, was in a tough spot economically.

"Ron got up in the middle of the field and without hesitation told fans to 'fly Canadian.' He told them Canadian Airlines was supporting the sport they loved, and deserved their patronage in return. It was, he added, their Western airline and they should all be proud of that fact.

"I've never seen that done anywhere else in the world," said Charles. "Ron Southern is definitely the master and has set an example for the rest of the global riding community."

Companies become involved in sponsorship programs for many different reasons, some of them knowing from the outset that no commercial benefit will accrue to them from the relationship.

The Ritchie family of Edmonton financially endorsed junior jumping for almost fifteen years and sought nothing in return other than the satisfaction of helping young riders.

Donna Marshall, the personification of calmness in Central Communications at Spruce Meadows, said she and her husband decided to corporately sponsor a class as a way of returning something.

Promotion for the family's energy company, Blake Resources, was very secondary in their minds, said Donna.

"With four daughters riding, we felt very privileged to have a facility like this in Calgary. We just felt like giving something back, and while it wasn't a huge sponsorship, we enjoyed doing it."

Ian Millar reflected back to a press conference presided over by William Mulholland, now retired, but at the time Chairman of the Board of the Bank of Montreal.

He made a couple of points regarding the sport and sponsorship that impressed Ian, points that still hold a great deal of validity.

"Show jumping," said the Bank of Montreal executive, "is a sport where Canada is perceived to be internationally competitive. . . as opposed to something restricted only to national prominence." His bank valued a connection with something that Canadians did on a world-class level, "

The second point, he touted, focused on show jumping as a sponsorship bargain. If a company put an equal amount of money into tennis, he suggested, the impact would hardly have been noticed.

But in show jumping the money went a lot further and presented the bank as a major sponsor.

Since that meeting, the sport has captured substantial global television coverage out of Spruce Meadows, as well as international attention from the print media.

Bill Mulholland was bang on. The worldwide exposure, when compared to the dollars spent, was the advertising bargain of the eighties and nineties.

"That," emphasized Ian, "is how the sport must continue to be sold to new advertisers. Of course, there's nobody better at it than the Spruce Meadows team."

Jeffrey Norman, a Vice-President of Sunlife of Canada, remembered that his company's introduction to Spruce Meadows also began in a very small way.

"But then Marg and Ron dropped by my office in Toronto for a casual visit. Before it was over we had written a sponsorship contract out in long hand," said Jeffrey.

"And that was it. No lawyers . . . just a handshake. To this day that is still our contract."

Such closure would normally never occur in today's business climate.

"But they are so remarkable. It just seemed like the most natural thing in the world to do. I've never even considered doing that with anyone else."

Texaco Canada, before being absorbed by Imperial Oil, sponsored ninety per cent of all events in the old Spruce Meadows JUNIOR and Spruce Meadows INVITATIONAL

The world class level of competitors and sponsors is reflected in this attractive MASTERS advertising.

tournaments. After the merger, the sponsorship commitment continued and actually expanded to include several pony, junior and amateur events as well as the Grand Prix in Phase I of the NORTH AMERICAN.

Ernie Wood, Director of Public Affairs for Texaco at the time, negotiated that original sponsorship with Spruce Meadows and worked creatively to find new ways of involving as many employees as possible.

Texaco became the first company to fully exploit its sponsorship as a means of rewarding workers. Company picnics during the junior competition were huge successes and large hospitality tents played host to a wide cross-section of employees rather than just executives and selected guests.

Other corporations soon picked up on the Texaco experience and sponsor-hosted

Today, twenty years later, Marg Southern still writes personal letters to every official, every volunteer and every sponsor. Even her own daughters and their husbands get a note of gratitude from Marg at the end of each tournament.

receptions for employees are now commonplace at all tournaments. For Ernie Wood, the most accurate measurement of sponsorship success is the number of pluses or "add-ons" that you can get out of it.

"It's very easy for any corporation to give money and say 'here you are, now do your own thing.' If you want real value, however, you've got to build on that money."

He recalled a conversation with du Maurier's Wilmat Tennyson who advised him to spend $2 for every $1 actually put into a sponsorship.

"He was right. You have to be prepared to do that sort of thing," said Ernie. "Make people feel good about your company and the products that you're selling and at the same time involve the employees and make them feel good about it as well."

The value of a dollar, yours or someone else's, is something the Southerns respect. They take nothing for granted and deeply appreciate the personal sacrifice and commitment that must be exhibited before there is any corporate or personal profit. Marg said they also learned very early in the game that if you want to ask for funding, no matter what the purpose, you had better be ready to thank those who provide it.

She recalled a phone call in 1978 from one of the sponsors she had written to thank for supporting that first year of competition.

"He told me he had been involved in another sponsorship for ten years, yet had never received so much as a thank you. They'd always ask for more money, but no one had ever taken the time to write him a letter and simply say 'thank you,'" said Marg.

Today, twenty years later, Marg Southern still writes personal letters to every official, every volunteer and every sponsor. Even her own daughters and their husbands get a note of gratitude from Marg at the end of each tournament.

"That is extraordinary," said Ron, "but that's the definition of excellence Marg follows - going far beyond what anybody would ever expect."

New opportunities and ideas were presented to potential advertisers and sponsors during a unique Advertising & Promotions Symposium in the transformed Spruce Meadows Riding Hall.

Nancy Southern says there has been a noticeable "shift of intent" when one begins to compare the motivation behind sponsors who join the fold now and those who came on board in the seventies and early eighties.

As examples, she draws on the richness of the experiences shared with people like the late Wilmat Tennyson of Imperial Tobacco and Bill Mulholland of the Bank of Montreal - certainly the flagships of the Spruce Meadows sponsorship fleet.

"I believe that Mr. Tennyson came here as a bit of an opportunist, which is not a bad thing," said Nancy. "He was looking for the right thing for his company.

"But what he found quite shocking was an alliance that went far beyond just a good business opportunity. He discovered care and sense of belonging. I think the relationship really changed the lives of both he and Mrs. Tennyson, and it certainly changed our lives."

With the Bank of Montreal, show jumping sponsorship was something the bank was already into, so becoming involved with Spruce Meadows loomed more as a continuing obligation rather than as a unique and new opportunity.

"But the same thing happened. Mr. Mulholland (an avid rider) found a place to belong and something he really enjoyed and wanted to be part of.

"There are," Nancy concluded, "two types of sponsors at Spruce Meadows: the ones who felt obligated, and those who are looking for a different opportunity.

"Today's sponsors," she suggested, "begin the sponsorship process by looking for business opportunity. It's the way the Spruce Meadows experience enhances that process that elevates its sponsorship program above all others.

"And what is truly wonderful, is the continuing visibility at Spruce Meadows tournaments of most of those earlier traditional patrons.

"Many of those men who started off with us are still around and they have an esteem about them that does not go unnoticed in the eyes of the next generation of businessmen," said Nancy.

The presence of corporate mentors, and the way they relate in such a uniform and comfortable fashion to Spruce Meadows, serves as a valuable learning tool to the anxious crop of younger executives.

"They quickly understand that this is much more than just a business opportunity. It's wonderful that we have the two generations now while my Mom and Dad are still so active. New people can see for themselves that it isn't just a matter of dollars and cents and the competition," said Nancy.

"That's the thing that Linda and I will have to try and create . . . to make certain that the new understands why the old are still here . . . and why that is so vital to our success and viability."

Britain's Ronnie Massarella casts a sensitive eye toward sponsorship. He strongly feels that, at least on a global basis, the sport of show jumping does not treat its sponsors very well.

"Having said that, the best in the world are Marg and Ron Southern and their staff. They're artists at looking after sponsors, absolute artists. Look at the comfort provided, the food. Always give them value for their money and send them home with sweaters, a jacket . . . always something special to remember the day."

With very little coaxing, his riders spend more time with sponsors at Spruce Meadows then at any other tournament in the world.

Why?

"Because the Spruce Meadows sponsors have more time for our riders than anywhere else. A lot of people come in with their company's money, give it to you, and that's it. But here they are interested in you.

"And don't ever think you can fool a sponsor into believing the sport or venue is something it isn't," warned Ronnie.

"These people with money, they earned it the hard way. They are on top because they are tough, astute businessmen. As much as they love the sport, they also must know that the man who is in charge will give them value for their money."

Sometimes it's the little things you do for people, that when stacked, make you significantly taller than your competition.

Riders cannot put coolers on their horses for presentation ceremonies or ride with

Paul Hulburd of King City, Ontario salutes sponsor during the traditional Victory Ride.

coolers on their horses during parades at Spruce Meadows. It wouldn't serve anyone's interests if the president of a company handed out a cheque to a rider whose horse was decked out in his competitor's blanket. The best way to avoid that embarrassment is simply not to give it the opportunity of happening.

No rider is ever excused from a presentation ceremony or a parade. At Spruce Meadows you compete for more money than offered anywhere else in the sport. That money comes from sponsors who should expect no less than having riders turn up in person to accept it. No excuses, thank you very much. Miss a presentation and your winnings are automatically forfeited.

> Those who use only dollar signs to measure the success of Spruce Meadows are destined to fail miserably in their attempt to emulate that success.

All competitions will begin on time. Sponsors are business people and they're used to keeping appointments. If you tell them the class will end at a specific time, make sure that happens.

All salutes will be taken by the event sponsor, not judges as at every other tournament. Officials at Spruce Meadows' tournaments are professionals and they are paid to be the best. Why would you salute them and not the people who are providing the money that makes all of it possible? Saluting the sponsor has great public relations impact, yet costs nothing.

Spruce Meadows announcers don't wait for official scores to be calculated by judges before making the announcement. Announcer Bill Kehler is quite capable of counting faults, and if he is wrong, he will correct the error immediately. If he hasn't announced fault totals within twenty seconds of the completed ride, Ron Southern is on the radio wanting to know why.

The managers and staff of Spruce Meadows take great pride in the relationship they share with sponsors, and it is a relationship where nothing less than exceptional will be tolerated by the Southerns.

Ron and Marg never waste an opportunity to remind riders of their unwritten obligation to the sponsor, but the message is always delivered in an uplifting fashion as opposed to idle threats.

Take, for example, this excerpt from a Riders' Meeting at one of the early MASTERS.

"I'd like to talk about the people that made this venue what it is today," began Ron Southern. "This is the best prize money tournament in the world and those big companies come here to support you. During the course of the week you're going to get a chance to meet many of them.

"I've always been impressed with your attitude towards people, each and every one of you. It's a very unique thing in our sport, the way we involve the athletes. So if you get the opportunity to meet some of the sponsors . . . take the time to thank them or talk with them a bit.

"There hasn't been a year at Spruce Meadows that the sponsors haven't left here and asked, 'What more can we do for you?' The Chefs really help us with that and it's a great way to ensure that the prize money next year will continue," he concluded.

Those who use only dollar signs to measure the success of Spruce Meadows are destined to fail miserably in their attempt to emulate that success.

"Certainly you need the people like the Southerns who have the ability of putting together the money and attracting the backers," said Ronnie Massarella. "But you also need their vision.

"What is special," he explained, "is not that the presidents commit the money to Spruce Meadows, but that they fall into line and love every minute of it."

Marg and Alfonso Romo Garza of Monterrey, Mexico.

The Future

Mexico's Alfonso Romo Garza is identified by many as the one person who comes closer than any other to sharing Ron Southern's futuristic vision for this sport.

A man of wealth, Alfonso is also committed to giving something back to his community and country. The community is Monterrey, Mexico where he is creating a show jumping complex as distinctive in its own right as Spruce Meadows.

Because of an even greater isolation factor than that which faced Spruce Meadows, Alfonso has also struggled in his bid to attract international riders. To succeed, he knows that like Spruce Meadows, he must find ways of enticing the world's best to his doorstep and then across it.

Initially his company financed almost one hundred per cent of prize money at his Monterrey tournaments. By 1994, three years later, he had found enough sponsors to absorb forty per cent of that expense.

In his search for ways to make the sport more exciting for the fan, Alfonso sponsored a world-wide Grand Prix series, the Professional Jumping Association (P.J.A.), that ultimately failed because it couldn't gain the support of enough riders.

The P.J.A. rewrote the rule book in a dramatic fashion by allowing the top eight riders from the first round of competition, regardless of faults, to start with a clean slate in jump-off rounds.

The premise, depending upon whom you spoke with, was either basic and sound or fanciful and destructive. From the crowd's perspective it was appealing since they were guaranteed a jump-off shoot-out involving at least eight gunners, all on an equal footing. The jump-off is the overtime of show jumping and the more action the better.

And as much as fans appreciated it, the riders, except for those who won it because of the second chance, hated it. Why even bother with the first round, they argued? This is a sport of skill, yet this concept allowed riders to escape penalty free for what could have been a sloppy ride.

"It was very difficult to convince the International Equestrian Federation (F.E.I.) that we needed three years to prove that the concept was valid," said Alfonso. "When I started my business I started from nothing, and then I started to learn. Maybe it was not the perfect idea for the first time, but I still think the idea is fantastic."

After a year of struggling to keep the concept alive, Alfonso told the F.E.I. he was in the sport to help, not to fight. It was time to move on to something else.

"I told them if they didn't want us to do the P.J.A., then we wouldn't do it. We left it at that but I hope someday someone will pick it up."

Alfonso is convinced that once all of the international bonds have matured, show jumping will become one of the top four spectator sports in the world.

"We have to revolutionize, to get the attention of the media and the public. Then we will attract more riders and better horses."

Prize money may be vital to any sport's success, said Alfonso, but don't ignore reputation. "The Olympics has no money, but it has a huge reputation. It has to be both."

His dreams for show jumping do not stop there. Alfonso would also like to introduce team sponsorship into the sport, the way it is done now in auto racing.

"If we want to attract the biggest sponsors and the world media, we must have team competitions. And if I'm going to build a team for Pulsar, I want access to the best in the world which means maybe an Italian, a German, a Canadian and a Mexican.

"The problem with Nations' Cup competitions," he said, "is that a few very strong nations traditionally dominate. It doesn't do much for fans from the weaker show jumping nations who seldom have reason to get excited.

"Germany has hundreds of great riders, so does France and Holland. But in other countries there may be only one or two, and what chance do you have of developing the sport there? It is not fair.

"But I will guarantee you something," said the man who amassed his fortune starting with the purchase of a bankrupt cookie company. "If the big teams are coming, which means the big money is coming, everybody will know about it. All of the major newspapers, CNN, ESPN and the Sports Channel, as well as the major European networks, they will be talking about the big stars.

"I would never say eliminate Nations' Cup competitions as they give such pride and involvement by the citizens of each country. I am only suggesting we add another level."

The team concept could extend to individual competition as well. Each rider would still be on their own in the competition, but they would also be earning points for their team depending upon where they finished. A team title, as well as individual honours, could then be recognized.

> "We're getting people saying that show jumping should be more like pro-tennis or pro-golf. But show jumping shouldn't be like anything else - it should be itself."
>
> (Peter Churchill)

"Fantastic, no? If we can do that, then we can revolutionize the sport."

But what chance does Alfonso have in pushing this through the F.E.I., an abstemious body which, as he has already discovered, does not take to change easily? Most would suggest, "not much."

The F.E.I. knows his feelings about its hesitancy toward rapid change at the international level. He made certain of that when given the opportunity to address an F.E.I. meeting.

"If you want to put this sport in the top four in the world, you have to have visionaries," he told them. "You have to show those in the sport that you want to change, and if you want to change you have to bring the best people on board.

"If we don't, this sport won't change at all," said Alfonso. "But if they ask me now to become a member I would say 'no way' because I don't want to devote my time to politics. I prefer to work on new ideas."

There are two sides to this coin, however, and British journalist Peter Churchill warns that too much change could be very dangerous.

"We're getting people saying that show jumping should be more like professional tennis or golf. But show jumping shouldn't be like anything else, it should be itself," said Peter.

"The sport," he continued, "has a classical format that makes it easy to understand. You knock down a rail, you get four faults. You get a clear round and you go on to a tie-breaker. You're the fastest with the lowest faults, and you're the winner.

"When you take riders with faults and still move them into a jump-off against those with clean rounds, you are confusing your crowd, not entertaining it.

"The sport does not need it, I've seen the attempts before, and they've failed because they interfere with the simple format," said Peter. "There's something about human nature. We can never leave something simple."

Course designer Pamela Carruthers is among the many who offer up the name of Ron Southern as one who would bring leadership and excitement to the F.E.I. structure. She adds Alfonso's name, suggesting it would then be "even more exciting." She would also throw in some of the older riders, "people like Nelson Pessoa."

Ron, who has gracefully declined all attempts to get involved in the Canadian Equestrian Federation, is not eager to tackle the problems of the F.E.I. It would, however, serve up a titanic clash of ideals.

There is little doubt that show jumping has the potential to become far more global in presentation and concept than it is now. It is part and parcel of more national sport cultures than any other sport with the possible exception of soccer, yet it lags far behind in terms of international cohesion.

Show jumping desperately needs an identity shock, and the best prod may be some sort of a super circuit that will allow the world's best horses and riders to compete under sensible scheduling.

But the sport must also find a way of paying its best riders enough so they can abandon time-consuming tasks that rob them of the time and energy they should be applying toward competition.

Such a circuit, in fact, would not represent any revolutionary structuring. It would merely parrot what is already in place for golf, tennis, motor racing and even bowling. In fact, virtually every other sport, from snooker to bike racing, has been able to create a showcase portal through which the world can observe its finest.

It is a difficult dream to create, most riders will suggest. Perhaps even impossible given the complexities and expense of moving horses and riders around the world.

British coach Ronnie Massarella also warns such a circuit would remove all of the top riders and horses from many of the existing shows, many of them established institutions.

And you can't expect a horse to be competitive at the super level if you are also jumping it at a dozen or so other major competitions each year. Some venues, obviously, would suffer severely.

"Very few horses could take that pace year after year. Even with the best rider in the world, there's no horse that can jump at all of those places and do that," said Ronnie.

Despite the positives swarming about the sport, there is a growing camp convinced that show jumping will never escape its image as an ancient game swathed in modern problems.

There is no doubt it still faces its most momentous step in any evolutionary march to international greatness, but sceptics no longer have the power, or right, to hamper its augmentation.

Show jumping now belongs to the public, not to a privileged few. The word is out as more and more recognize the sport for what it has always been: a competition of strategy, excitement and danger that requires perfection of performance from not one, but two superb athletes.

It has taken a venue like Spruce Meadows to unveil its potential to the North American viewing market, the fastest growing sports audience in the world. The curtain has been flung open and it's unlikely the masses will ever allow it to be closed again.

Things are still far from perfect. The sport must be marketed better and television must continue to improve its presentation, although the CBC and Spruce Meadows Television do a far better job than most others in the world.

Education leads to a greater appreciation of the sport. On this day, an attentive young crowd receives a lesson on how to judge a water jump.

Spruce Meadows beckons as an oasis away from the concrete trappings of nearby Calgary.

Most of all, the sport must be allowed to test the resiliency of the experimental edge that beckons. If there are limits to be imposed, challenge the contention by walking to that precipice.

And if there is consensus that Spruce Meadows stands as a testimonial to what the sport should become, ways must be found to distract those who insist it will never happen elsewhere.

There is no magic to what the Southern family has done. It can all be explained in simple words like commitment, work, belief and sacrifice. They did not originate and then act upon a secret plan.

Nor are they created differently from those around them. But they have taken their God-given talents and applied them to the fullest. Their starting point was the same as that of millions of others. It's where they've ended up that is so exceptional.

To understand the success of Spruce Meadows it is imperative that one has a feeling for the personalities of the two main characters: Marg and Ron Southern. This is done not to promote envy, but to share the warmth of their success.

Both Marg and Ron are extremely modest people. They do not see themselves as being special and balk at those who try to pin such distinctions upon them. But they take enormous pride in what has happened with Spruce Meadows, always crediting others for the bulk of the success.

And if Spruce Meadows is the best, said Ron, it is not for him to define what that means. That definition must ultimately come from the athletes, the fans and the media.

"The great enjoyment I've always had, even as a young man, is coaching. I've brought a lot of people on to management from some unlikely places . . . and I marvel at their successes within ATCO and now at Spruce Meadows."

Even though there were times he wasn't sure how Spruce Meadows could succeed, he was always confident it would.

"Throughout it all, my approach with the riders and with the people at Spruce Meadows, has been to really be encouraging and enthusiastic while trying to show them the way strategically that they could do it."

Although Marg and Ron may not agree on everything that happens at Spruce Meadows, there is definite unanimity when it comes to decisions about the sport.

"The two most important things in both our minds are the horse and rider," said Marg. "From there we may not agree, but we always come to a compromise."

There is a common goal between them, said Ron, and Spruce Meadows is better for it. There have been some battles, he said, but once a decision is reached each has the full support of the other.

For Marg Southern, the perception of what Spruce Meadows was, is now, and must be in the future, has never been threatened.

"People must always know they can come out here and feel both welcome and comfortable. They must want to come because of the beauty of the facility, and because of the horse. Spruce Meadows will always be for the horse."

Nancy Southern sees in her father a man who will go out of his way to give people a chance to make or break a situation themselves.

"He'll give you the chance, the opportunity and the responsibility, and then it is up to you. Because of his generosity towards people he just can't find a way to say 'No,'" said Nancy.

The only thing that truly hurts him, Nancy said, is when somebody he believed to be loyal or his friend, somebody he has deep respect for, does something to lose that trust.

"That's the only time I think he really gets hurt. Many people think he's beyond that, but they don't see that side of him at all."

Anne and Bas French are among the Southerns' closest friends, and therefore know them better than most. Anne suggested that much of what they have done has been motivated by the fierce pride each has in being born and raised in Calgary. They did, in fact, first meet as students of Calgary's Crescent Heights High School.

"I think Spruce Meadows is their way of paying back the land, the people, the city, the province and in turn, the country. They truly are such strong Western Canadians," she said.

It is amazing, added Anne, to see how much enjoyment the Southerns get from ordinary people, particularly the handicapped, seniors and the young.

Ron Southern is a man you can learn from, said Pedro Cebulka whose rags-to-riches life is graphic proof of his contention.

"He certainly is a man who can judge a character," said the British Columbia land developer who started his Canadian career on the maintenance crew at Spruce Meadows. "He taught me a great deal about judging people for what they were, not what they appeared to be.

> "The great enjoyment I've always had, even as a young man, is coaching. I've brought a lot of people on to management from some unlikely places . . . and I marvel at their successes within ATCO and now at Spruce Meadows."
>
> (Ron Southern)

"You can do anything you want in life. That's what his philosophy has always been, and I'm sure he's afraid of no one. Work hard and whatever you do, do it one hundred per cent, because anything less is not good enough."

People describe the attributes of Ron Southern in many different fashions, but none see him as an individual bent on 'power.'

"He doesn't want 'yes' men around him. That does not impress Ron Southern," said British journalist Peter Churchill. "He equally does not like arrogant, self-opinionated people who think they're going to change the world in ten seconds.

"He also has this wonderful pride in Canada, particularly the West. It's not a narrow pride nor is it chauvinism. It's an absolute natural tribal pride," said Peter, who has attended more Spruce Meadows tournaments than any other foreign journalist.

There is a sensitive edge to Ron Southern that he conceals quite well, suggested the late Wilmat Tennyson.

"He has a very gentle person inside him. Some say the 'gentleman's gentleman' comes from Marg, others say it's from his mother," said Wilmat.

"Ron is most proud of Marg and her achievements in the business world, particularly those at Spruce Meadows."

In an interview conducted just months before his death, Mr. Tennyson presented a personal insight into Ron Southern which placed him far above most others. It came during the opening of an ATCO plant in Budapest, Hungary. As an ATCO Director, he attended the ceremony with Ron.

"It was very nicely done with a marquee and microphone and all the officials and translators and tents with lovely food. The officials," said Wilmat, "went through all the gyrations of an opening ceremony until it was time for Ron to speak."

But before taking the microphone, Ron strode to the rear of the factory where workers had been shuffled into the background. They were dressed for work, not a party.

"Ron insisted they all join him at the front, and only then did he speak.

Ron will never pass by a group of fans, young or old, without stopping to speak with them.

"These are the people who are going to build the ATCO trailers, and I will not have them stand in the background while I open this facility."

As he spoke, the translator broke into tears and told the audience he could not go on.

"I was almost in tears myself," said Wilmat.

Nancy remembers that the way her father handled one of his toughest days also personalized his greatest strength.

"He had to go down to the ATCO factory in Calgary to tell hundreds of people they no longer had a job. He didn't send an executive to do it, he knew he had to talk to them himself."

It was his responsibility, said Nancy. Most companies would have passed on the bad news through notices or supervisors.

"He went down and gathered everybody in the middle of the factory and talked to them and told them how sorry he was and disheartened this had to happen. And he told them they could rest assured that he was going to work harder than anybody to get their jobs back.

"You know," said Nancy "when it was over those men cheered him."

That is the sort of commitment both her parents have brought to Spruce Meadows, said Nancy.

"It's an intangible thing, but it's a personal commitment and a feeling of responsibility. It's a lot of weight, but they're pretty incredible people."

There is little doubt that the most hurtful moment of the Southerns' lives took place early Sunday morning during the 1992 MASTERS. Horses belonging to the Lord Strathcona's Horse (Royal Canadians) were tethered in a temporary corral away from the permanent stables. That is the way the army preferred to keep the horses, always under battle-field conditions.

Something, however, frightened them midway through the night, and fifteen terrified horses bolted down a sideroad after breaking out of the paddock and straight onto Highway 22X.

A van containing two young men collided full on with the horses. One of those men, twenty-nine-year-old Charles John Leptich died instantly, while the van's driver eventually recovered from the serious injuries he sustained. The driver of a second car, which also hit the horses, has also since recovered from injuries. Seven horses either died instantly or were later humanely destroyed as a result of the tragedy.

The Southerns were devastated by the death of Mr. Leptich. Although the family was unknown to the Southerns at the time, Marg insisted that she visit the young man's mother, not as the president of Spruce Meadows, but also as a mother filled with grief.

More than thirty people involved with Spruce Meadows attended the funeral, for it was a tragedy deeply felt by the entire Spruce Meadows family.

Ron and Marg Southern would never ask anyone to do anything they themselves haven't done. Both have been on the good and bad end of virtually every assignment and job ever associated with Spruce Meadows.

There have been countless occasions when, during presentations, the rain and wind have been so fierce Ron's hair was plastered straight down his face and his hands were so cold he could barely hang on to the microphone.

Yet when it came time for the actual award presentation, he always removed his parka or raincoat. It is done out of respect for the sponsor and exemplifies his spirit of "excellence."

"You want Spruce Meadows to have attention to detail," he once said, "and to go that extra mile for it. You want it to go far beyond what anyone thinks it can be, and that gives excellence."

Spruce Meadows Riding Master Albert Kley sees the lessons Ron dealt to Nancy and Linda as part of a character-building process that paid great dividends.

"He has taught them to learn, to fight for themselves, and work hard," said Albert. "They have come to understand that if they want something, they must get it for themselves. And, because of that, they feel better about it."

There were times Albert felt both Nancy and Linda deserved better horses.

"But buying the best horses doesn't usually work out. People then expect you to always win, and sometimes a horse that went well for one rider just won't perform for another. It is better the way Linda has gone. She has some outstanding horses now that she has worked hard to develop herself."

Tournament Secretary Joanne Nimitz knows that no one has ever worked harder for what they have.

"By most people's standards they have so much," said Joanne, "yet I don't believe Marg views herself as a wealthy person. I don't think Ron does either."

"They both know they must continue to work hard for Spruce Meadows and when people suggest they relax a little more, both will ask 'Why?' since they love everything they do.

"And it's not just Spruce Meadows," added Joanne. "It's everything they do.

"Ron," she said, "is a master at analyzing situations and then understanding where they will lead to long before anyone else.

"He's also the world's greatest at motivating people. That is why I believe he lives on a different level than the rest of us. Even when he is angry with me, and over the years we've had rows when he's been spitting mad, he is still motivating me. You only have to sit back after it's all over and think about what he actually said."

And while Spruce Meadows has been a wonderful thing for the Southern family, Nancy will tell you there have also been some difficult times.

"I don't believe any of us would ever criticize or say the ideas that my Dad has, and wants to try and implement, are wrong. They aren't. When he explains them and he says 'this is my concept, let's pursue it,' you know it is the right thing to do."

What's hard, said Nancy, is that her mother also has her passion, and that is a desire to have things feel the way they did when Spruce Meadows first opened.

Those around in the early years truly became members of the Southerns' Spruce Meadows team. They revelled in all triumphs, and worked countless hours to help bring them about. They were also made to believe it was their efforts that made the difference.

Her hours at Spruce Meadows are long, but there is nowhere else Marg would rather spend them.

That same touch is far more difficult to maintain now. Spruce Meadows, and the entourage of volunteers, staff and sponsors surrounding it, is just too large.

"But my mother is concerned that for things to happen and be successful, people must continue the way they once did, and she is right. Jaded New Yorkers come here and feel they've found heaven the way they are treated. They want to be part of it.

"It worries me sometimes just how hard she works," said Nancy. "I think it worries everybody that works with her or knows her. How can she keep it up? Because it's something she loves, needs, and wants to do.

"So as long as she is able to do it, why shouldn't she? Better to live life to the very last minute than sit and twiddle your thumbs as you wait for your kids to take you out of a job."

Marg, of course, had no trouble at all justifying her long days at Spruce Meadows.

"I know that I spend hours and hours at Spruce Meadows, it's my hobby, it's my love and it's my life," said Marg. "People might say I'm a workaholic, but that really isn't true. It isn't work for me, it's fun."

Ron burns his own share of midnight oil at Spruce Meadows, but he knows better than to count on Marg for a ride home. He would miss half his early morning appointments if he did.

He confessed that one of his greatest pleasures in the business world is derived from the creation of strategies.

"I always think strategy," he said. "My first recollection of books was the five volumes of the *History of World War I*. I loved those books, not for the war part of it, but for the strategy that was contained in them."

As an outside director of ten major corporations, the committees he is most asked to serve on are related to strategic development. Even at Spruce Meadows, the projects that excite him the most are those requiring the development of approaches for the future.

"I find you must try and conceptualize or visualize, and then develop strategies with fall-back positions. You must evaluate the strategies in the position of both their up-side and down-side potentials, recognizing that you can fail, but also understanding what's at risk if you do fail."

He said many people who want to think strategically couch the process in a Las Vegas atmosphere.

"The psychology of Las Vegas is you've got to win or you lose," said Ron. "The good strategy is to have an evolution where the up-side potential is great, but the down-side is small."

Personal or business backgrounds are of little concern to either Marg or Ron. Neither cares what other people do for a living, and therefore they never ask.

"It doesn't matter what they do," said Marg, "because it's nice to know them as people, not as a category. Ron has taught me that. We've never asked if someone is a doctor, a trucker, a lawyer or an Indian chief. It doesn't matter."

Nor are they impressed by those who try to impress them. The story is told about two prominent hunter judges who, on their first visit to Spruce Meadows, arrived ten minutes late for a competition.

They hadn't met Ron as yet, but that was about to change since he was waiting for them at the gate. They approached with hands out-stretched, flashing broad smiles. But before a miffed Ron Southern could utter a word, one of the men suggested he and Marg had to come to California where he would introduce them to Paul Newman.

Ron never did shake either man's hand. He politely, but firmly, told them they were late and explained that at Spruce Meadows competitions always started on time.

As the two humbled judges turned to leave, Ron was overheard to mumble: "Why the hell do I want to meet Paul Newman. Why doesn't he come up here and meet Bas French (Spruce Meadows' Competitions Manager)?"

Retired CTV kingpin Johnny Esaw remembers Marg as "the greatest greeter in the world."

"She made you feel like you weren't just another person when you did business with Spruce Meadows," said Johnny. "You were a part of the family and she made you feel so comfortable, you felt good going there."

Those who worked beside her in those early hectic years had the greatest admiration for her devotion to Spruce Meadows, and to the people who helped piece it all together. These special talents have also made her a sought-after candidate for membership on Canadian corporate boards.

Christy Lindskog was Tournament Secretary in the early eighties and remembers the night she dragged herself out of the office toward the parking lot at about 3 a.m.

"I was feeling like I was the only one in the whole world still awake, and all for a horse show," said Christy. But as she was going out the door she heard a noise from one of the washrooms. It was Marg plunging the toilets, 'because she didn't want to wake anybody else up to do it.'

"That wasn't an exception," said Christy. "There's never a job she wouldn't take on, and if something needed to be done, she was there to do it."

In searching for words to describe the two, Christy suggested that the greatness of

> "There's never a job she (Marg Southern) wouldn't take on, and if something needed to be done, she was there to do it."
>
> (Christy Lindskog)

Spruce Meadows was certainly the primary goal of Ron Southern, while Marg appeared more focused with the sincerity of its presentation.

"I think perhaps she's brought all of this greatness into perspective by giving it a genuine warmth."

The Southerns have a private side to their lives that includes an altruism few seldom hear about. They see a goodness in people that transcends all barriers. The stories of their generosity will never be confirmed by family members, simply because it is the one dimension of their characters they will not share.

Only one such story will be repeated here, and this is only because it reflects so much of Marg Southern's belief in the precious relationship between children and horses.

It is told by Christy, who left Spruce Meadows to ultimately raise a family of five little girls. She came by Spruce Meadows one January with the children to show them the horses. Marg saw them and mentioned that it didn't seem right that five little girls didn't have a pony to ride, particularly since they lived on a small farm.

"I didn't think anything about it until one day that spring a trailer pulled up and out pops two ponies. The kids had a great time all summer and we returned the ponies in October."

They're 'hands on' people, explained Bas French, and that's probably why people work so hard on their behalf.

"If they had been like most and delegated everything, I don't believe they would have generated the spirit they have."

Special Projects Manager Randy Fedorak suggested that Marg probably enjoys the sport even more than Ron.

"He enjoys the event, she enjoys the sport," said Randy. "That's why Marg won't move her office out of the Riding Hall. She wants to be close to the horses."

On his first visit to Spruce Meadows in 1977 Ronnie Massarella said the wind and rain were so vicious on the Saturday that Ron asked him if he should call it off.

"I told him there was no point in making Spruce Meadows famous if he was going to call the second show off just because of some bad weather," said Ronnie. "He knew then by my attitude that it had to go on."

Ronnie wasn't all that anxious to go to Spruce Meadows in the first place that year, but having gone and seen the effort that had been made, he wanted it to be a success.

"What I remember most," he said, "is that Ron had the kick-start to somehow bring out the best in me. I don't know what it is, but he had something from the word 'go' that made me want to help him and Spruce Meadows and everybody there."

He, like many others, always endeavoured to give the Southerns the best he could deliver.

"I could tell from the start that if somebody helped him along the way, and when I say 'help' I meant putting good performers on the plane, it would work out. That first British team wasn't a good team, it was third rate for us. But after that I said to myself the man needs the best and that's what he'll get."

Ian Millar remembers a Riders' Meeting where Ron began by once again explaining the importance of the sponsors to the sport. Just into the talk, he was interrupted by one rider who said: "OK, fine Ron! Yes, we'll do whatever it takes.

"But I haven't finished, Ron said, bewildered by the interruption. You haven't even heard my whole pitch, so why are you agreeing?

"No, replied the rider. It's fine! We're committed and we're going to do it. It's not what is being asked for, it's who is doing the asking."

That, said Ian, was a huge compliment to Ron Southern and to Spruce Meadows.

He suggested that the spirit of Spruce Meadows is Ron and Marg and without their spirit, the facility is like any other, just "bricks and mortar."

"The strength," he continued, "is the spirit, the drive, the intelligence, the vision, the daring, the commitment and the determination of Ron and Marg and their whole team. "I've always felt that you could take Marg and Ron and the Spruce Meadows team and drop them down anywhere in the world and when you came back you would find that something pretty amazing had happened there."

The future continues to beckon without signs of restraint, yet no one dares to predict just how much more growth the complex will absorb.

It is unlikely Spruce Meadows will ever go beyond three major tournaments each year, but it is certain that ways will be found to make existing presentations even stronger, particularly the mid-week portions of them.

"I believe our focus in the future will always be to ensure we have the best riders, the best footing and the best crowds," said Linda Southern-Heathcott.

She also knows that Spruce Meadows is no longer just about tournaments, but is the sum of many parts which she emphasizes must all stand on their own.

"Our horse program must produce better horses than we do now," said Linda. "It is equally important that we find new and innovative ideas for Special Features, as well as ways of giving even more coverage to our sponsors and their events."

Linda sees huge potential for Spruce Meadows as a meeting place for the business community . . . not just for Round Table discussions twice yearly, but as a year-round destination for many different conferences.

As more support structures and systems are created, the level of horse-related commerce will skyrocket and ultimately there will be a horse-related event of some description every weekend.

Winter jumping, wrapped into a Christmas production, looms in the immediate future. Turn your imagination loose on what it could become . . . a sparkling winter wonderland complete with sleigh rides, horse-drawn skiers, Santa's village that includes a post office with its own commemorative stamp, skating ponds, hotdog roasts, and of course, some kind of jumping competition. As green and clean as Spruce Meadows is in the summer, now think white and bright.

"The quality of the competition will continue to improve," said Ron, "but I believe the major change at Spruce Meadows will be its dramatic evolvement into a place of great beauty."

David Broome is possibly the best all-round horseman this sport has ever known, so it seems quite appropriate to close this book with some of his observations.

"I don't think we've learned the lesson that Ron's given us with Spruce Meadows," David said. "You see, you take a couple like Ron and Marg who are outstanding in this world, and you have them put their minds toward running a horse show. They then take this cattle feedlot in the outback and turn it into something that attracts 120,000 people.

"I mean, if you're sponsoring or organizing horse shows, it's your duty to study what they've done," concluded David.

Mexico's Jaime Azcarraga is clear in the first round of the 1994 du Maurier International.

Final Competition

Thomas Fuchs of Switzerland finishes second in the 1994 du Maurier International after an exciting two-horse jump-off.

Fifteen minutes before the start of the du Maurier International, a ravenous sun devours the last of the cloud layer that has corralled Spruce Meadows since early this morning.

It truly is uncanny how often this happens. Just when you are certain the day will be a weather disaster, a breeze blows away all signs of discomfort and the sun explodes on the scene.

The rain has not hurt the course at all. Medium corks will control any slickness, as aptly demonstrated in the just-completed $60,000 Pulsar Internacional Parcours de Chasse.

Nick Skelton wins the speed class aboard Everest Limited Edition, beating teammate Michael Whitaker by almost three seconds. You know how bad he must have wanted it when he can beat this field by that much time. It was once said of Nick that if he had so chosen, he could have become the world's best steeplechase jockey. No one can read a competitive situation as quickly, or with more accuracy.

It's interesting to see the Brits start well on the closing day after yesterday's disaster in the Bank of Montreal Nations' Cup. Ronnie Massarella's pride suffered a brutal wound and he hopes good performances will serve as the healer today.

Nick is asked what he and others would do if the big money was not available at Spruce Meadows any more.

"We would still come," says Nick. "We owe the Southerns that much."

In the first round of the du Maurier, eight of the twelve making it to the second round are clean. What a talented list they comprise: Thomas Fuchs of Switzerland, Eric Navet and Michel Robert of France, John Whitaker of Great Britain, Jaime Azcarraga of Mexico, and three German riders: Franke Sloothaak, Ludger Beerbaum and Soren Von Ronne. If you chose the top dozen riders in the sport today, at least six of those names would be among them.

The second round is tougher than the first. With the exception of John Whitaker and Thomas Fuchs, all other clears pull a rail to set up a jump-off between those two.

Wouldn't you know it. Just seconds before the first rider enters the ring the skies have opened up. Not one soul, however, appears to have left the packed stadium.

Thomas Fuchs holds a slight edge since he has the luxury of watching John Whitaker go first. John, therefore, must go quick enough to at least worry the Swiss rider, but his primary objective is still to ride clean.

Riding Everest Grannusch, the same horse that gave him a faultless performance in yesterday's second round of the Bank of Montreal Nations' Cup, John takes off in a quest to become the first rider in history to win three du Maurier Internationals.

Eric Navet of France shows world championship form during the 1994 MASTERS.

His ride is classic John Whitaker. Not a wasted stride as he asks only for what he knows Grannusch can deliver. It is a third faultless performance in a time of 55.80 seconds: eight seconds quicker than the time allowed over the shortened jump-off course.

If there is an advantage to riding second, Thomas no longer has it. He now faces the pressure of having to ride clean and at break-neck speed. At the midway point of the nine-jump course he is within a tenth of a second of John's ride, and still clear.

Turning into the final vertical, Thomas still has a chance. But as he clears the top rail the clock tells the tale: 56.94 seconds, a full second longer than John.

John's reward is $225,000 for a little more than three minutes of work. Thomas Fuchs picks up $120,000 for second and Eric Navet, the best of the four-faulters, bolsters his bank account by a tidy $75,000. Ian Millar, missing his super partner Big Ben, is still the top Canadian finishing eleventh on Future Vision.

The course for the du Maurier was a touch slippery, John tells reporters, but it didn't bother the riders since the fences were so big they didn't have to turn really quick.

"It was more power jumping than speed," he explains.

John is very surprised he ended up in first place. He tells reporters he didn't think he had much of a chance at the start of competition.

"But in this game you keep trying. Horses are not machines and they don't always jump the best when you want them to."

His wife, says John, owns Grannusch, but "it's going to be difficult to get the money off me when I get home."

Thomas says he honestly believed he would beat John in the jump-off since his horse is known to be very fast and "John hadn't really gone crazy quick."

"It didn't work out," he stresses, "but there is such good money for second - I mean there's better money here for second than you would win in any other Grand Prix, or two or three Grand Prix together."

The Spruce Meadows MASTERS is over. Competition was again exceptional, perhaps the best in almost two decades. Fans have already stripped the jumps of flowers and crews are carefully breaking down fences to tuck them away for one more winter.

And when the next spring erupts, all of those who have worked hand-in-hand with the Southerns to mold Spruce Meadows in the image of the family dream, will rise collectively like the mystical Phoenix to soar confidently into the next year with boundless enthusiasm and vitality.

That's the way it happens each and every year.

An explosion of color marks the end of another competitive year.

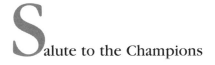

Salute to the Champions

MASTERS TOURNAMENT

Bank of Montreal Nations' Cup

1995	Ireland	Peter Charles
		Trevor Coyle
		Capt. John Ledingham
		Eddie Macken
1994	United States	Anne Kursinski
		Tim Grubb
		Darlene McMullen
		Leslie Lenehan
1993	France	Hubert Bourdy
		Michel Robert
		Herve Godignon
		Eric Navet
1992	Great Britain	Nick Skelton
		John Whitaker
		Michael Whitaker
		Tim Grubb
1991	Great Britain	Nick Skelton
		John Whitaker
		Michael Whitaker
		David Broome
1990	Great Britain	Nick Skelton
		John Whitaker
		Michael Whitaker
		Emma-Jane Mac
1989	Great Britain	Nick Skelton
		John Whitaker
		Michael Whitaker
		Joe Turi
1988	United States	Peter Leone
		Leslie Lenehan
		Joan Scharffenburger
		Katie Prudent
1987	United States	Anne Kursinski
		Debbie Dolan
		Joan Scharffenburger
		Beezy Paton
1986	United States	Robert Ridland
		Hap Hansen
		Joan Scharffenburger
		Jennifer Newell

1985	Great Britain	Nick Skelton
		John Whitaker
		Michael Whitaker
		Malcolm Pyrah
1984	Germany	Paul Schockemöhle
		Franke Sloothaak
		Peter Luther
		Karsten Huck
1983	United States	Norman Dello Joio
		Joe Fargis
		Katie Monaghan
		Melanie Smith
1982	Great Britain	Harvey Smith
		John Whitaker
		David Broome
		Malcolm Pyrah
1981	Netherlands	Anton Ebben
		Rob Ehrens
		Johan Heinz
		Henk Noorens
1980	Great Britain	Graham Fletcher
		Jean Germany
		Malcolm Pyrah
		John Whitaker
1979	Great Britain	Lionel Dunning
		Tim Grubb
		Caroline Bradley
		Malcolm Pyrah
1978	Great Britain	Caroline Bradley
		Graham Fletcher
		Mark Phillips
		Michael Saywell
1977	Germany	Herman Schridde
		Heinrich Schulze
		Norbert Koof
		Ulrich Meyer

du Maurier International

1995	Michael Whitaker	Everest Two-Step	Great Britain
1994	John Whitaker	Everest Grannusch	Great Britain
1993	Nick Skelton	Everest Dollar Girl	Great Britain
1992	John Whitaker	Henderson Gammon	Great Britain
1991	Ian Millar	Big Ben	Canada
1990	Otto Becker	Optibeurs Pamina	Germany
1989	Michael Whitaker	Next Mon Santa	Great Britain
1988	George Morris	Rio	United States
1987	Ian Millar	Big Ben	Canada
1986	John Whitaker	Next Milton	Great Britain
1985	Nick Skelton	Everest St. James	Great Britain
1984	Heidi Robbiani	Jessica V	Switzerland
1983	Norman dello Joio	I Love You	United States
1982	Malcolm Pyrah	Towerlands Anglezarke	Great Britain
1981	David Broome	Queens Way Philco	Great Britain

NORTH AMERICAN TOURNAMENT

North American Show Jumping Champion

1995	Laura Balisky	Easy Boy	Canada
1994	Hap Hansen	Fairway	United States
1993	Hap Hansen	Fairway	United States
1992	Mark Laskin	Sullivan	Canada
1991	Candice Schlom	Kodiac	United States
1990	Barney Ward	So Long	United States
1989	Hugh Graham	Sirocco	Canada

Queen Elizabeth II Cup

1995	Hugh Graham	Money Talks	Canada
1994	Hugh Graham	Money Talks	Canada
1993	Fernando Senderos	Rivage	Mexico
1992	Hap Hansen	Mirage	United States
1991	Rich Fellers	El Mirasol	United States
1990	Alice Debany	The Natural	United States

Chrysler Classic (Derby)

1995	Laura Balisky	Easy Boy	Canada
1994	John Anderson	Scirocco	Canada
1993	Hap Hansen	Fairway	United States
1992	Ronnie Freeman	Starlet	United States
1991	Mark Laskin	Volia T	Canada
1990	Laura Balisky	Lavendel 48	Canada
1989	Ian Millar	El Futuro	Canada
1988	Ian Millar	Big Ben	Canada
1987	Ian Millar	Big Ben	Canada
1986	Ian Millar	Big Ben	Canada
1985	Doug Henry	Big Bird	Canada

NATIONAL TOURNAMENT

Canadian Show Jumping Champion
(Officially Sanctioned in 1989)

1995	Eric Lamaze	Cagney	Canada
1994	Beth Underhill	Monopoly	Canada
1993	Ian Millar	Big Ben	Canada
1992	Mario Deslauriers	Alemao V	Canada
1991	Ian Millar	Big Ben	Canada
1990	Ian Millar	Czar	Canada
1989	Ian Millar	El Futuro	Canada
1988	Ian Millar	El Futuro	Canada
1987	Ian Millar	Warrior	Canada
1986	Ian Millar	Big Ben	Canada
1985	Lisa Carlsen	Kahlua	Canada
1984	Lisa Carlsen	Kahlua	Canada
1983	Ian Millar	Warrior	Canada
1982	Michel Vaillancourt	Marcato	Canada
1981	Barbara Kerr	40 Below	Canada
1980	Bo Mearns	The Flying Nun	Canada
1979	Bo Mearns	The Flying Nun	Canada
1978	Albert Kley	Gambrinus	Canada
1977	John Simpson	Texas	Canada
1976	Jean-Guy Mathers	Pomme D'Apie	Canada

Royal Bank World Cup

1995	Mario Deslauriers	Alemao V	Canada
1994	Beth Underhill	Monopoly	Canada
1993	Beth Underhill	Monopoly	Canada
1992	Ian Millar	Big Ben	Canada
1991	Ian Millar	Big Ben	Canada
1990	Ian Millar	Czar	Canada
1989	Hugh Graham	Sirocco	Canada
1988	Laura Balisky	Lavendel 48	Canada
1987	Ian Millar	Warrior	Canada
1986	Ian Millar	Warrior	Canada

Shell Cup (Derby)

1995	Eric Lamaze	Cagney	Canada
1994	Eric Lamaze	Cagney	Canada
1993	Ian Millar	Big Ben	Canada
1992	Ian Millar	Big Ben	Canada
1991	Ian Millar	Big Ben	Canada
1990	Mark Laskin	Voila T	Canada